Genny

with love and
best wishes

Bryan

advent 2001

Born into 'trade' - his father ran an electrical business - the author grew up as a wartime country lad. Not a particularly adventurous beginning, but service in the RAF started a more surprising and interesting future. Twenty-five years with the innovative and pioneering Decca Navigator Company provided experience of the world that stood him in good stead when he answered the call to be ordained as an Anglican priest. Thirty years of full and part-time Ministry was crammed with experiences worth recording as it gives an unseen - and perhaps unexpected - picture of the varied and demanding life of a parish priest. Now approaching eighty, he lives happily with his wife in the beauty of Mid Devon.

SCENES FROM AN ERRATIC LIFE

Bryan Strange

Scenes From An Erratic Life

Vanguard Press

VANGUARD PAPERBACK

A CIP catalogue record for this title is
available from the British Library

Front cover. BS at the age of eight. Drawn by his father, Leonard
Strange, using a pencil form of pointillism.

ISBN 1 84386 269 7

Vanguard Press is an imprint of
Pegasus Elliot MacKenzie Publishers Ltd.
www.pegasuspublishers.com

First Published in 2006

Vanguard Press
Sheraton House Castle Park
Cambridge England

Printed & Bound in Great Britain

Dedication

This book is dedicated to the three women in my life
Marian, Claire and Fiona.

Acknowledgements

This book would never have seen the light of day and could have lacked some accuracy without the memories and records of several people who came to my aid when dates or details eluded me. In particular I would like to thank my sister-in-law Dorothy Strange for setting me straight about dates and events associated with many trips to see my brother's family in Scotland. To the RAF Records Office in Gloucester for copies of my Service Records. To Janet Gillham, cousin, for details of some of my relations and of family outings in my Sussex childhood days. To Dennis Hendley, Chief Engineer, for certain technical information concerning the Decca Navigator System. To Harry Mellor, one of my churchwardens at Kewstoke, Somerset, for details of the Oldfield Trust. To David Stone, military history author, for much help and guidance in setting about my task of writing this book. To Lisa Birdwood, granddaughter, and her publishing colleagues for assuring me that I could write basic English and did have something to tell. To Joan Horn who kindly read and helped correct the final proofs.

To my daughters Claire and Fiona for dates and details of many happenings throughout our life together and since their marriages. And last but not least to my wife Marian who has kept me on the straight and narrow with this narrative and who came to my rescue on countless occasions when I couldn't spell and when I pressed the wrong keys on this horrible thing called a computer!

CONTENTS

Bryan Strange

INTRODUCTION

Having written the first two Scenes of this book, I find it necessary to include an Introduction. Here is an early example of erraticism! The reason for this addition is that I suspect I am getting into some difficulty with my task.

The initial driving force to write this account has always been that I can see the many differences between young people's lives today and my childhood lot, especially before the Second World War. It is the nature – the weft and warp – particularly of my early years, that I want to record for the younger members of my extended family. Family life and the social structure in general are undergoing radical change at an ever-accelerating rate. I believe that in, say, twenty years time, life will be so changed and different from my early experiences, as to be totally unreal – was it actually like that? My hope is that the book will be some sort of record, not just as a family affair, but also as a means of recapturing and recording some of the foundations of life in previous generations. I also hope it will reflect some of the thinking of present day older people.

So what is my problem? It is my memory! It is a well-known fact that the brain is more able to retain the distant past than the immediate present and I remember far more detail and small happenings of my first twelve years than of more recent ones. It is a gradual change, of course, but it will mean that my later Scenes may have differing complexions. The account of my life as a clergyman may not come as such a great surprise to the members of my family as so many of them became 'children of the vicarage'. However, the public image of the Church of England today may not be the one I tried to foster and so I hope my record might rekindle the position of the church as having a strong influence in the community. As I sit in front of my computer, at this moment, I am flirting with the very thing that is responsible for so much of the disintegration of community and family life today – the small screen.

The only records I have of my life, or of my past family members, are my work diaries from 1989 till the present time, the odd registrar's certificate and a motley collection of unsorted and unlabeled photographs that help to jog the memory. Perhaps it's all a reflection that as life proceeds it becomes starker and the simplicity and freedom of spirit of young life is slowly overtaken. However this is not all bad news for me, nor I hope for you. It was those first years that were the foundation of how I have lived the rest of my life and I hope the following Acts and Scenes will bear out what I am trying to say.

ACT 1

Scene 1

In The Beginning

It all started in Cranbrook – a small town in the middle of the Garden of England. I can never remember if I am a Man of Kent or a Kentish Man but the atlas does show Cranbrook located south of the River Medway.

When I say it all began in this little Kentish town, I am not being strictly accurate – many things had come together before my appearance there in 1926, the details of which I have only limited information. I think my parents were married in 1922 – but where I am not sure. Perhaps in Beckenham, where my mother Madge Isabelle Lake lived, or in Sevenoaks where the newly-weds had lodgings and where my brother Edward Stanley (Teddy) was born in 1924. Madge was the third child of William and Jessie Lake. Jessie's maiden name was Harris. William, by profession a marine engineer, was always known in the family as 'Kaiser' – the moustache and Christian name no doubt being responsible for linking him with the German monarchy. I have few details about the early life of my mother who was brought up as a member of the Plymouth Brethren and as a rebellion against this austere regime used to escape out of her bedroom window to visit the house of the devil – the cinema! She earned her living in a City of London office. My father, Leonard Stanley Strange, was the second son of Francis and Charlotte Strange. Charlotte's maiden name was Weston. Leonard was never known by this name within the family – he was always Buller. What was his similarity to General Buller I do not know, except that 1899 was the year my father was born and the General relieved Ladysmith during the Boer War.

Francis Strange owned an electrical retail and contracting business (Strange Electrical Co. Ltd.) in Tunbridge Wells with a branch in Sevenoaks. Originally the company was a building contractor and the spa town was home to many Strange families most of whom owned some sort of business activity. And this is where Cranbrook is about to come on the scene.

My father was working as an electrician from the shop in Sevenoaks when one day he was called into the office by my grandfather. "Go to Cranbrook and open a new branch of Strange Electrical Co. Ltd. – I've been told the electricity supply company is taking the overhead cables there and we want to be ready to wire-out people's homes and sell them fittings." Grandfather had spoken. Electricity, for some, at that time was 'new-fangled' and still not available in all areas of the country, so here was a chance to exercise entrepreneurial abilities.

Before we leave for Cranbrook, there is one occasion that deserves recall. My father was working at Ightham Court, near Sevenoaks, installing a 'plant' – a petrol driven generator for charging up banks of acid accumulators. This produced 'the juice' – a non-technical term used for electricity in those days. Obviously the overhead cable supply hadn't arrived there. Ightham Court was a large country house that delighted in putting on tennis parties for weekend guests – it was pretty upper class – but on one occasion the assembled company was short of a player to make up a foursome. So my father, who was only 'trade', was dragooned into making up the number. Unbeknown to the regular players, he was something of an all-round sportsman and at the end of the day he walked off with a very nice canteen of cutlery. Which reminds me of one other sporting occasion, when as a spectator at a local football match, he was dragged off the touchline by his elder brother Frank and as an unregistered player – again to make up the numbers – scored seven times. He was quickly escorted from the pitch before the opposing team could get their hands on him.

I must confess that the dates for these early years may not be accurate – a year or two 'either side' must be understood. There are no diaries or family records to confirm dates but at least I can be fairly sure that the details of what happened are in the right order. I also believe that what I write comes from my memory of the facts – well, after the age of about four – and not from the retelling over the years by members of my family. Of course I could get off my bottom and visit various record offices and registrars, but somehow that doesn't quite fit the character or objective of what I am trying to relate.

The year 1925 saw Buller and Madge and baby Teddy arrive in Cranbrook. Sevenoaks to Cranbrook isn't all that far in today's terms, but when the transport was only a motorcycle and sidecar it must have been quite an adventure especially with a young baby. Previous visits had identified premises in the High Street with living accommodation 'over the shop'. This was to be my birthplace – not quite as sparse as 'no room at the inn' but not exactly ideal. My arrival on 22nd February 1926 is recorded in the Cranbrook Congregational Church Register of Baptisms and I share that birthday with George Washington and with the Girl Guides' Thinking Day. However I wasn't christened George nor did I become known as Baden. My father hoped this second child would be a daughter so maybe his disappointment was responsible for spelling Bryan with a 'y' and not the usual 'i' when registering the birth.

This is all I can relate about Cranbrook, except that the hoped for company expansion ended in disaster – and not just because I was a boy and not a girl, nor because my father couldn't spell. Maybe I was some compensation to my parents for what was planned to be the start of a new venture for Strange Electrical Co. Ltd. but which in fact never materialised. Well, not in the Garden of England.

So what went wrong? It wasn't for lack of energy on the part of my father but for want of energy on the part of the electricity supply company. In their wisdom someone finally decided that Cranbrook at that time was not yet to be blessed with electricity winging its way down cables suspended on poles across the countryside. If the reader has the stamina to persist in reading this account, you will finally discover what really happened! Anyway, without 'the juice' my father's house wiring would remain inanimate; there would be no sale for bulbs and fittings in the shop; Strange Electrical Co. Ltd. would become even more limited. However, someone must have gone back to the drawing board and discovered that poles had been seen some twenty five miles south west of Cranbrook. "Go west my boy and open a shop in Heathfield" was the next order from my grandfather. And so it was.

Scene 2

A Country Boy

Heathfield was what I would describe, perhaps a little unkindly, as being a hick place. It was unsophisticated, not a town and yet a bit more than a village. It had little to attract attention except that it was perched on top of the Weald of East Sussex and commanded wonderful views of wooded country to the north and the South Downs to the south. There was a railway station for stopping-trains on the single track so-called Cuckoo Line that meandered from Tunbridge Wells to Eastbourne. With a tunnel, so that the rails didn't have to climb over the final Wealden summit, and an approach gradient of one in fifty, the line was quite an engineering feat, but did little to make the service anything approaching 'express'. The line does have one small corner in the annals of railway history – a derailment just outside the station, late in the last century, resulted in many of the local populous running to the scene, applying a certain degree of self-mutilation, before lying down in the wreckage and then claiming compensation!

Heathfield spawned three streets with shops – The High Street, Hailsham Road and Station Road. A small single-fronted shop on the hill down to the station became the site of Strange Electrical Co. Ltd. Shops with an address in any Station Road are usually cheaper and far less pretentious than those in The High Street, but it was a start.

The largest building in The High Street was made of corrugated iron and housed the local cinema. It was never known as a cinema but was called 'the pictures'. It was 'talking pictures' of course but it had added built-in sound effects – the tin roof amplified the sound of falling rain, which was great for some scenes, but not so appropriate for the large number of sunny Western films that were shown. This disconcerting feature was worth enduring as my father displayed posters of the week's screening for which he received free tickets for the family. The only other public buildings of any size were the Union Church, built at the beginning of the century in red brick and commanding attention at the junction of the main shopping roads and, again in red brick, the Anglican Church dedicated to St Richard of Chichester. Union Church was to play an important part in shaping my life although the seeds sown there took many years to germinate –and into unexpected fruit – and St Richard's became the final resting place of my mother and father.

An odd feature of Heathfield was that the shopping and business parts, built near the station, weren't in the Parish of Heathfield at all, but in the Parish of Waldron – a small village some three miles away. The original Heathfield had become Old Heathfield, also a very small village two miles away. The confusion came about because railway engineers always go for the easiest, and therefore the cheapest, route which was up the little valley between the two existing villages. It was the railway that produced the development of the new part of Heathfield. Parish boundaries can have serious effects on one's life, as you will find out later.

Did Heathfield have any claim to fame – was there anything to commend it apart from having electricity? Two things perhaps in those 20's and early 30's.

The railway station was unique because its lighting didn't come from the new electricity, nor from the little local gas works, but from methane – natural or marsh gas – which bubbled up out of the ground hard under the beginning of the down platform. It had been hoped that this cheap source of power would be exploited commercially to other customers but these dreams never came to anything. As adventurous kids, playing in the nearby woods, we lit the marsh gas after driving a stick into boggy ground, but because of its low calorific value we were never in any danger of being blown skyward.

Then there were chickens. The railway station despatched far more dead hens than living humans. These birds had been helped to their final journey by having enriched food forced down into their crops by a machine called a crammer, invented by Mr Neve the local ironmonger. Whether this was crueller than modern day battery feeding is hard to tell but Heathfield was well known for its poultry production to feed the hungry mouths of Londoners. Heathfield certainly had no supermarkets, and apart from a couple of banks and a Post Office, like all places in those days every business was owned and run by local people. There were already two other electrical businesses in the High Street, resulting in a very definite frosty relationship between them and this new upstart who had started trading in their territory.

So this was the place to which we were despatched. Well, not quite. My father set up his business in Station Road, Heathfield but the family was housed in Cross-in-Hand which is a small piece of ribbon development along the main road to the west of Heathfield and also a part of the Parish of Waldron. You would be correct in thinking that the area seemed to be muddled up, administratively, and even more so when I tell you that the school for Heathfield children was in Cross-in-Hand – in fact right next to the house my parents bought in 1930. The purchase of St Michaels – and there seemed no ecclesiastical attachment for our house to claim a saintly name – came about by the generosity of one, cousin John (a relative of my father) who, with a lady we will meet later, played a major part in providing much that was beneficial for we two boys' material upbringing. John was an albino and a chain smoker; a piano tuner working in London and a wonderful improviser on the piano. Cigarettes and music are strong memories of cousin John, with his white curly hair deeply tinted smoke-yellow at the front.

My memories of life at St Michaels are almost entirely

bound up with the school next door – apart from one instance. Steam traction was widely used in 1930 and the local council had what I would describe as a bull-nosed steam-driven open lorry. It snorted and squirted out hissing steam from orifices all over its metal body. One day it stopped right outside our front gate and a grease-smeared driver got down to make some adjustment to his charge. I was playing in the front garden and upon the appearance of this terrifying machine with its menacing attendant, I ran indoors shouting "Mummy he's come to get me!"

Cross-in-Hand school. A brick single-storey four classroom building in which, term by term, about a 150 five-to-fourteen year olds attended to learn little more than the three R's and religious education, it being a church school. Four rooms, in which sat seven classes according to age and taught by five teachers. We were kept warm in winter by open coal fires and in summer refreshed by water taken from a bucket, with a tin mug, placed in the playground. There was no running water in the school at all, so it was carried in buckets from the headmaster's house that stood guard on the opposite side of the playground from St Michaels. The absence of water, as you may not want to imagine, caused great difficulty in providing hygienic disposal of bodily waste products. An attempt was made by building outside privies – a row of wooden cubicles, without doors, connected by a half open horizontal drain down into which the waste was collected. The system was pumped out at the end of each term!! The inside of the school too had its own peculiar smell. All the floors were bare wooden boards that were washed with carbolic soap and giving the place a kind of damp odour coming from dirty water. Oil lamps provided lighting, when required on late winter afternoons, and all the windows were high so wandering eyes could not drift into the world outside.

I cannot remember the names of all the teachers – and of course they came and went like any other school. There was the headmaster and his wife, Mr and Mrs Marsh, very forceful disciplinarians, held in much awe and not to be tempted by childish behaviour. Then Miss Huckvale – a lovely lady who, because she was unqualified as a teacher, had no pension to enjoy on her retirement after a lifetime of service to her charges. Mr Coutanche came from the Channel Isles and, maybe because of some French blood, he found it a lot easier to make pets of the girls rather than the boys. Others came and went, including Miss Weston who found lodgings with us at St Michaels. It was a great honour to be chosen to stand guard over the cloakroom door as Miss Weston cleaned her teeth after dinner! Then there was Mrs Beckley, a very large lady with beads falling down over her ample bosom, who loved to stand in front of the fire while we all got colder and colder. But they all had one thing in common – they were good at driving home the nuts and bolts of the three R's into our thick heads, so that by the leaving age of fourteen everyone could read and write and do the necessary sums for life in the wide world outside. Only one boy stands out in my memory and that was Billy. His claim to fame was that he came from a very poor family and was constantly exuding a smell resulting from perpetually wet trousers. Girls of course played little or no part in my life – at that time!

1935 saw the silver jubilee of King George V. As part of the celebrations the whole school paraded down the road to St Bartholomew's Church where we gave thanks for his majesty's twenty-five years on the throne. The service concluded by singing the National Anthem, so this public singing had to be well practised beforehand. And this is where the eccentricities of parish boundaries came into play. Because by this time we had moved from St Michaels and out of the Parish of Waldron, where the school and church were, and now living in the Parish of Heathfield, we were not allowed to participate in the pre-service practices. I cannot remember if there was any embargo on my singing capabilities at the service but most certainly I – and half of the rest of the school I suppose – were not given the opportunity to get in tune beforehand!

School life wasn't all sitting upright in pairs at a double desk in a rather dingy classroom – there was a lively and often very robust folk culture in the playground. Games of all sorts were played, depending on the time of year. Marbles, conkers, hoops, spinning tops, yo-yos, each had their turn – their 'season' – as well as ongoing tag and 'lines' where those caught joined hands to form a line to chase and trap those still free. Ash Wednesday wasn't just a day to start remembering the Passion of our Lord and stop eating sweets; it was a day when if you were found without a sprig of ash tucked into your sock, you automatically qualified to be pinched on the bottom by anyone who was correctly equipped. Hence the day was known as Pinch Bum Day!

A day not to be looked forward to was the visit by the school dentist. He set up his torture chamber in one of the cloakrooms and put a large number of children through the pain of extraction. I think drilling wasn't on the menu, as he couldn't transport the necessary equipment. Any little tooth that showed signs of deterioration was OUT. By the end of the day the dentist had collected a bowl of red-smeared teeth that on one occasion he threw over the hedge into our garden! I am not sure if this unpleasantness prompted my parents to think about moving, but after about two years at St Michaels we moved to a new bungalow in Collingwood Rise, Heathfield. Most importantly our new home had a view of the railway station.

And so we came to Mudros – that being the name my father gave to our new home. Those with any geographical knowledge will know that Mudros is the capital of the Greek island of Lemnos in the Aegean Sea. During the First World War, Mudros was the home to a large Royal Naval Air Service airship station, to which the high-ups at the Admiralty had sent my father to fight for his country. When he wasn't holding on to an airship tethering-rope he helped keep Turkish prisoners-of-war from escaping across the sea back to their native land. To prove his contribution to the war effort he brought back to England a bright red Turkish fez that for many years languished in a box in the attic alongside other war memorabilia. Mudros – in Heathfield – was to be the family seat for nearly fifty years.

I suppose for its day, Mudros could be described as a modern building – a bungalow with two bedrooms, a sitting-room, a scullery (later to be converted into a kitchen), a bathroom, a living-room with a large black range which provided heating for the room, hot water and two ovens in which to cook the food. A large plot of land developed into a wonderful source of fresh vegetables and a joy to my mother who had the greenest fingers possible. However, the most intriguing feature, for we two young boys, was the attic which was as big as the whole of the ground floor of the bungalow. Initially this was just an open space under the rafters but soon my father was boxing-in most of it with 'hardboard' (did they have hardboard in those days?) to make another bedroom. The problem with this arrangement was that to get upstairs required a loft ladder to be installed in the tiny hall in the middle of the bungalow. This ladder was always referred to as 'the trap' – and with good reason. Whenever it was down it cut the bungalow into two separate parts so that to get from the back door and scullery to the rest of the rooms one became an extremely agile contortionist to circumnavigate it. For fifty years it was the bane of our existence and many was the hour spent in trying to device another way to reach the attic. The sitting room too had its own characteristics. It was placed between the two bedrooms and the little hall. The front door opened directly into it, so that with four opening windows and the three other doors, and draught-proofing being an inexact technology in those days, its large open brickwork fire had its work cut out to provide any semblance of warmth for the family. Once the fire really got going, gathering around it was a most cosy affair. These occasions of course only occurred on a Sunday or some high day or holiday. My parents rented this newly built dwelling from a local builder for one pound every week.

ıe only other feature to note about Mudros was the from the attic window. I have spent countless hours g out of that window. Looking down the hill I saw the railway goods yard and station and all those lovely steam trains. I knew the timetable of arrivals and departures like the back of my hand. I knew when to expect a tank engine and when an engine with a tender – these latter being much more important and exciting even if they still only pulled the standard three coaches. Then there was counting the number of wagons, which came up from Eastbourne as the morning goods train, and the mystery of shunting as wagons were sorted out and made up into a new train leaving for 'up' stations and ultimately Tunbridge Wells. The greater the number of wagons arriving, compared to those leaving, the better, as that increased the activity of Heathfield's railway goods yard – we really were a place of some importance after all on the Cuckoo Line. I thought this name a bit degrading but it did have some local connection. Heathfield boasted an annual 'cuckoo fair' to coincide with the arrival of that bully-for-nest-space bird. The fair was a 30's version of the modern-day agricultural show. The railway never was a version of anything modern. Beeching had it in his axing eye and by the early 60's it was just a scar on the landscape. Fortunately, by that time I had long left Mudros and didn't have to suffer the constant reminder that my beloved railway was dead and buried. It never was more than a country sideline – a sideshow – compared to those flashy electric trains that I knew sped along the bottom of the South Downs that framed the backcloth of my view. I said 'standing' at the attic window –well actually it was kneeling because under the window stood a large metal trunk that had a specific job in the yearly cycle of childhood life. Not only was it the right height for my small body to see the wonders of Victorian railway engineering, but was storage space for the half-yearly clothes changing ceremony. On May 1st out came the summer clothes and in went the winter's, with a reversal of procedure on October 1st. It is only in recent years that we imagine the weather to be unreliable! In those days, summer and winter were far more dependable, or was it that my mother didn't like unnecessary work?

Mudros was built almost at the top of the south side of the Wealden Ridge, which ran west to east. From the attic window there was open country sloping down and away for some twelve miles until the land was suddenly pulled up by one of nature's most beautiful features – the South Downs. I had a panoramic view of these fabulous hills rolling west to Mount Caburn near Lewes and across the Ouse Gap and past Firle Beacon to the east. The scene was ever changing – not by the seasons, but by the light. The Downs are a series of beautifully folding curves in three dimensions and as the sun moves from east to west so the shade formations change – the most spectacular occurring just as the sun sets in the west. It was like a piece of Vaughan Williams music with ever moving light and shade, or like the poet – I cannot remember which one – comparing the Downs with a whale's undulating back.

Life wasn't all looking out of a window, so we must get back to the real world of young boys – school and playing and getting dirty and getting into trouble.

Moving to Mudros meant that school was now a mile and a half away. The journey was made on foot with my brother but unaccompanied by any adults. We walked all over the place in those days without fear of attack or mugging. There was no 'school run' by mum driving the second car. Long holidays were spent playing in the nearby woods; tracking, these days called orienteering; damming up little streams; lighting the marsh gas and collecting 'food-for-free' from the hedgerows; getting into trouble which, on at least two occasions I can remember, could have ended in disaster. I still have the scar in the middle of my forehead to prove it, as I threw a cricket bat up in the air and then watched it come down! One day my mother observed my brother standing near me in the garden – he had the garden rake poised, with the prongs downwards, above my head. What his intention was, I am not quite sure, but my mother's dilemma was similar to the policeman confronted with a man about to jump off a high building. I survived and so did my brother – but only just!

Talking of survival reminds me of washing days – always on a Monday. There was no washing machine and not even a boiler. It was just hard graft for my mother. The wet clothes and linen, after being passed through the large wooden rollers of a mangle, were all hung out on a long line in the garden. This required meteorological information on wind direction as the things had to be pegged so the wind could blow into them. If after all this labour there was a change in wind direction, then everything had to be re-hung round the other way. When we were home, dinner on Mondays was only thick lentil soup cooked with large whole onions. I say 'only' – but I loved it.

And so my life proceeded peaceably and without serious discomfort or disaster from the age of five to eleven. At school it passed through the hands of Miss Huckvale, Mrs Beckley, Miss Weston, and finally to the somewhat dreaded Mrs Marsh. Later in my story we will discover why I never came under the immediate attention of headmaster Marsh.

I think I was about ten when there occurred a unique event in my infants' school life. It was not the practice in those days for country schools to issue yearly – yet alone termly – school reports; but on one occasion, for some unknown reason, the powers in control decided to issue reports on the progress of the young pupils for whom they were charged to instil knowledge for life. So it was that I found myself carrying a brown envelope for delivery to my parents. Having been told that under no circumstances was I to open the envelope, I, of course, opened it before arriving home. I understood the ordinary sort of remarks about how Bryan was coping with the three R's and various other activities but what really attracted my attention was Mr Marsh's comment at the bottom of the page – "Bryan is erratic in his work." To a ten-year-old 'erratic' was an unknown quantity but it sounded rather posh and important. Not knowing the meaning of this strange word, but being so excited by it, I forgot all about not opening the letter and burst in upon my mother when I got home; "Mummy, mummy, I'm erratic, I'm erratic!" I cannot remember how erratic my mother's hand became at this exclamation but I am sure that I was soon disabused of any ideas of grandeur. However the word erratic passed into our family history, as the title of this book bears witness. In many ways I think the headmaster had a good understanding of some of the fundamental characteristics of his pupils – including me.

At home my parents worked tirelessly to transform the quarter acre building-plot into a garden of some complexity and beauty with vegetables and fruit bushes taking a slight priority over flowers and lawns. My father built a circular pond in the front garden and stocked it with goldfish. A visiting heron caused some excitement until it was discovered it came for fish suppers. It soon had its chips as well. My father set about the task of building up the business of controlling electricity once it had entered people's homes so that heat and light could be had at the flick of a switch.

We enjoyed a happy life with occasional holidays and trips to Eastbourne, Hastings and Tunbridge Wells – and not so happy occasions with Sunday morning visits to hear long sermons and prayers at the Union Church. Sabbath afternoons saw Teddy and me in Sunday school but unfortunately for the church treasurer, a chewing-gum slot machine opposite the church was often the beneficiary of the penny collection provided by our parents. Although my father was part of a family business, money was always very 'tight'. However, a holiday to Herne Bay brought some unsolicited largesse by my father. First he told the garage attendant when he had finished winding the petrol pump handle to 'keep the change' and then he gave half a crown each to my brother and me to spend at Dreamland funfair!

Many breaks were enjoyed at Pevensey Bay. All holidays were self-catering or in rooms where my mother bought the food and the landlady did the cooking. Often holidays at Pevensey were shared with aunts and uncles and cousins. On one occasion we were treated to a grandstand view of the new German Graf Zeppelin (airship) flying in from over the sea. It was another sign of German airpower resurgence – was this sleek cigar-shaped monster already secretly photographing our shores? To a little boy it was just an object of wonder and I asked my father "Is it going all over the World?" – another utterance of mine that has gone into family history. Children have unlikely thoughts coming into their minds. On another Pevensey holiday my brother was under canvas at a nearby Cubs camp and my father, who was often not short of self-confidence, promised the fifty strong pack that he would catch their supper one evening. He had no need of Jesus' command to put the net out on the other side, he just cast his line from the shore and found a waiting shoal of whiting who couldn't resist his bait, enough to fill the empty tummies of all the cubs. I don't know how many baskets of scraps they collected.

When I was about seven years old a lady came on the scene who was to play an important role in our family's life and mine in particular.

Mrs Stanford was an American grandmother of some considerable wealth whose first home was in Philadelphia. Fate would have it that she had decided that each summer the bungalow opposite Mudros would make a pleasant change from the heat of the American eastern seaboard. For four months a year Mrs Stanford became our neighbour and although there was no obvious common ground between her and our ordinariness, she became intensely interested in us, and especially in me. I spent many an hour in Ahrone, as her bungalow was called, often playing cards with her. What exactly was the attraction for me I cannot remember, except perhaps that everything about her and her standard of life was so different from my everyday family life. This relationship was everything that was good. Perhaps it was just that we became her 'summer family' because she missed her

American one. It added much to my life and no doubt contributed to our financially restricted life. Mrs Stanford was a rich lady willing to use her money in a charitable way without any maternal overtones or strings. Her interest in me was particularly evident at a time when I became ill with symptoms not dissimilar from those associated with infantile paralysis or, in today's terminology, polio. To understand just what she did for me and my mother and father at this worrying time, we must first record something else that was to influence my life, in an adverse way, for many years.

For reasons that I never fully understood, my parents put up a barrier between me and everything that was remotely 'medical'. I was not to be privy to anything concerning my health and visits to doctors or dentists or hospitals were shrouded in mystery. I was not to be told any details about the reasons or remedies for illness. The whole subject of the body, its working and putting right when in need of repair, was totally taboo. All this medical silence did two things to me – it made me fearful of the slightest ache or pain and stamped me as being of a nervous disposition. My parents' attitude had nothing to do with leanings towards the Christian Science approach to ill health nor from a lack of love and concern for me. I suspect it came from something in their own upbringing. Visits to doctors and the like became times of mental torture, as can be illustrated by one particular occasion. Eastbourne was our nearest large town and periodically the family set out in our Ford 8 for a trip to the shops and, if we boys behaved ourselves, to an ice cream and a visit to the beach. However, on this particular day we diverted from the usual route into town and parked outside a large forbidding building. We all got out and entered a strange place of long corridors and high ceilings. We had arrived at The Princess Alexandra Hospital – for what reason I had no idea, but I was soon to find out! I was taken into a large room in the middle of which was some sort of machine on overhead rails with cables attached. Under this contraption was a bed and I was told to undress and then lie down on the white sheet. No explanation had been given me in preparation for what a strange man in a white coat was about to do with me. In reality it was nothing more than going for an X-ray! To a little unsuspecting boy of seven it was a nightmare. From that day onwards, till many years later, all men – and women – in white coats had only one thing on their minds and that was to subject me to fear and bodily pain.

This lack of common-sense openness about medical matters and the nature of how the body sometimes goes wrong, was to make every ache or pain in my body a life-threatening event and turned those ordinary people, whose job it was to make me better, into nothing more than torturers. It was many years later in my life that two things happened that finally changed all this.

Back to Mrs Stanford and those suspicions that I might have polio. Presumably the doctor had not yet been called, but our American guardian angel had. Polio was far more prevalent in America and so maybe it was assumed that she knew more of the signs of this crippling disease than my parents. She, without wearing a white coat, pushed, twisted and exercised every joint in my body and declared me free from polio. It all sounds most odd now but as I have said, things medical in our household were always far from normal. No doubt my parents were reassured, but I cannot remember if the diagnosis was confirmed by a man in a white coat. Anyway I didn't have polio.

Mrs Stanford continued to be part of our life every summer until the wartime German U-boat Commanders persuaded her to stay in her American home. She never returned after the war but in her great generosity she gave her bungalow to the Strange family. My parents thought about moving into Ahrone but in the end they sold it and with the proceeds became the proud owners of Mudros.

Until the age of eleven, life went on quietly in Heathfield. My father built up his business of exploiting the virtues of electric light and heat in many homes in the district. He set up an accumulator charging service in the larger premises that he took in the High Street. The reception of wireless waves in those days required a far more cumbersome outfit than today's high-tech package. No transistors or integrated circuits – but they had moved beyond 'cat's whiskers' to power-hungry valves and wireless-sets which required a shelf or corner in the living room all for itself. The power was provided from an acid accumulator and an even bigger high-tension (voltage) dry battery. This non re-chargeable item when dead had to be replaced from The Shop. (The premises of Strange Electrical Co. Ltd became known in the family as The Shop.) This periodic renewal of the wireless power supplies was tedious for the customer but good for trade as it meant people coming into The Shop at regular intervals and seeing many new fangled gadgets on offer as a result of 'the juice'.

Heathfield wasn't a place with a lot of money around – there were a few larger country houses but it was nothing like the Surrey stockbroker belt so the business ticked over without any rapid profits. The Shop was the junior part of Strange Electrical, and much to my mother's annoyance, my father was only the manager at Heathfield and not a director as was my grandfather and my father's brother Frank. Many years later due to dead man's boots he did become the senior director. But in those early years before WW2 things were 'tight' for the family.

In 1937 – or was it 1938? – there was great excitement as my father became the first person in Heathfield to acquire the very latest in advanced technology. Television had arrived! The transmissions from Alexandra Palace just about reached over and down the hill to Mudros but only with the aid of a large H-aerial and a piece of free-standing furniture in which was housed 'the works'. The picture was five inches square – black and white – and only visible after adjusting at least six controls and much shouting of "there it is daddy – don't touch it any more." Viewing, that often looked more like a snowstorm than anything else, was limited to two or three hours each evening.

During this pre-war period my grandparents really only played a minor part in the lives of Teddy and me. Gran Lake and grandpa Kaiser were living some fifty miles away in Beckenham – a distance not lightly undertaken in a Ford 8 – so any visits were by train and these very rarely. They lived in a wonderful Victorian terraced house of four storeys in Aldersmead Road. The very top rooms were approached up a narrow staircase and so they became a kind of secret hide-away for we children. From the back window we had a panoramic view of south-east London with the Crystal Palace spread out across the background. But perhaps the best thing about visits to Beckenham was the regular noise of the electric trains that rumbled away quite close through Kent House Station. This sound summed up the glamour and excitement of London to a small boy more used to the chirp of birds and hum of dragonflies – trains always gave me a special excitement.

Gran Lake's kitchen was full of old-fashioned and very solid cooking and food preparation utensils. It was a bit dark, but it had one thing that staked it out as 'Gran's kitchen' – an old-fashioned wooden coffee-grinder. I think Gran lived on coffee and burnt toast, as these smells were always present – and very nice too. She was a bit of a joker and leg-puller – on one visit our cousin Howard Tanton was also staying. He was about four years older than me and therefore considered himself slightly superior. I suppose he must have been around thirteen – that age when boys still had certain sensitivities about any association with girls. We were sitting at the table – and therefore unable to escape and hide – when Gran announced, "I know whom Howard is going to marry!" Howard's embarrassment and momentary loss of dignity was only restored when Gran concluded, after a certain amount of tittering between my brother and me, "Mrs Tanton!"

My father's parents were somewhat different. They too lived in a terraced house – quite big and Edwardian – in a 'select' part of St Leonards-on-Sea, which was not to be confused with Hastings, any more than Hove was to be coupled with Brighton. The house was solid, dark and foreboding especially for little boys. There seemed to be heavy draped curtains and brown paint everywhere and the living rooms were reached through a long dark passage from the outer front door, then inner door, then to the back of the house. Grandpa was quite jovial and had the Strange ruddy complexion and white hair (I have been white from about the age of thirty-five) but grandma Strange was almost a clone of Queen Victoria in her severity and dress. She was extremely large and so always covered her body with a floor-length black dress. I was certain her body went right down to the floor and that she had no legs because we never saw them. However in her youth (as Miss Weston) she was a champion ice-skater and no doubt in those past days she was something quite different to behold, but I did find it hard to imagine her in a leotard!

Visits to 42 Lower Park Road, St Leonards, were a mixture of pleasure and trepidation. My most vivid memories of these journeys occurred when my father drove a Renault car and we two boys rode in the dickey (rear uncovered seats). This car, with its wacky-shaped radiator, was more exciting than a Ford but it lacked the pulling power of the black metal box and, as there is one particularly steep hill coming up into the village of Dallington, many times we urged the car ever upwards as we got slower and slower. Once we had to get out to lighten the load and walk the last hundred yards up the hill.

Dallington was famous – well, to us locals anyway – for two features that we passed en route to Lower Park Road. First there was the 'sugar-loaf', an isolated cone built of grey stone about fifty feet high in the middle of a field. This edifice belongs in the category of 'folly' as it has no earthly use although it does have a heavenly connection. Many years before, the local squire – it is alleged – bet the vicar of Dallington that he (the squire) could see the church spire from his house. On closer investigation of the line of vision, the squire discovered he had made a mistake. To win his bet he ordered his tenants to replicate the church spire in the appropriate position. History does not reveal if the vicar was suitably impressed and relieved of his money.

The other object of interest was the wayside chapel at Dallington. Above its little door was a big sign that read: 'The Wages of Sin are Death'. I was convinced that this was a warning for the likes of me, visiting rather severe grandmothers!

The best thing about St Leonards was the boating pool in the park right opposite No. 42. We were usually given the 4d for a 'go' in a boat and allowed to do this on our own. On one memorable occasion this excursion ended in tears. No, we didn't tip the boat up or fail to come in when hailed by the attendant. You remember the description of the houses in Lower Park Road – tall, dark, an outer and inner front door, followed by a long passage to the back of the house and into the living room. We disembarked from our 4d trip, crossed the road, passed through the two front doors, along the passage and walked into the living room. We were confronted, not with parents and grandparents, but by unknown people – yes, we had walked into the wrong house! I said it ended in tears – the tears of two very frightened little boys. Still, grandma's teas made up for a lot of childhood anguish because they always included meat, salad, jam AND cake!

Scene 3

Trains and Grammar School

At the age of eleven I sat the scholarship examination for Lewes County Secondary School (although not in the title, this was a grammar school) I failed!

But all was not lost because half the pupils at that sort of school were fee paying and a place was available if an entrance examination could be passed and the headmaster liked the look of you. With these hurdles cleared, it was just a case of finding the money. Teddy had already been through all this and with the help of father's piano-tuning albino cousin was now a grammar school boy at Lewes. Mrs Stanford, our American neighbour, offered to be my provider and so at the age of eleven I escaped the future clutches of Mr Marsh and fell into the hands of headmaster Bradshaw. As a very young and new boy at grammar school, I am not sure who awed me most, Marsh or Bradshaw.

To understand the relationship between Bradshaw (known by everyone – including himself no doubt – as The Old Man) and myself, we have to go back several years to that formative time when I became fearful of all things medical and my state of health. In my parents understanding I was always classified as a 'nervy child'. This information was offered to Bradshaw, by my parents, at my interview, to ensure that I was not subjected to any physical chastisement. In other words, please don't cane our little boy!

No doubt Bradshaw noted these protestations and when the time came several terms later to mete out punishment he had a cunning method to circumvent my parents demands – a method specially selected for me.

But first to relate more of my translation from old-

ıuntry infants to modern grammar. For me the
ıent and expectation wasn't the fitting out with
; and school blazer; school cap and rugby boots;
vallet for money. The attraction was the twenty-
n journey from Heathfield to Lewes. Every day I would travel on my beloved trains – steam to Polegate and then a change into one of those flashy electric trains that I knew sped across the scene so familiar to me from the attic window. Within a short time I had memorised every signal and point and goods yard layout at all the stations. I knew where to expect waiting trains and shunting trains. I learnt the techniques of passing the staff (like a large metal baton), employed between station signalmen and the engine-drivers, to ensure that on our single track railway opposite running trains waited at stations and did not find themselves in a hissing confrontation down the line or even worse in a mighty crash. I knew the location of every milepost and the posts in between. I could have run the railway myself. I knew when to expect the train to slow down because of a rising gradient and there were some pretty steep stretches as the line climbed up to the top of the Weald. Gathering all this information necessitated much leaning out of windows and regularly collecting smuts in my eyes from the puffing funnel of the engine.

One particular excitement often occurred at Horam (or Horeham Road as it was sometime known). Express Dairies had a depot at Horam from which railway milk-tankers carried large quantities of milk to help make cockney cuppers. Our evening train was backed down into a siding and three or four milk-tankers coupled on to the rear carriage. This of course greatly increased the load the engine – usually a small tank engine – had to pull up the 1in 50 gradient starting immediately outside the exit from the station. When the milk-tankers had been coupled on, our train was then shunted down the station approach section of line to then gather speed and so take a 'running jump' up the gradient towards Heathfield. The final excitement was to see if the train would 'make the grade'. (I wonder if this is where the saying comes from)? More than once it didn't – we came to a grinding halt with slipping wheels and great clouds of black smoke and so had to back down the hill and start all over again. I don't think Dr Beeching would have been impressed, and many years later he did close the line, but for me it was great fun – even if we were late home for tea.

The education authority in its wisdom provided reserved compartments for we school children. Each morning and evening we ran up and down the platform to find the reserved-labelled compartment. I was never sure if this arrangement was to protect the travelling public from noisy and uncouth children or to protect us from marauding adults. Whichever way, there was the business of finding the reserved notice, stuck on the inside of the carriage, and transferring it, if possible, to one of those compartments that included a lavatory. Now this wasn't a precaution on our part against the results of drinking too much tea or being overdosed with liquid paraffin oil – it was so we could participate in the favourite pass-time of pushing the end of the toilet roll down the pan, flushing the cistern, and seeing it stream out behind the train along the line! The only mitigating feature of this disgraceful activity was that it didn't work while the train was standing in the station!

Reserved carriages also provided private facilities for older boys to inflict various tortures on younger bodies. Armed with a pocket knife (every self-respecting boy legally carried such a weapon in those days) the window-opening leather straps could be cut and made available for chastising the weaker members of school. The most excruciating pain and discomfort could be administered to a junior by sitting on the victim's lap and then putting ones shoes on the edge of the opposite seat. By forcing your legs increasingly against the seat, the little boy became compressed against the back of the carriage until his breathing was all but stopped. I can tell you; those school train journeys were pretty lively times! Exciting as they were, we had to face up to arriving at school before the nine o'clock bell and start the serious business of learning for life.

Schooldays are the happiest of our lives? Well, for me, they weren't really unhappy but I wasn't over enthusiastic about academic life. Parts were bearable such as geography, woodwork and games. Some 'subject-liking' was dependent on the master who was charged with driving the information into our brains. Mr Auld, whose unenviable task was to teach me French, frightened me beyond belief. He was a little man and he would tightly wrap his gown round himself and, sitting hunched up on his stool, survey the assembled class and say "Je marque mon homme." This would be followed by a long pregnant pause and more glaring round the boys. The tension would heighten and he would ultimately say "Mon homme est marqué" – and the chosen name would then be announced – "Monsieur E'trange." He would then demand what was required in the way of translation. I failed French School Certificate.

Woodwork was a different matter altogether. I liked Mr Larwood – he was a brilliant craftsman and teacher, having a wonderful Sussex accent, slow speaking and very 'broad'. Known by everyone as Gluey, one day a young boy burst into the woodwork room and shouted "where's Gluey?" Hidden behind the open door came the reply "ere I am!" I managed a credit for woodwork in the School Cert. All forms of games were a great pleasure to me and I think it was cross-country that I looked forward to most of all. Behind the school were miles of flat boggy land criss-crossed with dykes and ditches. I am not by nature a solitary type of person but it was by one's own individual effort that you came in first or last. The only problem with school games was the trains! Games, as a subject, was only allocated the last period of the day so full-time came by playing into after-school hours. As my train home left at 4.29pm, games for me were cut short, and other passengers on the station would see a mud besmirched schoolboy dive into the nearest compartment – reserved or unreserved.

Bradshaw – the Old Man – taught us history in our first year. No doubt this was to make sure he personally got the measure of every boy at the start of their time at his school. I cannot remember what breakage of school rules resulted in my being paraded before Bradshaw in his study, but I do remember what the punishment was. Remembering my parents' request that I should not be caned – nervous disposition and all that – demanded something else to chasten this wayward pupil. At the front of the school was a large stretch of lawn that often produced an exceedingly good crop of yellow dandelions. My punishment was to pick these brightly coloured flowers. This no doubt saved grass mowing petrol and gardener's time but to me it was far more painful than 'six of the best' – not only did it save money but provided entertainment for a large number of boys! It only happened once – as I said, the Old Man made sure he got the measure of all his boys. Notwithstanding – or maybe because of – his general strict discipline, he reigned over a grammar school that turned out some of the finest young citizens that the education system of the time would produce. His boys were soon to take their part, with honour, in the Second World War. Many a time I have seen him walking up and down the playing field in deep conversation with a uniformed Old Boy. After the war Bradshaw raised enough money to build a school chapel in memory of dozens of boys who never returned to walk those playing fields of England.

Scene 4

War over Sussex

The broadcast words of Neville Chamberlain on September 3rd 1939 have probably been repeated more times than any others – we were at war with Germany. They are almost mandatory for any programme about the Second World War. To me, on that Sunday morning, they sounded like trouble but to my mother and father, who only twenty years before had breathed a sigh of relief at the end the First World War, they must have filled them with total despair. My father, the year before, had volunteered to serve as an Air Raid Warden and there is a family photograph of him hanging up a row of cleansed gas masks to dry on the garden line. We had already heard the local air raid siren sounding, in practice, but it was not till September 3rd that it produced that sinking feeling deep in the stomach every time it wailed up and down to warn us that our end might be nigh.

There had been other local signs of the impending conflict – on our journeys to Hastings we had seen mystifying new masts appearing out of the flats of Pevensey Marshes. There were strange and exciting stories about death-rays and car engines suddenly cutting out and warnings not to stop and stare. These tall latticed structures rising out of the land were in fact the pre-war brainchild of Robert Watson-Watt – the technical and political driving power that produced the Chain Home radar system which saved England, along with a few young pilots, from being bombed out of existence. Little did I know that later in life I would become familiar with the inventions of Watson-Watt. Those masts, with the red-bricked Heathfield Union Church, perhaps could be described as icons pointing the way to my future working life. How often can unrelated objects – or events – unknowingly become an intimate part of later life?

In the above two paragraphs I have used three phrases which perhaps sum up what the war meant to me. 'That sinking feeling'; 'strange and exciting'; 'not to stop and stare'. My kaleidoscope of events in those war years largely fit into those three slots. There is no doubt that for the likes of myself – young and living in the country – the effect of those times and the experiences we went through, was barely coloured by all the horrors of war. As the war progressed the whole tenor of the community life in Heathfield quickened with the arrival of hundreds of soldiers. Canteens were opened in church halls; dances were organised; families were encouraged to befriend individual soldiers and there was a buzz of activity everywhere.

The first few months of the war were rightly described as the Phoney War. Nothing much happened – perhaps if it were all to be like this, then there wouldn't be too much of 'that sinking feeling'. The excitement was limited to the arrival of soldiers in the district and the rumble of khaki-coloured convoys of assorted vehicles with more soldiers driving along the High Street. Where were they going – where had they come from? What hidden hand had ordered them to pass through Heathfield? The nearest active military establishment to Mudros was in a field just over the other side of the Wealden Ridge. It was a searchlight accompanied by a dozen or so soldiers. The 'not to stand and stare' bit applied here but didn't prevent we boys from spying through holes in the hedge and trying to hear the orders of a soldier with two stripes on his uniform that resulted in the searchlight turning heavenwards. It wasn't till darkness fell that we saw the results of our unauthorised collection of information, as the beam searched for the non-existent enemy planes.

From spring 1940 onwards things were to change and I was to witness one of the most desperate, but to me exciting, battles of modern times – the Battle of Britain. Meanwhile life was radically changing before that crucial time. It was a life that must have been so hard and bewildering for countless numbers of children. No doubt for soldiers posted to foreign parts it wasn't a very happy time either, but for young souls to be suddenly uprooted from home and family must have seemed like the end of the world. Yet this was the lot of the evacuees.

Heathfield had its share of these waif-like young humans from London. They arrived at the station with their pathetic looking cases and every one adorned with a brown cardboard box slung around their neck in which was the ever-present nasty rubber smelling gas mask. A long snake of these bewildered children shuffled to St Richard's church hall where their destiny would to be decided.

My mother was a volunteer evacuation official and had the task of allocating the new arrivals to appropriate homes in the district. We had one, Alan Letts, whom my mother had selected to be our evacuee. He was younger than my brother and me and so on the first evening with us his bedtime came earlier than ours, but he was to be treated just like one of the family. He got his cup of cocoa and an invitation to make a selection from the biscuit barrel before our turn came. Unfortunately my mother hadn't checked the background of Alan and how his family made a living. His father was a London East-End grocer and rationing for Alan hadn't become a reality. This piece of vital missing information resulted in the biscuit barrel being empty when later my brother and I came to get our last bite before bed! It was a very bad start for we brothers but, I hope, our displeasure wasn't the reason for soon driving little Alan back to the bosom of his London home. Like many other evacuees, the rigours of country life were too much for him – the prospect of death by bombs was to be preferred to death by separation and boredom. We never heard if Alan survived the war.

In the spring of 1940 we increased our living accommodation although it would not pass the most rudimentary modern building regulations. It was small, dark and damp. Inside were wooden slatted seats against three walls and in the months and years to come was to be our shelter from marauding enemy bombers on many a long night and at times of extreme daylight danger. 'The Shelter' was made of arched corrugated iron sheets sunk into a hole that we all helped to dig in the garden and then covered with a thick layer of the excavated soil. A wooden floor with an earth wall in front of the entrance and door completed the structure. Although we weren't any part of a military or industrial target, it was a wearying and nerve-racking experience to sit night after night in The Shelter listening to a single German bomber roaming around in the sky above us. But thousands of these Anderson shelters did just as was claimed for them – they withstood everything except a direct hit and saved countless lives. Ours remained for many post-war years and became my father's homemade wine cellar as well as a flower-covered garden feature.

The spectre of evacuation was to rear its head in a more dramatic way for Lewes County Secondary School than that of the arrival of a grocer's son to one family. Within a few weeks of Chamberlain's fateful words, several hundred boys descended on my school from Tooting Bec in South London. It must have been a nightmare for Bradshaw but somehow everything was slotted into a new timetable and we didn't suffer much loss of schooling. At the same time huge circular concrete drains and thousands of bricks were delivered to the school that workmen soon turned into air raid shelters. Air raids, practice and reality, with the whole school decamping into the shelters, were times which raised the pulse rate and the chance of missing a French test!

I am not sure when the decision was taken, probably after a raid by a low flying Messerschmitt 109 (a nasty little German fighter-bomber with a swastika on its tail) on a train, that it would be safer to travel to school by bus. You can imagine how this took me. Abandon the train for a bus! The war was beginning to have a serious effect on me at last. Buses provide no privacy in which to practice schoolboy pranks or administer pain to smaller boys. There was no glamour in a smelly old bus and they went so slowly. The only good thing to say about the arrangement was that the bus left Lewes twenty minutes later than the train which meant extra time playing games or getting muddy running cross-country.

As 1939 went into 1940, so the number of troops around us increased. Big country houses and estates became barracks and headquarters and parks for large numbers of a variety of military vehicles. Sometime early in the war, one of these soldiers was my uncle Eric, my mother's younger brother. He was a Royal Engineers officer and he often visited Mudros to continue his courtship with Phyllis, who was lodging with us, and who later became my aunt. On one occasion he had a forty-eight hour leave pass and so could stay overnight. This presented my mother with a problem, there being only one spare bedroom for them both. I am not sure if her solution to the situation was a reflection of a limited knowledge of contraception or was to satisfy her need to uphold a moralistic stance, but she placed a large long bolster down the middle of the bed and left the couple to get on with it – or not get on with it, if you see what I mean!

The evacuation from Dunkirk through the calm seas of the English Channel brought even more activity. The countryside I knew so well and through which we passed on visits to Eastbourne, Hastings, Pevensey and St Leonards now became the potential battleground on which would be fought a desperate battle between a bedraggled English army and the might of Germany. So the coastal resorts had become restricted areas and we were banned from visiting them. Apart from an army with very little surviving equipment there was the Local Defence Volunteer force consisting of long-retired army officers delighting to be in uniform again and young men masquerading as soldiers but only armed with pikes or sometimes wooden rifles. Across open ground appeared metal poles, with wire strung between them, to snare and crash German gliders. Looking carefully across some field, or in the curve of a riverbank, or on the edge of a wood, small squat concrete structures could be identified. They had no windows – just narrow horizontal slits – just large enough through which to point a machine gun. These were the pillboxes that the military wizards thought would halt, or at least slow down, the impending German onslaught. At the time we all thought that 'Dunkirk' was an act of divine intervention with the calm water – all said and done, God had on another notable occasion manipulated the waters in favour of the Goodies! A greater miracle surely was the decision of Hitler not to invade our green and pleasant land and put to the test those little concrete boxes.

However, it wasn't what was happening on the ground that attracted our greatest attention, but what was going on in the air above us. It was those hot sun-drenched days of early summer through to late September 1940 that brought the greatest excitement – and danger – to our lives up to then and probably ever since. We were to witness from a grandstand seat The Battle of Britain. Heathfield wasn't in the coastal front line of aerial defence, nor was it a prime target, but it was underneath the path of the Luftwaffe as it flew and fought its way to London and other targets of military and industrial importance. I am glad to say we were largely ignored by the bomb-aimers except when, in desperation to escape our hurricanes and spitfires, they dumped their lethal loads at random. Random for us on one occasion almost meant Mudros. We were in the garden watching a German bomber flying high towards us, when it was suddenly pursued and attacked by an RAF fighter. We watched, literally spellbound, as a black object rapidly became larger and larger, coming nearer and nearer. It was a bomb that looked increasingly destined for our address and as we finally realised what was about to happen we all dived into The Shelter and landed in a heap on top of each other. Fortunately it fell short of Mudros into the front garden four doors away. Nobody was hurt but it was a narrow escape, that being the way of things in life, especially during a war.

It has always been a bit of a mystery to me, why we

never saw white vapour trails before the Battle of Britain. Perhaps the British hurricanes and spitfires, although capable of flying high enough to produce trails, didn't fly that high until the German Junkers and Heinkels forced them up to greater heights – civilian planes never flew high or fast enough. Anyway these thin fluffy white lines in the sky were a wonder to behold. I still find today's vapour trails, against a brilliant blue sky, a wonder to behold. In 1940, however, there was the added attraction as the trails made beautiful circles; widening; becoming tighter; making patterns across the blue sky. There wasn't just one trail but several interweaving and accompanied by the stutter of machine gun fire. Up there a dogfight was taking place. Young men were pitting their flying skills against other young men with the deadly intention of killing each other. Well, I am not quite sure about 'killing each other'. One side – the Germans – were intent on pressing home their attack on English targets; on the other side the Allies (mainly English) were intent on stopping the Germans from reaching their targets. That is not quite the same as killing for the sake of killing. There had been a strange kind of camaraderie between Hun and British pilots during the days over the trenches in the First World War, when adversaries could almost literally see the colour of each other's eyes. Enclosed cockpits and greater flying speeds stopped that sort of close encounter, but even so there was still a largely gentlemanly way of behaving when fighting each other in the air. Dogfights, high up in a cloudless sky, became a daily spectacle for us; which ones were 'ours?' which ones were 'theirs?' At twenty thousand feet it wasn't possible to distinguish between a German swastika and the RAF roundel and the skills of aircraft recognition became ineffective. Amidst the chatter of gunfire would appear black smoke streaming out from a tiny dot in the sky. "He's got him – he's got him", we would shout but not always knowing if 'him' was friend or foe. The noise of battle would ebb and flow; a plane would spiral down spewing out black smoke; the firing would stop; the whine of aircraft engines fade away; there would be absolute silence; there would appear against the blue sky the white canopy of a parachute drifting down to earth. Perhaps we weren't as gallant as some of those pilots as we hoped and prayed it would be 'one of ours'. We never had the excitement of a parachuting pilot landing near us but as my father had transferred from Air Raid Precaution (ARP) duties to the Special Constabulary he was often called out to collect descending aircrew of both sides.

His duties included standing guard over crashed aircraft. Guards were strictly forbidden to tamper with the wreckage – let alone remove any small part for a souvenir. My father was a most law-abiding person, generally speaking, but when no harm was intended he didn't allow the law to make a total ass of him! Crashed aircraft engines were a good source of chunks of aluminium from which could be turned, on a lathe, some most attractive souvenirs for use as ashtrays. His speciality was a small lighthouse and bowl. They became dotted round most of our relations sitting rooms. His mechanical skills had far more impact than just discreetly breaking the law – early in the war he purchased a rusty old metal-turning lathe for one pound. This was soon resurrected into a working piece of machinery and became the start of a most enterprising project. As the war got into its stride, The Shop had less and less products to sell and people had more pressing problems than thinking about improving their homes with extra 'electrics' and mains electricity was fast replacing the old accumulators and high tension batteries for the wireless set.

My father had an inbuilt natural bent for all things mechanical and so he set up a machine shop in the storeroom at The Shop and started to produce parts as a sub-contractor to an aircraft factory. His electrical staff became machinist and together they turned out thousands of high-precision components for Spitfires. A small showcase of these parts still exists in the home of Mark Strange's rectory in Elgin. Perhaps this effort salved his conscience about removing bits of engines lying across the English countryside. It also saved Strange Electrical Co Ltd from going bust and left them in a strong position to restart domestic trading when the war came to its end. As a tailpiece to his wartime effort, the lathe he bought for a pound, and which helped him put the food into our mouths, he sold for twenty pounds.

By the autumn of 1940 the war in the air changed from an exciting spectacle to one of worry and restless nights. For us, under a kind of aerial no-mans-land, we suffered from long periods of air raid warnings with German bombers passing up and down the country, some on route and then returning from London, and others that just circled around keeping everyone in a state of fear of sudden death. They would come and go and then return again.

This nightly drama was heightened by what was called The Blackout. No lights of any sort or intensity were allowed to escape from any window or door. All street lighting was switched off for the duration of the war. The only concession to this watertight exclusion of light was that car headlights were fitted with a grill that defused the beam and so (supposedly) became invisible to those German bombers. Enemy agents were a constant concern of the local constabulary and many is the story of a light, caused by a draught intermittently blowing open a curtain, being interpreted as someone signalling to the Germans! Rumours and strange happening were all part of wartime life and helped to lighten a dark uncertain existence.

The bombers made a distinctive throbbing noise, easily identified by their twin unsynchronised engines. Long nights sleeping cramped and apprehensive in The Shelter wasn't good for morale and life became a grim and endless struggle. That struggle also centred in the kitchen and on The Ration Book.

I cannot remember the exact quantities of all the basic rationed provisions, but if I were to say two ounces of butter; two ounces of margarine; four ounces of sugar; two ounces of bacon; 1/2d (6p) of meat; two ounces of cheese; one egg;

these are the sort of quantities each person received each week. We were still in the era of food being individually weighed and wrapped by a man or lady behind the counter wearing a white apron. These tiny amounts were wrapped in grease proof paper by a grocer who was being closely watched to make sure the full ration was given. As the war progressed, so all foods came to be rationed. A large group of the non-basic items were rationed by a points system. Each person was allocated so many points each week and we could choose, for example, whether we had a tin of fruit or sardines. Everything was in short supply – some products, like bananas, almost disappeared. I was to learn much later from my wife, who worked in a hospital, that special appeals were made for bananas, as they were useful in the treatment of nephritis in children.

No wonder large areas of our school playing fields were dug up and the Dig for Victory campaign became a vital activity. Some class-time was allocated each week to actual gardening to help the school dining-room supply a dinner each day. My mother's green fingers really came into their own and, with her cooking skills and culinary imagination, greatly helped to keep the family fed and healthy. Most of the food was far from Cordon Bleu and even my mother's camouflage strategies failed to disguise some of the origins of the dishes that appeared at the table. Whatever she did, nothing could remove or hide the fishy taste of whale meat served up as a delicious meat casserole. It was disgusting! One concoction of hers, however, I did enjoy mash boiled potatoes (no milk or butter or margarine) and mix with one Oxo-cube and spread (thinly) on a slice (thick) of bread; this made a good supper! And I came to realise that our family's rations were not evenly distributed amongst its members – like most mums she often 'did' with a cup of tea – "I'm not hungry" – to ensure we others had enough nourishment. Recent medical research has concluded that the wartime rations were not all bad news. We were fitter and leaner than many present-day couch potatoes. Even so, I was always pleased when my father came home with a few extra sweets from his friendly manager at the Co-op. The black market was very big business for the unscrupulous, but everyone was just that much happier for a little under-the-counter extra.

Clothes too were rationed, but I don't remember this being too much of a hardship for the family. We weren't used to a lot of new clothes – a hole appearing in a pair of trousers or a vest was no reason to visit the outfitters shop – mend-and-make-do had long been a family slogan.

By the age of sixteen – the war had been going for three years –I began to have ideas about what work I would like to do. Train driving had had its turn but was not a serious contender. I was developing an interest in maps and how they were produced, no doubt encouraged by my favourite role model, surveyor and civil engineer, Uncle Eric of bed bolster fame.

In spring 1942 I sat the School Certificate examination that I managed to pass with a smattering of credits but not with the intention of staying on into the sixth form to study for the Higher School Certificate, let alone going to university. I suppose the war confused any long-term thinking about the future and there was no family tradition or history of graduation, apart from Uncle Eric who received a BSc from London University.

I did take 'a year out' between finishing my education and starting work. Well it wasn't a year but exactly ten days! Leaving school at the end of July, I set out with a classmate on a cycling holiday around the Home Counties. We sampled the delights of staying at Youth Hostels that were popular in those days. Only those who arrived by foot or cycle were offered shelter and food at a most reasonable charge and in exchange for an hour's housework. Being trained to contribute to the daily chores at home, ("do the washing up before you can go out to play") this part of the payment did little to detract from the style of accommodation on offer. However, as my holiday progressed I became desperately home sick and was glad when the adventure was over.

Perhaps leaving school, cycling off into the blue, and the impending return to face the new world of work was rather a lot for a lad of sixteen to cope with. I said 'home sick', but I am not sure if that is the right description of how I felt. It was more a sense of deep unease, not being able to cope with new and unknown places, wanting to get back to familiar surroundings and routine. No doubt today research doctors would annex my feelings to some syndrome or other. Perhaps it was an offshoot of my fear of the medical world. Whatever it was, its intensity and effect was something all embracing – it drove oneself into oneself and that could be quite disturbing. Unfortunately this malaise was to dog me, intermittently, for many years – not that every new situation affected me in this way and within a few days of an attack, when I returned to normal routine, everything would be fine again. There must have been some trigger that set it off but I have never been able to pin down what it might be.

Wage earning began for me in August 1942, through my employment in Lewes by the Land Drainage Department of the East Sussex War Agricultural Committee. The task of the department was to build up food production for the beleaguered nation by increasing the yield of the land. With two other boys from my form at school, we were interviewed and all offered jobs as junior draughtsmen, each for the grand pay packet of one pound every week. Draughtsman, even junior, was rather an exalted description of our work – in truth much of the time we were only tracers of Ordinance Survey maps. We produced large-scale copy maps of farmland, used by the department's surveyors, to help plan land drainage schemes. Compared to present-day printers and copiers, our method of producing multiple copies of our work was primitive in the extreme. The maps, drawn on tracing linen, were placed in a folder, with a thin perspex front, on top of a sheet of photographic paper. The folder was then taken to a window and exposed to the light for a period of time, after which the paper was removed and dipped in a developing solution. The financial outlay for this piece of technology must have been almost nil, so the results depended on the skill of the junior draughtsman to estimate the light intensity of the sky outside!

We so-called draughtsmen were supervised by a most extraordinary man by the name of Smith. Smithy (as known behind his back) was a cross between a country squire and Colonel Blimp. He always wore immaculate brown riding breeches and boots; had an equally immaculate waxed moustache; had a ramrod back and chain-smoked. He had a deep educated voice. He wasn't, however, an unkind or over strict disciplinarian – in fact I came to have great respect for him – but then he made life for me more pleasurable than just sitting in the office tracing other people's work. When farmers had completed their drainage schemes, the government handed out a fifty per cent grant and it was part of Smithy's job to measure up the work before payment. I became his assistant in this task – a chain or tape measure requiring two people to manipulate. In the eighteen months that I worked for the 'War-Ag', I think I visited nearly every farm in East Sussex and walked over some of those restricted areas that the military were so keen to keep hidden from public view.

The time in the second floor drawing-office nearly came to a premature end when a Messerschmitt 109 fighter-bomber flew level past our window. Unbeknown to us, just before its appearance, he had released a bomb that exploded a few yards from the corner of our building. We all escaped unharmed but it was far too close for comfort.

My classification of draughtsman at the time seemed 'over the top' but four years later was to have a most unusual, but welcome, repercussion.

With the war seemingly set to go on for some time, most boys of my age had other things on their minds other than work and I don't just mean girls! Which of the three Armed Services would offer the most excitement and glamour – the Army or Navy or Air Force – when called up at the age of eighteen or even a little earlier? To help ensure you got into what you wanted required volunteering and not waiting to be conscripted. Joining the Air Training Corps also helped my chances of becoming an airman, as my first choice was the Royal Air Force. Airmen were kitted out with collars and ties and blue was far more attractive (sexy in today's parlance but never in those days) than army khaki or navy bell-bottoms. Unless one aspired to becoming aircrew, the chances of getting shot at were reckoned to be less in the RAF than the other two services. My brother was already a member of the ATC with the exalted rank of corporal but it wasn't he who had the most influence on my training. Our flight commander was about the least military looking person you could imagine –he found it hard even to stand really upright – but the warrant officer was something different. Being a past member of a Scottish Highland Regiment, he had all the qualities of a traditional regimental sergeant-major. Warrant-officer Borne had two great abilities – he could change the doziest recruit into a heal-clicking guardsman before you could say 'quick march'. It was a mentally and somewhat physically hard process but he turned out a very fine flight of cadets. His other outstanding feature was his ability to fart louder and more often than a foghorn in winter. If there is a Guinness Book of Records section for this activity, I am sure his name would be included!

Two years of marching and parading; grappling with the navigational calculations of airspeed and groundspeed and wind direction; visits to RAF stations and flights in warplanes; aircraft recognition; all these and more, prepared me for call-up. Before my eighteenth birthday I presented myself to the recruiting officer in Brighton and after being told to drop my trousers in front of a medical officer and cough I was duly signed up as a volunteer reservist. I was given a number – 3206018 – a number, which unbeknown to me at the time, was to decide the nature of my wartime service.

At this point in the war, there was an enormous demand for coal to sustain the vast industrial output of munitions, but not enough miners to satisfy this demand, let alone for the family grate. The Minister of Labour and National Service at that time was Ernest Bevin. Not only was he a member of Churchill's government but also a Welsh Baptist lay-preacher and therefore no doubt he knew his Bible better than most. Perhaps he had recently read Acts chapter 1 verse 26, when considering how to increase the number of men at the coalface. Bevin, like the Apostles, decided to solve a problem by means of a lottery. Each month a number from 1 to 0 was chosen, at random, and if your service number ended with it, then you went down the mines and not into your chosen part of the Armed Services. Hence for me the number 8 became very important! Fortunately and by sheer good luck I never drew the short straw. For those who did, they became known as Bevin Boys and experienced a very unpleasant way to serve their country. There was nothing glamorous about getting filthy and tired down a coal mine – and you didn't even get a uniform with which to impress the girls.

So, by my eighteenth birthday, England considered I was grown up enough to serve my country in the Royal Air Force. My father had already played his part in bringing me to this state of adulthood and readiness. He was a smoker, like nearly everyone else, so when I was discovered puffing a Woodbine behind the garden shed he suggested that a pipe might be more manly – advice which I heeded. I am not sure how manly this really made a fresh looking sixteen year old appear, as I had barely started to shave. Removing my facial hair also came under my father's attention. He, being a life-long user of the cut-throat variety of razor, felt I should become the same. Manliness to my father was important although in no way could you describe him as macho. My preparation for the evil world outside also included his version of sex education. His total instruction could be summed up in about one sentence; if you 'play with yourself' (his words not mine) you will grow hair on the palms of your hands and you will go blind and stop growing! Fortunately relationships and activities with girls was a constant subject of exploration amongst my school friends. When he heard me use a four letter swear word, his reaction was to tell me that he would rather cut off his right hand than tell me what it meant!! His instruction must have had a deep impression on me, as today I can quite plainly remember his words.

One girl in particular was playing a part in my life at this time. Compared with today's 'relationships' our time together could be described as nothing more than platonic and like many young romances was to end in tears but with only very temporary broken hearts. On the last night before leaving to join up, I remember gently laying the palm of my hand on the outside of the front of her blouse for the first time. What next!

Scene 5

War and Peace in the Royal Air Force

February 22nd and February 23rd 1944 must have been two terrible days for my mother and father. The 22nd was my eighteenth birthday and the day I left home to join the RAF. The 23rd had no yearly significance but in 1944 it was the day my brother was called-up, also to join the RAF. Can you imagine how our parents must have felt? I cannot remember to where Teddy was ordered to report, but it was to an RAF station for trainee aircrew. I had no inclination to fly and so I was to train as an aircraft armourer. Why an armourer I cannot remember – maybe when I first volunteered there was a shortage of that trade but all I cared about then was to become a 'boy in blue'. Events were to turn out differently and so change a great chunk of my life – as you will find out later in this book.

What I do remember, however, is the place to which I reported. There must be tens of thousands of ex-RAF personnel for whom the word Padgate conjures up the most dire memories. Everyone of them, I am sure, would agree that RAF Padgate was the dreariest and least inviting place in the World. In February it had the added disadvantages of being very wet, cold and often shrouded in fog. The camp was a sprawling mass of wooden huts built to house the likes of me training for war. It was situated near Warrington, Lancashire, and suffered all the traditional characteristic of 'Manchester' weather. Life at Padgate was to last for eight weeks – eight weeks of square bashing; of being shouted at by sadistic jumped-up non-commissioned officers; of food that was almost uneatable at times; of being afraid to report sick for fear of loosing time and so extending the length of training.

Bryan Strange in wartime airman's uniform. Padgate 1944

The huts were the normal RAF version – each holding about thirty beds and two of the ubiquitous round iron solid fuel stoves. Those whose beds were next to these sources of heat kept the warmest, but had to suffer the inconvenience of the bodies of sundry airman using their 'pit' (RAF slang for bed) as a fireside chair. The bedding consisted of three 'biscuits' – thin hard mattress in three parts – a sausage shaped pillow and three dark-coloured blankets. There was no issue of bed linen and because the blankets had to be kept folded during daytime, the huts didn't exactly smell of roses. The prime use of this bedding wasn't to keep out the night cold from our weary bodies but to act as material with which to test our ability to keep things immaculately in order and within RAF regulations. It had to be folded exactly and precisely to a pre-ordained shape each morning for inspection by an NCO who was specially trained to observe the smallest of irregularities. One evening each week was designated 'bull night'. Bull was short for 'bull shit' – an RAF term for any activity that was not strictly utilitarian by normal human standards – and one of its manifestations was the production of a hut that gleamed all over, especially the floors. This condition was achieved by hours of cleaning and polishing. Each airman was responsible for his own bed area but the inspection the next morning resulted in the collective result of the whole hut passing or failing. This, of course, was a ploy to ensure everyone pulled their weight and engendered that most important commodity, esprit de corps. It also produced a certain amount of abuse and violence towards the less energetic members of the hut if the cleaning wasn't acceptable to the inspecting officer! The weekly cleaning of our home was coupled to an inspection of our issued kit. Now it wasn't good enough for the 'powers to be' to observe and count all the bits and pieces – knife, fork and spoon (irons they were called) and all our clothing ('RAF issue, airman, for the use of') – that wasn't what it was all about. Kit inspections were further exercises in precision – everything had to be laid out on your bed in an exact pattern. Failure in this activity officially went against the whole hut but afterwards unofficially against sloppy individuals.

Food preparation and eating facilities for the recruits all took place in the cookhouse, which was the airman's version of the more elite sounding officers' mess. The two places bore little similarity, although we all ate our food for free. Officer messes were places controlled by etiquette and expected good manners – cookhouses by the law of the jungle; those at the front of the queue got the best of the pickings. One of the cook's specialities was 'reconstituted egg'. I am not certain how much dried egg was included in the basic mix but what was slopped out on to our plates was a yellow rubbery substance that required a knife to cut. It was universally renamed 'prostitute egg'. Another regular evening meal was a lump of cheese with bread and a few slices of beetroot. After an exhausting day of square-bashing, often in wet and cold weather, this repast didn't exactly satisfy an airman's empty stomach. No wonder the NAAFI canteen did a roaring trade. The only other noteworthy item on the menu was the tea. This was always strong in taste but had an added ingredient that made our sex-drive weak! Drinking this beverage was a precaution, with regular FFI (Free From Infection) inspections of our genitals, as part of the system to ensure we didn't ravage the local girls nor spread or contract any unseemly desease.

After three weeks training we were deemed smart enough to be let out of camp and sample the local delights, which in wartime Warrington were somewhat limited.

My description of life at Padgate may have given an impression of unadulterated misery, but in fact in a strange sort of way, I thoroughly enjoyed those eight weeks. The instructions of WO Bourne (ATC) in the art of parade ground drill stood me in good stead and I became the squadron right marker. I had the honour of marching, solo, on to the parade ground after which all the other recruits lined up on me. After the passing-out parade we became airmen with a smart uniform that included a collar and tie and ready to proceed to the next part of our training. We had a 'rank' –even if it was only Aircraftsman 2nd class and there wasn't anything lower than that.

Before that final passing-out parade we sat a written test from which those in power concluded that I could probably cope with the mental rigours of training to become a wireless mechanic. Now this was good news for me, because this trade paid more than an armourer – my original allocation to the war effort. And so that simple test in dreary Padgate set the seal on my life for many years to come. The mystery of invisible radio waves was to take the place in my life of the drawing board and the surveyor's measuring instruments.

Stockport is a southern suburb of Manchester, home in those days to many cotton mills but with a broad high road leading south to Buxton and the Peak District National Park. Along this road in the centre of Stockport was to be found another RAF station – well, it wasn't strictly 'a station', as it was located in several requisitioned houses and the local Masonic hall, with the hub of activities at Stockport Technical College. It was to this seat of learning that I was posted in April 1944. I can remember the short train journey from Padgate to Stockport, carrying all my worldly and service kit. It was a 'journey of expectation' to be repeated many times in the next four years – what would the next posting be like – how much 'bull' (as mentioned before, short for 'bull shit', short for undesirable discipline) would there be, would the food be eatable? I needn't have worried. Stockport was completely different from Padgate. Our time was spent in classrooms and workshops and the military side of service life was kept to an absolute minimum. The food was vastly better – no doubt because there were only about one hundred hungry mouths to feed; beds became things to sleep on and not displays of military precision; NCOs were replaced by civilian instructors and life became academic. But for me life became harder than square bashing.

My knowledge of electricity was limited to experiments using iron filings and a magnet and the shape of one of my father's accumulators. What technological wizardry was required to capture unseen wireless waves out of the atmosphere and persuade them to give up their intelligence to mankind was one of the dark and deep mysteries for me on that first morning in a Stockport classroom. The course was labelled 'ab initio' – from the beginning – and how grateful I was for that. And how grateful I was for one instructor, Mr Middleton, who was a brilliant teacher and knew his electricity and radio like the back of his hand. His task was to transfer information and understanding into the brains of Aircraftsmen 2nd Class Wireless Mechanics U/T (Under Training). By a system of short rhyming phrases, he summarised principles of the subject in such a way as to make them easy to remember – well, easier to remember. Ohms Law – and more complicated fundamentals – became part of our knowledge through what were known as 'Middleton's Magic Methods'. His genius and perseverance finally bore fruit when one day each of us in the class finished constructing a simple wireless set. The quality of the radio-wave reception we had detected, amplified and wired into earphones would make a modern-day CD player curl up and die – but to me it was almost as wonderful as the Second Coming!

Life in Stockport was far from the regime of any large permanent RAF station. Intellectually it was worlds away from Padgate. Living in requisitioned houses was as good as staying in the Ritz Hotel when compared to an airman's hut. 'Bull' was absolutely minimal, but there were other delights to make a serviceman's life a pleasure. The people of Stockport were very hospitable and many a Saturday night I found myself, with a few other airmen, invited to a twenty-first birthday party or some other family celebration. I soon found the local Congregational church but I am not sure if the invitation to worship God or the invitations to Sunday meals was the real attraction.

Stockport was an out-station, for administrative purposes, of RAF Wimslow which in those days was a recruits training station for WAAFs (Women's Auxiliary Air Force). When we visited the doctor or dentist at this station we were accosted by the girls-in-blue from their huts with wolf cries worthy of any macho male. Young female recruits here were also kept in camp for some time before being let out and their pent up romantic desires were given something of a release as we marched past to sick quarters. As I was still 'going out' with the girl at home, I put a self-imposed limitation on my amorous activities but looking back I am not convinced that that was a sensible thing to do!

However, it was sensible to swot extremely hard at mastering the principles of electricity and wireless because the next posting would depend on passing all the examinations. When examination results were posted our one great fear was the two letters CT – Cease Training – which meant being re-graded to some lesser trade with its reduced pay. FT – Further Training – gave a reprieve to try again. At the end of six months I was considered educated well enough to go on to the next stage of wireless training but there was a surprise in store for us all. Usually the brightest trainees went on to become radar mechanics and the less skilful to be wireless mechanics. There was a certain mystique about radar, it was highly secret and those who worked with it were 'on to' something that really set them apart. So my pleasure on learning that I was to be posted to No 2 Electrical and Wireless School at RAF Yatesbury, the ground radar training establishment, knew no bounds.

What was in store for me, however, wasn't all to my liking.

RAF Yatesbury, built on the Downs east of the Wiltshire town of Calne, was a sprawling mass of wooded huts, parade grounds and service police. Put these together and you come up with something as different from Stockport as chalk and cheese. This was the place I had to endure for four months while digesting the inner workings of complicated radar transmitting, receiving and display equipment. As if this wasn't hard enough, there was a high level of 'bull' and the guardroom at the station gate was famous for housing keen eyed service police looking for every deviation from Regulations, especially by brainy little erks like me.

Calne was famous for the production of Harris's sausages and pork pies so we had more than our fair share of this local produce in the cookhouse. It was in the kitchens at Yatesbury that I discovered the meaning of 'tin room'. This was the place where all the greasy cooking trays were cleaned and also the place where I leant the truth of rule number one for a service man – never volunteer for anything! Having volunteered for something that sounded good for me – I cannot remember what it was – I found myself working one week-end in the tin room, cleaning great piles of disgusting greasy pans that had been used for feeding hundreds of airmen.

One Sunday evening I was walking the streets of Calne looking for a church to go to. (Remembering the Service's canteen and other hospitality activities at Union Church Heathfield, I came to realise that church wasn't only a place for feeding the soul but it could also feed the stomach.) I saw a nice young girl and asked her if she could direct me. She said she was going to church and would I like to go with her. My luck was in! Unfortunately my non-conformist upbringing didn't stretch as far as the Plymouth Brethren, but later when she invited me home for supper, I thought the PB's couldn't be all that bad if she was a member. But my anticipation of good things to come took a turn for the worse when cold sausages and pork pie were served up for supper! My pursuit of the girl and church and free suppers in Calne ceased that very night.

After sixteen gruelling weeks working with cathode ray tubes, pulse transmission and reception, the great day came when I passed out as a fully trained airman second-class radar mechanic and the coveted sparks badge could be sewn on to the sleeve of my tunic. I then went on leave and I am not sure who was the proudest, my father or me. I was now ready to play an active part in detecting those German planes that had plagued my family for over four years. It was spring 1945, but events don't always live up to expectation.

By the time I was ready to be posted to a radar station the enemy had retreated back into the Homeland and for all practical purposes the air war over south-east England was finished. I was posted first to RAF Ventnor and then, after only a couple of weeks, to RAF Beachy Head. On a fine and clear day I could see Heathfield from the window of my hut but I never saw a fine and clear enemy blip on the radar screen. Even so, the station was still on full war alert and I joined the shift system to maintain the station in an operational state. I had entered those strange and forbidden portals that had so mystified us before the war and I would be able to tell my children and grandchildren that I had 'fought in the war'! I cannot imagine a more beautiful spot than Beachy Head for an RAF station and with it being so close to home, my few weeks service there couldn't have been better. Working a shift system meant that I frequently took the beloved train from Eastbourne to Heathfield and home – and to see the girlfriend. However, the high-ups at the Air Ministry had more pressing things to think about than a young airman enjoying himself on the Sussex coast; there was still a war to be fought and won across the other side of the world and their plans included providing radar cover for the battle against the Japanese.

During these fifteen months of life in the RAF I had enjoyed some time at home on leave between postings and the romance with my girlfriend continued. My brother had started flying training and my father continued to make aircraft parts, although that activity was soon to finish. The end of the war was obviously close to hand and that was the signal for my father to look ahead to restart domestic electrical work. By the end of the war all the machine shop equipment was sold, at a profit, and The Shop was ready to resume normal service.

In May 1945 came VE Day – Victory in Europe – and there was a great national celebration and the 'letting down of hair'. I was still stationed at Beachy Head but by now the need for enemy aircraft detection was over for the south east but not for the Far East. So it was, that in June I received notice that my services were required overseas. I would enjoy seven days embarkation leave before reporting to the RAF in Blackpool, where hundreds of us airmen were gathered together and made ready for service abroad. We weren't told where our destination was to be, but the issue of tropical kit and anti-malarial tablets made it unlikely we were destined for Iceland or to occupy Germany. Our stay in Blackpool lasted about two weeks in which time we experienced the fame accrued by the Blackpool landladies, who provided us with a bed and cold spam and a lettuce leaf for our suppers. It was at about this time that the realities of war were beginning to seep into my brain. I was going to some unknown destination to confront the enemy – and all the glamour of wearing RAF blue 'at home' was about to be replaced with the 'away' drab of khaki. And so it was, that with some sense of apprehension, one night we slipped silently down the Firth of Clyde on a journey into the unknown. Our troopship – SS Bussvane – had seen better days plying the seas around the Dutch East Indies. The fact that she was flat bottomed had serious consequences later, but for now the feature that concerned me most was that H deck was far below A deck and daylight. The hot, airless, H deck and a hammock were to be my eating and sleeping quarters for three weeks – but there were compensations as literally a whole new world was about to unfold before my eyes. We were told nothing of the route we were sailing, but one morning, after two days steaming, I climbed up from H deck into fresh air, a brilliant dark blue sky, hot sunshine and the magnificent view of a wedge of towering white cliff just across a short stretch of clear blue sea. We were anchored off Gibraltar.

This was the first piece of overseas land I had ever seen and it couldn't have been more impressive. We were at the gateway to the Mediterranean Sea and as we soon streamed away, with the land near to our port side, The Rock behind us, I didn't need any navigation instruments to tell me we were sailing east.

There followed several days of glorious sunshine and the first airing of our tropical kit. We saw flying fish skimming over the sea and the stars at night were so bright. Even with the rigours and discomfort of H deck, it was a Mediterranean cruise – and I was being paid for the privilege.

Our next landfall took us down a very narrow waterway – the land had changed into sand and the trees become tall with spiky leaves sticking out at the top. We could see people dressed in long white shifts – men and women – and animals with humps on their backs. It was extremely hot and the salt-water showers, even with salt-water soap, did little to alleviate our discomfort. We had arrived at Port Said and were about to sail down the Suez Canal. No one was allowed off ship but we were surrounded by dozens of little scruffy boats and even scruffier men trying to sell us all sorts of merchandise. The trading was negotiated via ropes and baskets between the sellers below and the travellers above. It was all so different and exciting, even if a little daunting, especially after nearly five years of rationing and almost bare shop shelves.

A day or so later we left the Land of the Pharaohs, and the sea across which Moses had escaped with his tribe of grumbling Israelites, and headed out into open water. By this time we were sufficiently near to our destination to be told where we were heading and given the information that we would be serving with the South East Asia Air Force (SEAAF). In a few days we would be docking in Bombay on the central west coast of India.

Unfortunately the climatic conditions of the Indian Ocean were under the influence of the winds of the summer monsoon that was gathering its strength and rain on its eastward journey to India. Our flat-bottomed ship didn't take kindly to such rough treatment and nor did any sailing in her. She wallowed and bucked – and not being seasoned sailors, so did we – to such an extent that the keels of the lifeboats on the upper decks were washed by the heaving waves. Food became an irrelevance but the singing of 'Eternal Father strong to save' at the Sunday church parade took on a new and immediate meaning. Our arrival at the Gateway to India was a great relief – H deck was now a thing of the past – and solid ground beckoned me, even if it appeared to be covered with the signs of a population suffering from rampant TB. What I thought were the spittings of an unhealthy nation, were the remnants of chewed red betelnut seeds. Our town streets have the white marks of a gum-chewing population – Indian roads are more colourful. I was entering a country that was to unfold many new things to a young airman.

I was also entering a time of much uncertainty about where I was to be posted and what duties I was to perform. It seemed that as my stay in India began, nobody was issuing the answers to these questions – certainly not to me nor to the many others travelling with me. Of my ten months in India, most of it was spent in soul-destroying transit camps, 'sitting on our arses doing nothing'. It all started in a huge transit camp on the outskirts of Bombay at a placed called Worli. The only memorable thing about my short time there was swimming in the warmth of the Arabian Sea and beginning a life when the nasty little malaria-carrying mosquito became enemy number one. Anti-malarial mepacrine tablets had turned us all a pale shade of yellow but colour didn't deter those nasty little biters.

When my posting arrived I was in for a real treat and the start of the main feature, for me, of my stay in the sub continent – travelling hundreds of miles on Indian railways. This form of transport encapsulated much that made up the nature of Indian life as I was to experience it. The railway line was like a magnet that attracted great crowds of the poor and lowest castes of the population. The stations were teeming with people of all ages trying to beg a living by offering services of different kinds. Trade –or more correctly bargaining – was conducted in a conglomerate of the Urdu and English languages. The char-wallahs offered dubious cups of tea, served from an old urn on a broken down trolley, and many willing hands competed for an anna or two (less than 1p) to carry all our belongings. Hair cutting and shoe shining were available without having to find a shop – life and trade were all available on the platform as we waited for the transport police to get us on to the train. I was about to start on my first Indian journey.

The servicemen's compartments were reserved, which limited the number of bodies to the number of wooden slatted seats. This luxury was essential as the remainder of the train made a crowded London commuter train look almost empty! Not only were the compartments bulging at the seams with humanity but it was virtually impossible to see the outside of the train for more bodies standing on every step and ledge and even sitting on the roof. The railway staff made little attempt to remove this seething mass before the huge monster of a steam engine gave several shrill blasts as we slowly drew out of Bombay station on our journey of discovery.

We were travelling to Belgaum, nearly three hundred miles south-east of Bombay. Why we were destined for this place, or what we were to do when we arrived, had not been revealed to the lowly ranks of the RAF but what was revealed was some of the most spectacular scenery I have ever experienced.

Bombay is built on a south-facing peninsular, so the railway travels north for several miles before turning south and starting the ascent up the northern end of the Western Ghats – a forested mountain range running down the western Indian seaboard. As it was the monsoon season, with intermittent torrential downpours of rain and hot sunshine, the vegetation was at its lushest and with very high humidity it was an extremely steamy journey. As we climbed higher and higher we servicemen followed suit with our fellow native travellers and sat outside on the train steps and watched the beautiful green mountainous country unfold before our eyes. The railway engineering, of course, interested me and I made many comparisons with the Sussex

Cuckoo line. My journey was long before continuous welded rails and I think the engineers must have left extra wide expansion gaps that gave a noisy and uncomfortable ride. Looking down deep ravines, the flimsy looking bridges didn't offer much confidence to one used to the gentler slopes of Sussex.

Our first stop was at that famous Anglicized military town of Poona where we had time to walk into the town and sample the equally famous hospitality of the English memsahib – only their tea and cakes in a canteen I would hasten to add! Poona had the genteel atmosphere of any Edwardian English spa town. A short stay, then onwards south to Belgaum.

I have little memory of Belgaum as a town and not much more as a military camp, except that the rain was almost continuous and extremely heavy. Our accommodation was a six-bed apartment made of canvas on a concrete plinth, the whole surrounded by a shallow ditch to keep the water at bay. We stayed here several weeks doing absolutely nothing. This lack of activity was, I think, indicative of the state of uncertainty of our commanders in high places to decide how to proceed with the war. But better things were to come as finally we entrained again and rattled further south to Bangalore.

My aging encyclopaedia says of Bangalore; 'it stands on a healthy plateau 3000 feet above sea-level and is one of the pleasantest British stations (administrative and military centre) in India'. I agree with that.

I was soon to discover that at last we had come to a place for a specific purpose and that our brains were finally to be exercised. RAF Bangalore was home to No. 51 Radio Direction Finding School (RDF being an older description for radar) and was another of those radio schools at which the mysteries of magnetic transmission and reception are uncovered to enable the likes of myself maintain military equipment in efficient working order. Yatesbury had given me information about ground radar and the interception of enemy planes. The purpose of Bangalore was to introduce me to the inner workings of airborne radar sets. This made some sense because it was in August that VJ Day was declared, after the A-bombs had been delivered on Japan, and so ground radar for defending our own territories became unnecessary. By this time, however, much of the enthusiasm of the training staff to impart information had been replaced by thoughts of 'demob' and returning to home comforts. My understanding of airborne radar barely germinated but fortunately, for some unsuspecting pilots, this deficiency never caused any dire results – I never came within a dozen miles of an RAF plane.

For myself, this lack of purpose did nothing to dampen my pleasure in almost everything that Bangalore offered me.

By August the monsoon had dispensed all its rain and together with the high altitude of Bangalore, the climate was almost perfect – hot and dry. Playing tennis in 90F was just great! Our accommodation was in native-style wood and rush huts, called bashers, housing twenty airmen, with one shared Indian servant. Each of us paid him one and a half rupees (about ten p) each week, for which he did all the usual barrack room chores. He demonstrated one skill that was almost beyond belief. He would collect up in his arms twenty pairs of black air force shoes – deliberately manufactured to all look alike – take them away for polishing and return them to each bed space and their correct owners. He was a gentle man who worked to keep a very large extended family on about two pounds a week. I often wondered what happened to him when the British lost control and left after independence?

Another pleasurable memory of Bangalore was the beauty of the Anglo-Indian girls –offspring of mixed unions somewhere down the line of British rule. We were strongly advised not to emulate any such relationships as they usually ended in tears for many reasons. We came in contact with these dark beauties who worked in the cafes and shops in the British cantonment. Keeping apart from them was made all the harder by the exotic perfume of the tropical flowers and warm nights as we wondered back to camp after an evening at the local cinema. Life could have been very romantic!

One final memory of Bangalore comes from that much maligned institution – the cookhouse. Being only a small RAF station, the man in charge of the catering was not an officer but only a sergeant. I say 'only' but he was a chef of the very highest order. It so happened that he had been in charge of catering at Stockport. He produced the most wonderful cold buffets as an extra with 'tiffin' – the midday dinner. Produce was probably cheap and plentiful and with his skills and imagination it was an object lesson in what can be provided with a limited budget.

Towards the end of 1945 my happy time at RAF Bangalore came to an end with a posting to Calcutta. Why to Calcutta I never knew – VJ Day had been declared but I suppose that even if the fighting had finished there was much still to be done, not least to repatriate thousands of servicemen, many of whom were conscripts and who had been away from England and loved ones for four years. I met some of them in Calcutta and they were extremely bitter about being part of a forgotten and underrated army. I cannot imagine what political rows and Parliamentary questions would be asked if present-day servicemen and women were expected to stay abroad for so long, even in time of conflict.

Calcutta turned out to be another of those awful transit camps, but the travelling there from Bangalore had more excitement in store for me. The train journey of eleven hundred miles took three days – including a stop in Madras long enough to take a rickshaw trip around the city. The eastern seaboard of India tends to be flatter and less forested than the Western Gnats so our journey wasn't so exciting except for one experience – a trip on the footplate of the engine pulling our train. Indian railways have always had a fair number of Scottish engineers and operating staff and so my driver turned out to be of jock descent. Having never ridden anywhere in an engine before, I cannot make comparisons, but my trip on that Indian engine was dirty, hot, steamy, and extremely uncomfortable. It was like being rattled around in a metal furnace. Railway engines, I discovered, have no suspension and the jolt over every rail gap was transmitted directly into my body! Going over points was even worse, with an increase in noise and vibration – I began to understand that the expression 'going off the rails' had a basis for its meaning, even if we did stay 'on'. Still, it was a marvellous experience and I thanked the driver for his kindness. The carriages were little better and the wooden seats added only a minimum of comfort especially when one was stretched out to sleep at night. My other vivid memory of that journey was the audacity of the shite hawks – these birds would swoop down and steal out of our hands the food we had bought on the platform. I seem to remember they had a particular taste for egg sandwiches. Travelling for OR's (Other Ranks and therefore not officers) wasn't particularly comfortable and would have warranted about a fifth class classification in England. Still, compared to the hardships suffered by the native Indian travellers it wasn't all that bad, even if, as I suspect, many hadn't a ticket in their pocket.

Calcutta stands on the western bank of the river Hooghly that in turn is a branch of the wide and filthy Ganges. My memories of this huge city are ones of contrast. Perhaps the most vivid was to walk down the broad and best known highway named Chowringi. On one side of the road was dumped a disgusting shanty town and on the other fine European buildings. Here were beggars and the poor and deformed and the dying living in the gutter and here was the famous Firpo's restaurant where the well-off and well-nourished – the likes of me – met for afternoon tea. Had Jesus been an Indian, this surely must have been the place he had in mind when telling the parable of the rich man in his castle and the poor man at his gate. This was the place where years later Mother Teresa ministered to the sick and brought dignified dying to many. Near to our transit camp was Victoria Park with a beautiful swimming pool that attracted our attendance on most days of the weeks as we waited to be posted. Life was hot and sticky and mostly boring. Here in this place of waiting, we crossed over with airmen whose demobilisation number had come up and were returning home, many of them after a gruelling war in the Burmese jungle. My 'demob' number was fifty-nine so I was destined yet for a long stretch serving in the RAF.

It was at this point that something odd happened. The government in England had decided that to speed up reconstruction of war damage, servicemen with certain skills and trades would be given what was classified as a Class B release. Irrespective of their 'demob' number they got out immediately to start drawing up plans and laying the bricks and mortar of post-war Britain. Called to the orderly room, I was offered one of these quick tickets home. Who imagined that a lad of nineteen, with an equal number of months experience as not much more than a very junior draughtsman, could contribute anything to raise England from the ashes of war, I shall never know. However, when I saw the application forms for my release, it was written in a freehand most surprisingly like my father's! Within a week I was rattling my way across Central India on the last leg of my free railway journey around the sub-continent.

What were my abiding impressions of India? At the time I was probably too young to have any immediate views, but on reflection I found it a country full of contrasts – poor and rich living side by side and not caring much about the great divide separating them. Of course I was part of the British Empire and British Raj that since 1858 ruled this vast country and teeming population. All that in two years time was to change with independence and the partition into India and Pakistan. I saw few signs of unrest or evidence of hatred against the British – but then most Indians I came in contact with depended on the likes of me for their living. I have a feeling that they knew which side their bread was buttered even if politically dry bread was ultimately to be preferred. Most Indians seemed to have an inbuilt gentleness and culture, but then we so often forget that they were a great civilisation centuries before the British East India Company began to plunder the land at the expense of the population.

Those nine months remain as one of the great experiences of my life – now it was coming to a sudden end – and I began to wonder where else the high-ups at the Air Ministry would have posted me if number fifty-nine hadn't been circumvented?

The return sea journey from Bombay on SS Duchess of Richmond saw me scrubbing decks for my twentieth birthday. Slowly as we sailed west the weather changed from the blue of the Orient to the grey of a Biscay gale and an English winter. Having escaped malaria and many other nasty tropical diseases, at Liverpool I was carried off the ship on a stretcher suffering with flu. Hardly a triumphal homecoming, but it was home.

After exchanging my RAF kit for a demob outfit – that was as far from Saville Row as Mudros was from Madras – I finally arrived at Heathfield railway station. My first observation on getting out was how small everything appeared – Station Road and Collingwood Rise looked as if they had shrunk – I suppose it was after the wide-open spaces I had visited in the last nine months. Gone were the milling smelly white-dressed crowds on the platform, now only a couple of porters in their black Southern Railway uniforms, and everything seemed so quiet and slow moving. I am sure my parents must have been overjoyed at my return but I don't remember any special welcome-home party. Although the war was over, all the restrictions and rationing were still in operation and these seemed to me to make life grey and unattractive especially after the colour and glamour of the Orient.

My next move was to report to the Labour Exchange in Hailsham and receive my posting to reconstruct England into a land worthy of those servicemen who had spent years overseas really fighting for my freedom. But there was to be no such luck – the officials were not expecting me and on examining my qualifications decided that I was no fit person to undertake such difficult work. I was to go home and await further instructions. In the meantime I was unemployed and receiving no wages, which was not good for my mother's weekly budget nor for my spare time. Our next door neighbour Jim Hamper, who owned a butcher's shop and ran a smallholding producing pigs and vegetables, offered me work on the land. Jim took a philosophical outlook on life and one day when I was very cheesed-off waiting to hear my fate from the Labour Exchange, he pointed to a cabbage so large it was splitting open. "Look at that" he said. "It's so happy and full of life it's splitting its sides with laughter." A few days later I was ordered to report back to the RAF and to my second instalment of service. I felt like that cabbage but I still wonder who made out that Class B Release Form?

In March 1948 my brother Teddy married a most delightful girl – a WAAF from Holmfirth near Huddersfield – a lovely Yorkshire lass. Dorothy Tinker was to become a lifelong 'sister' to us all. My longstanding girl friend, who was the only bridesmaid, and my mother and father and I travelled to Huddersfield by car for the wedding. My father always was a bit of an 'arranger' – he organised things particularly to suit his (and our) needs. A few weeks before the wedding he sold his rather nice Austin saloon car to a buyer in Heathfield and bought a Ford 8 (of 'you can have any colour as long as it is black' fame). This deal no doubt put a few pounds into my father's pocket but left him with a car unlikely to survive the long journey to Yorkshire. So he asked his buyer if he could borrow back the car he just sold to make the wedding journey! This ploy wasn't as successful as he had hoped – we had four punctures and as there were no motorways, the twelve hour journey north through the centre of many large towns was extremely tedious.

It was soon after the wedding that my longstanding romance ended. I think the whole affair had gone stale and both of us, to use modern parlance, wanted to 'move on'. (Or was it the sound of wedding bells that frightened us off?) Anyway, it didn't end in a great number of tears like those we had been warned of in Bangalore.

One of the great advances in radar technology during the war was the British invention (NOT American!) of the magnetron and other miniaturized components. The magnetron produces very high frequency power in a small space and so the wartime requirement to fit radar systems into aircraft and still allow the plane to leave the ground was achieved. Today the magnetron is the gizmo in all our microwave ovens. These revolutionary techniques also made it possible to fit complicated radars into trucks for many different kinds of identification work. My first posting back into the RAF was to discover and learn the mysteries of such a system.

One associates Stratford-on-Avon with the romances, plottings and machinations of Elizabethan drama, but for me, nearby RAF Honiley was to be the stage for learning about Ground Controlled Approach (GCA). There developed, however, a connection with everyday life for me in the bard's home town – a whirlwind romance which resulted in my buying the young lady an engagement ring. Within a few months, this really did end in tears for her and, as I later was to realise, a lucky escape for me! She could have sued me for breech of promise.

It took three months hard slog to learn the intricacies of the GCA system that enabled controllers, in a truck at the end of a airfield runway, to talk down an incoming aircraft in almost zero visibility.

Then once again came that time of expectation and excitement – to which airfield in England would I be posted to help in the safe landing of planes in bad weather? For many reasons the decision of some postings officer couldn't have been more profound, for St Eval on the rugged north coast of Cornwall was to be a defining place in my life – as you will read later.

St Eval was the middle aerodrome of a trinity, with St Mawgan to the south and St Mirren to the north. Cornwall delights in its Celtic saints. All three stations were built close to coastal headlands and across undulating ground. Although this was September 1946 the RAF still flew meteorological flights far out over the Atlantic and it was these aircrews that GCA was there to help, especially when the weather suddenly closed in. At last, I felt that I was really making a worthwhile contribution – even if it was post-war. As my experience with the equipment increased, I was promoted to the dizzy heights of Leading Aircraftsman with a much-needed increase in pay – to about six shillings (30p) per day. Most of this money went on extra food in the NAAFI (Navy Army Air Force Institution) and in a little tearoom we discovered in our nearest town of Newquay. Food was still rationed and hard to come by, but the dear lady in this cafe had something going with a local farmer and she served a wonderful fry-up, including steak, especially for 'her airmen'.

The winter of 1946/47 was one of the coldest in living memory and snowfalls made travel extremely difficult. Coal was in short supply so the two famous round iron stoves in our hut were kept alight by burning all sorts of scrounged wood and even furniture we considered expendable. But it was a great life and, with 'bull' being a very low priority, we worked hard and played hard. Perhaps the best times were when I was in the radar truck and the controllers were talking down an aircraft in bad weather. Much depended on the operators interpreting the echoes on the screens correctly and passing instructions over the radio to the pilot. But all their efforts would be in vain if the likes of myself hadn't set-up the equipment (calibration) accurately beforehand. The main runway started over the brow of a hill – this meant that when an aircraft landed, even in good visibility, we at the other end saw nothing. There was no greater relief, as the talk-down ended in the hoped-for safe landing, and the plane appeared passing us to taxi to its dispersal stand.

My 'playing' at this time didn't seriously include girls – I was wary of any close encounter with the opposite sex after two recent failed episodes. Football and cross-country running got rid of my excess energy and I represented the station on several occasions including matches played away and requiring air travel. There is a family photo (somewhere) recording me, the goalkeeper, spectacularly diving to save a goal; unfortunately the ball can clearly be seen in the back of the net. The chance to fly in one of the station Liberators couldn't be missed and so team selection became very competitive. Ultimately my sporting activities produced a serious pain in my right foot that necessitated a trip to Truro hospital. The X-ray department by this time held little terror for me and the broken metatarsal resulted in a plaster up to my knee. This obviously had serious implications for my sporting activities, in one sense of the word, but in another was my passport to other activities of what was commonly known as 'sport' i.e. activity with the fair sex.

It was September 1947 and the RAF had inaugurated the annual Battle of Britain Day to commemorate those combats I had witnessed over the Sussex countryside seven years before. St Eval was opened for this special day to a public that included hundreds of holidaymakers staying in Newquay. Amongst this temporary population were two young ladies from Surrey on a fortnight's holiday. On the morning of Battle of Britain Day, one of them wanted to spend the day pursuing her favourite pastime of swimming and taking advantage of the famous Newquay surf, while the other was all for sampling the airmen at St Eval. With three other male holidaymakers, the swimmer lost out and so found herself on a glorious September afternoon inside a hot radar truck, being introduced to the mysteries of aircraft control by a young airman with his foot in plaster. I had met Marian, my wife to be!

I am not sure how interested I was in educating a young lady in the science of radar, but I am certain I was interested in fostering good relations with this member of the public. I had just become an uncle for the first time (Gregory had been born to Dorothy and Teddy in Salisbury) and maybe I wanted to show off to someone. After the lesson was over, hoping of course that I had suitably impressed the lady, we went, with her friend Beri and another airman, to the YMCA for cups of tea. There it was arranged we should all meet up again that evening. Sometime later Marian admitted to me that she had agreed because she decided that if I got a bit too fresh with her, she would be able to run faster than an airman with one leg in plaster! So as I said, my plaster was my passport to some sport! Later still, she confessed that in fact it was, for her, almost love at first sight. My intentions towards her were a little more open-ended and undefined. Here was someone who was very nice to be with but memories of other recent girls were still nagging in my mind. We met several times in the following week before she went home, both of us agreeing we would write to each other. So what was it about her that in the end led me to ask her if she would marry me? She was slim with reddish brown curly hair – not a glamorous film star beauty but nevertheless pretty and attractive. In no way was she brash or flashy but had a delightful simplicity in appearance and character. There was a natural honesty about her looks and what she said and all that she was. Over the coming months, then over the years, I was to discover her absolute reliability (not in her timekeeping, I would add) and her faithfulness. She never spoke an unkind word about anybody. She had a taste for the right sort of dress – very smart but never over the top. She was everything that I would be happy to introduce to even a strict chapel-going grandmother. St Paul says in one of his epistles, concerning marriage, that we should not be 'unequally yoked' – meaning that if a man and woman have the same religion, then the obstacles to a happy and successful union are greatly reduced. I believe that it isn't just in the matter of religion that this is true. Marian's and my family backgrounds were the same. We had been educated in the same kind of school. Without being snobby, we were not marrying outside of each other's class or creed. Good marriages are made without these conditions, but with them the tensions and pressures that can develop are minimised. We were both, in a mild sort of way, Christian believers so the only hurdle I had to jump with Marian was the work that she did. She was training as a hospital haematology technician – she dealt with human blood! In the end this profession of hers was, in large part, my saviour from the fear of all things medical and she was able to take the black (or would it be white?) mystique out of the medical world. A marriage made in heaven? Yes I believe that is the way it was to turn out to be. But back to St Eval!

No 59 was beginning to take on some significance for me – that was my demob number and by the end of 1947 it was clear it would come up early in the New Year. However, having served nearly four years and become reasonably proficient at radar maintenance, my CO decided that I should be elevated to the exalted rank of Acting Corporal Paid. How one only acts as a corporal, without actually being one, has always been a bit of a mystery but it was with some pride that I sewed two stripes on my tunic and again the extra money came in handy. The only change in my life-style was that now I could eat my wads (cakes) and drink my tea in a different NAAFI room from all those lower ranks.

During the autumn and early winter I met Marian several times in London. We sat in various parks but found it much darker and cosier in the back row of the News Cinema at Waterloo station! She further expressed her continuing interest in me by sending to St Eval large home-baked fruitcakes… the way to a man's heart!

Leaving the RAF threw up the question – what next? Did I really want to leave? What job could I get? What qualifications had I? How was I going to keep on seeing Marian?

From early days maps and surveying were on the cards as a way of earning a living, but I had no qualifications and at the age of twenty-two I 'needed the money'. I discovered that as I had been in gainful occupation (earning a pound each week) before volunteering for the RAF, I did not qualify for any more free education at a college or university. I had some training and experience of electronics, but was this RAF variety sufficient to get work in Civvy Street? My father offered me a job with Strange Electrical. I would live at home and be paid three pounds a week. His proposition didn't fill me with enthusiasm and there was one other reason for not wanting to accept his offer. Working with my father would create certain tensions that could not be easily overcome – he found it difficult to tell me off in a straight blunt sort of way. He would huff and puff a bit if I did something wrong and then go silent on me. I could have coped with a straight forward 'don't be such a bloody fool' and then allowed to get on with the work.

The question of work was finally solved by applying for, and being accepted as, a wireless mechanic with the Ministry of Civil Aviation. I was to become a Temporary Civil Servant. The pay was five pounds each week – about right in those times – and I had to be prepared to work anywhere in the UK.

In January 1948 I was demobbed for the second time, but as I had already been given one splendid outfit of clothing two years before, I did not qualify for further hand-outs from His Majesty's Government. That wasn't quite the end of my relationship with the RAF. A letter from the Air Ministry demanded that I return all the extra money I had received after being promoted to corporal. My St Eval CO did have the authority to make me 'acting' but not 'paid'. I didn't reply and I still owe the money.

Act Two

Scene One

Manhood and Electronics

By the age of twenty-two I had lived a tranquil childhood and six years of wartime fear and excitement. I had come through, survived, and was now about to embark on the next period of experience that life could throw at me. I had served my country in the armed forces – albeit in a benign way – I was young, healthy and full of expectation which is more than can be said for one of the boys who had accompanied me through childhood, two schools and a place of work. Brian Cornwall had been my friend since the age of about four. He opted for the army and was killed a few days after taking part in the Normandy Landings. He was picked-off by a German sniper. He was never to experience all the fulfilment that was to be the good fortune coming to me over many future decades. Whether we concur with a heavenly plan in which everything is decided in advance by God, or in life decided by random happenings – luck – or any other system of belief, I shall always be grateful that life has been so good to me.

So, let us stop, before going on with the journey, and consider what were the principles by which I tried to live and to make decisions about my future? I had pretty much abandoned churchgoing after many hours of boredom and discipline sitting on a hard chair in Heathfield Union Church. RAF church parades were not about finding God but conforming to Kings Regulations – except of course when I felt God might save us from sinking in the Arabian Sea! But the teaching and receiving of the Christian faith and virtues has a strange way of imperceptibly seeping into ones life however small and Bolshie may be the response at the point of delivery. My parent's adherence to chapel life and

Christian ways permeated their upbringing of we two boys and although temporarily rejecting formal church attendance, the teaching influenced our characters in all aspects of our life. In practical terms how did this work out? Openness and truth were paramount (although I have related the failure of my parents in matters medical). Telling lies or concealing the truth just wasn't on – and it makes life so much harder having to keep making up consistent untruths! We were taught and accepted the Biblical injunction 'never let the sun go down on your wrath' – in other words always make-up an argument the same day. Respect and concern for the well-being of others was very important. The 'work ethic' was a necessity – not because we lived in an acquisitive culture – but because wages were low and the fear of unemployment was never far away. You either found employment or you had a desperately hard time. No, I don't think all this made me a goody-goody; it held me in good stead and gave a firm foundation for a rattling happy life.

My application for a job with the Ministry of Civil Aviation was spurred on by knowing that Ground Controlled Approach units were in operation at various civil airports in the UK. I thought, when offered a post, that I would be sent to one of these units. For reasons beyond my understanding, the Civil Service decided differently and I landed up at the wireless station for Croydon Airport on nearby Mitcham Common. Apart from the very basic nuts and bolts of the theory of wireless telephony, the equipment was, and remained, something of a mystery to me, having been given no instruction or training on the specific equipment. So there I was, on shift, responsible for the wherewithal that kept countless passengers and pilots high in the sky safely in communication with the ground. I found the job dissatisfying, daunting and encumbered with Civil Service red tape. Living in rather drab digs, first in Croydon and then in Mitcham – where could be drabber – life was only lightened by the presence of Marian living half a dozen miles down the road at New Malden. This close proximity of the beloved had more going for it than just courtship. I said that living in digs was drab, but above that, landladies seem to have an aversion to providing anything approaching reasonable meals especially at weekends. They preferred their guests to make their own arrangements for satisfying the needs of the stomach on the Sabbath and this is where Marian's mother comes in. She (Ethel) cooked the finest roast dinners in all the world! They were absolutely marvellous – and there was still rationing. Her roasting potatoes were placed around the joint and became impregnated with all the succulence of the meat juices. How glad I was that in those days cholesterol was still to be invented. With roast dinners and the beguiling Marian, my visits to 25 Reynolds Road, New Malden continued apace but Marian's father (Fred) didn't always add anything to the meal. Being a gas engineer and having a bent for all things mechanical, he spent much of his leisure time with a great array of tools in his garage workshop. So often Ethel's call for lunch fell on deaf ears – and my rumbling stomach. Fred and Ethel were to become my in-laws and I can vouch that all the jokes associated with such relationships can be fun but are completely unfounded.

All love affairs have their problems – part of the work of courtship is to sort out these hurdles so they do not become insurmountable barriers after the ringing of wedding bells. Our problem – my problem – was that Marian worked in Hammersmith Post Graduate Medical School as a blood technician. Often when I met her after work she smelt! She smelt of hospitals! Nothing could be worse for me, with a deep-rooted horror of all things medical. Still, true love can overcome all obstacles and slowly but surely the terror of medicine began to loose its grip on me. I shall be eternally grateful!

My stay on Mitcham Common, with the unsolved mysteries of wireless telephony, was to last only a few months. New Malden was not only the home of the light of my life but also of a company with which I was about to start a long relationship – twenty-five years to the very day to be exact. The Decca Navigator Co. at 247 Burlington Road, New Malden, Surrey, was to be my place of employment for half my working life. I cannot remember how I first made contact with this company, but in June (24th?) 1948 I started work in its engineering laboratories as a junior technical assistant earning five pounds every week.

I will endeavour in the simplest terminology to explain what the Decca Navigator System did. But first I must declare something that was to bug me for twenty-five years. Coming into electronics via the RAF had its limitations. I was not professionally qualified, and the level of instruction I had received was sufficient to maintain existing equipment, but as I was soon to discover, barely good enough to carry out research or even development work on new emerging systems. During my first three years with Decca I tried to correct this disadvantage by attending evening classes at Wimbledon Technical College and passing the City and Guilds Intermediate Telecommunications Certificate. But there it ended as marriage and sleepless nights with babies took its toll of my determination to become fully qualified. I never did. However, as will be revealed, I possessed alternative abilities that in other ways enabled me to advance in the Company. We must also remember that this was in an age when there was a realistic expectation that if you 'kept your nose clean', you would have a job for life and 'a steady job' was necessary, amongst other things, to get a house mortgage!

So what was the Decca Navigator? It was (sadly, is no more) a radio transmission system using four stations electronically locked together, by receiving each others signals, to produce three sets of extremely stable position lines – an intersecting grid system something akin to 'lat and long'. To give an idea of the operational area of the four stations, the first civilian chain had transmitters located at Puckeridge near Bishop's Stortford (the master station); East Hoathly (green slave) near Lewes; Southam (purple slave) near Leamington Spa; Norwich (red slave). As the descriptions imply, Puckeridge controlled the other three stations. The coverage from these four stations included all the sea approaches around the south-east of England and the intervening land. When a ship or an aircraft, carrying a special Decca radio receiver, travelled through the area around the chain of four stations, three dials (red, green and purple) rotated giving the grid readings. The pilot or ship's navigator, provided with maps overdrawn with the grid, could then plot his position relative to the normal geographical features shown on the map. Later innovations (with which I was to be intimately involved) included feeding the receiver output, via a computer, to move a pen and roller-type map recording the track (where you have been and where you are now) and so indicating the position and heading of the vessel or plane. Unfortunately the positional relationship of the stations to each other and the circular nature of radio wave from a transmitting mast produced a lattice of hyperbolic lines and this of course meant that for a straight X-Y recorder the land topography shown on the map had to be distorted. Many and ingenious were the methods devised to reduce the effects of this distortion by interfacing electro-mechanical computers between the receiver and the display.

The Decca system was the brainchild of the American William (Bill to everyone) O'Brien who offered it to the British Admiralty in 1944 – after the American Navy had rejected it. The boffins in Whitehall saw its potential and contracted the system to be manufactured in time to greatly reduce the number of minesweepers blown up as they swept the seas off the D-Day Normandy coast. The transmissions and their reception gave the sweepers pinpoint accuracy of their position and so could record precisely the areas safe for the advancing armada. O'Brien's mate, Harvey Schwartz (another American, known by everyone as Harvey), was working for the Decca Record Co. at their factory in Brixton. Decca's chairman at that time was Edward Lewis (Ted Lewis to everyone and an English stockbroker). After the war these three men, of genius and irresistible energy, set up The Decca

Navigator Co. to which I was to become a member – not as a genius but with lots of energy.

When I joined in 1948 my first job was in the Systems Engineering Department, designing and producing equipment for the transmitting stations. The usual procedure in any production operation goes something like this:- requirement, research, development, pre-production, full production. Two factors prevented this normal arrangement. We were only making very small quantities of a complex and original system and we had in Harvey Schwartz a salesman who had the knack of being able to sell things before they were actually available! It was Watson Watt, of radar fame, who worked on the principle that half a loaf was better than none at all. The radar defence chain, only half finished and not working full blast in 1939, saved England from the might of the German bombers but half a Decca transmitting chain and receiving equipment in 1948, produced for hard cash, only caused the likes of me to work long hours and without overtime payment. But I can say that working with the likes of Bill O'Brien and Harvey Schwartz, engendered in the staff a sense of having something worthwhile and important to produce. We were prepared to work hard and long; innovation was part of daily life; we were working on something unique. So there were no rigid demarcations between different skills and staff grades; what you had to offer, particularly in innovation, was never rejected; the size of the operation (less than a hundred of us) made it a 'family affair'. Most of the staff was ex RAF 60 (Radar) Group or RN, so we all spoke the same language. We were working on chains of stations – it was like good old wartime – and I even wore my blue battledress to work but with the stripes and insignia removed!

One of my very first tasks was to assemble a small item of test gear for use in-house. I was provided with a circuit diagram and an empty box that was to house the finished unit. The rest was up to me. The last time I had embarked on such a project was to make a two valve wireless-set in Stockport

Technical College. I didn't have sufficient knowledge to design the circuit and only just enough to help in its testing when completed. For most of my time with Decca, this scenario was to prevail – with one notable exception later on. This test gear job was an exercise in what was called 'packaging'. Now, were the skills required an art or a science? Both. The more science you knew, the more likely the thing would work when tested by the engineer-in-charge. The more art you had, the more pleasing the thing would appear; the less likely to fall to bits when being used, the easier it would be to maintain and operate. There was always a healthy competitive spirit amongst the lower strata of the staff – we were all young and striving to make a mark as quickly as possible and so get promotion and more money. When I had finished this scientific work of art, one of my colleagues sidled up to my bench and had a good inspection of the results of my labour. "Not bad," he said. Pause. "Pity you had to rush it!"

This same technician was working on a large transformer for powering the red hazard light installed on top of the transmitting stations aerial masts. It was a long and tedious task of assembling coils of wire and metal plates so it had to be carried out in a careful logical sequence. One lunch hour we noticed John had missed out one assembly sequence and we were in the middle of having a good laugh at his misfortune and stupidity. Unbeknown to him, just as he was getting very annoyed with us all standing round and taking the mickey, Harvey Schwartz quietly walked in. Now Harvey was small and never said anything unless it was essential. John – the lowly technician – suddenly turned round and without looking said straight to the managing director "why don't you bugger off." Harvey never said a word – and he buggered off!

So life was all very exciting – Marian and Sunday dinners just down the road – and even more so when I found 'digs' in the street right opposite to 247 Burlington Road. Then there were Monday nights. Arthur was an ex radar operator from St Eval days and now living at home in Wimbledon. Together we always patronised Wimbledon Speedway Stadium on Monday nights. Why? I never really knew. Excitement, perhaps. It was noisy and smelly and for a whole evening's worth of our time we actually had seventeen minutes of racing. The rest of the time was taken up with waiting and watching men rake the track. Funny things we do when young and away from home.

Starting work at Decca coincided with a major upgrading of the English chain of four transmitting stations. It also coincided with a royal event. The current system – Decca not royalty – had certain limitations. It was absolutely essential that there never be a break in the transmissions. Also if you were flying or sailing into the area of transmission, it was not easy to set up the dials (Deccometers). The new upgraded system overcame some of these difficulties. Even so, all the various electronic units of the station were triplicates so that failures automatically switched in the standby equipment. My part, with others, in this grand scheme of things was wiring up the transmitters, power distribution units and aerial coils. This may sound fairly straightforward but I can assure you it wasn't! The excitement and interest lay in that fact that Schwartz had sold the system before everything was designed and drawn up. There were, in fact, few drawings and we were working alongside the top boffins 'making it up as we went along'. It was real hands-on stuff and increased my knowledge of electronics far quicker than any classroom instruction. Adaptability and being prepared to have a go at anything was what was required and ensured progress within the Company. By September 1948 the new equipment was ready and tested in the laboratories and workshops. And then more excitement. All the technical staff were split up into teams and detailed off to the four transmitting sites to install what we had produced and then commission the whole new system.

Now from that bedroom window in the attic at Mudros, from which I watched the trains, there was a new feature to behold – the transmitting mast of the green slave station at East Hoathly. So I spent several weeks living at home, with another member of staff, and installing the new equipment. It really was a most enjoyable and satisfying time. For the actual commissioning of the upgraded chain I was despatched to the purple slave at Southam in Warwickshire. It was quite a tense time for everyone making sure that everything would work smoothly when 'the switch was thrown' from the old to the new. So it was with some annoyance that one night I was awaked from a well-deserved sleep in a Southam hotel to hear church bells ringing. Why the announcement to the world that Prince Charles had seen the light of day had to be made in the middle of the night was beyond my comprehension.

On returning to 247 Burlington Road with a good report of my work, I immediately went to see my boss and asked for a rise. This was readily agreed and ten shillings (50p) was added to my weekly five pounds. I was on my way up!

My love affair with Marian had been continuing apace and at Easter 1948 I took her to meet my parents in Heathfield. Well, in a way, she only got there at that particular time by default. My friend Arthur was supposed to come with me but at the last moment he cried off and so I invited Marian instead!!

Marian has always had a liking for attractive clothes and so the first post-war fashion change called The New Look soon had her in its grasp. The short, knee-length, drab wartime fashion reflected the utilitarian need to use as little cloth as possible, but now was the time to break out and go a bit crazy. So what my mother saw coming up the garden path was a rather glamorous young girl in a very long silver grey coat with a fashionable bowler type hat swathed in net that covered her face. Fortunately first appearances don't always reveal the truth and my mother quickly discovered that Marian wasn't just a smart sophisticated Londoner, but an ordinary girl. She was in fact only the third young female, requiring a bed, to pass through the Mudros portals since the days of Phyllis and the bolster episode. As there were, on this occasion, enough bedrooms to go round with due propriety, the bolster remained unabashed in the linen cupboard!

Through the rest of 1948 and 1949 my life could be described as a period of consolidation, both on the romance and work fronts. I became something of an expert in the latter. More stations were being designed and assembled in the Decca laboratories, all of which required what were called aerial coils. These components were four feet diameter coils of wire, complexly wound round Perspex insulating formers that made up part of the link between the transmitters and the aerial mast. They were tuned, using large electrical oil-filled condensers, to generate high voltage radio frequency power to be radiated from the mast. Now the trick about all this technology was in the coil wire, which wasn't just one very thick wire, wound round into a coil, but 729 individual shellac-insulated wires. Mathematicians will immediately recognise the significance of 729 – it is 3x3x3x3x3x3. Bundles of 3 and 3, and so on, wires were spiralled lengthwise round each other in an increasing number to make one flexible wire with an overall covering of cotton thread insulation. The problem came when trying to solder the end of the wire to the condenser terminals. Each of the 729 wires was individually insulated by a coating of shellac varnish. The shellac had to be removed from the ends of 729 wires, each not much thicker than a few human hairs! Fortunately Bill O'Brien wasn't just a wizard at fundamental research and design (most of the day he sat with paper and slide-rule and a large packet of cigarettes) but he also had a very practical brain. He solved the problem of stripping the shellac by using an electrically heated ceramic tube, into which was pushed the plaited-up wire ends. When the wires were heated, the shellac and cotton burnt and flaked. At the critical temperature the wires were removed from the heater and plunged into methylated spirits to prevent them becoming brittle and breaking. They were then fanned out and carefully burnished with very fine emery paper. The result was 729 insulation-free copper wire ends that could be soldered together to make a single conductor and then soldered to a terminal. Sounds easy enough – but it wasn't! Too much heat and you ended up with less than 729 wires, which would cause the coil to overheat and burn out when transmissions started. Too little heat and the shellac remained clutching the wire. I depended on the Reverse Pontiff Effect to ensure that the wire was heated to the correct temperature. The signal that a new Pope is elected is a change of Vatican chimney smoke from black to white. For me a change in smoke from white to black signalled that my wire was ready to be plunged into the methylated spirits. So the Holy Spirit and meths do have something in common! I suppose that today the whole thing would be computer-controlled and where would the fun and the art be in that?

On November 17th 1949 Marian and I announced our engagement to be married. A couple of days before Marian was in the kitchen, with her arms up to the elbows in flour, making cakes for her birthday party, when I proposed to her. All very romantic, but then I am a very romantic person! I don't remember any bended knee or prior approval by her father, but there was great rejoicing all round. As a sign of my earnestness and lack of money I bought her a second-hand engagement ring.

The wedding day was set for July 29th 1950. At the time we didn't realise all the significance of that date. It meant that a golden wedding could be celebrated in the next millennium. Most preparations for a wedding fall on the bride-to-be and her mother, so thankfully I wasn't involved too much in the detail of what was to befall me. I continued to make progress at Decca but not progress with my landlady – well more accurately with her husband. She was a grandmother, but not withstanding, her husband got it into his head that she was giving me better attention, domestically, than him. I was ordered to quit my room and this just six weeks before the wedding.

Bryan Strange and Marian on their wedding day.
New Malden 1950

As we had no accommodation lined up to go to, after the honeymoon, we were going to live in the Burford house until we could find somewhere for ourselves. So a short time before the wedding I began to live at the same address as Marian and that meant that we both had the same address on the marriage certificate. That today is not an unusual occurrence and often means only one thing but then it was quite different. Sex before marriage was something that for the likes of Marian and me was just 'not on' – not that it didn't cross our minds and other parts of our body – sex was the great expectation in life when legally married. Some may argue that that way of thinking is man-made and against the natural instincts of human functioning, which of course is absolutely true, but a long time ago humans came to realise that if we were to live in a stable and healthy society, then sex shouldn't be casual but should be for those who agreed to live in a life-long public commitment. Mind you, such an arrangement helped to ensure that couples didn't hang around once they had decided to get married!

The ceremony took place at Christ Church, New Malden, on a beautiful blue-skied day and the reception held in a marquee in Marian's back garden. Compared with today's exotic multi-coloured canvas creations and hired loos as good as any five star hotel, our facilities were nothing more than a white army tent. The day was all very traditional even if unusual and difficult for my mother who had decided that the living came before the dead – her mother, Gran Lake, was buried on that day in Beckenham.

My bride and I caught the 5.30pm train out of Paddington heading west to Bideford in north Devon and our honeymoon. None of this evening disco or pig roast or fireworks that are all the rage for today's celebrations. Our minds were on much more exciting things than that!!

So there I was sitting in a FIRST class compartment – for the first time in my life I think – with a very glamorous wife speeding on an express train out of one of the great London termini. What more could a young man of twenty-four wish for? Not that we had boarded the train without incident. We had been escorted to the station by various friends and relations with devious minds who forced confetti down our clothes and wrote 'just married' in lipstick on the carriage windows. But there was more to come – we had dinner on the train. Looking back I am not sure how we afforded all that luxury. We changed trains at Taunton, but had a wait of about an hour before puffing off on the cross-country line to Barnstable, so we walked over to a pub just outside the station and on our return the little local train was getting up steam in the down bay. It was the practice to keep the carriages of this sort of train locked until near the time of departure. Perhaps the railway company directors imagined their profits going down the drain (but 'not while standing in the station') by people hiding in the lavatory compartments and so evading payment. Anyway an elderly porter saw us. Surely at that time on a Saturday evening, we being all dressed up in our finery, he must have guessed we were a honeymoon couple and after he had unlocked a carriage and helped us in, he relocked the door. I am sure as he moved away he gave me a wink!

The journey across west Somerset and north Devon was an exercise in labour economy. As ours was the last train of the day, the guard locked up all the stations en route before waving his green flag, having handled various items of freight, including getting a horse into the parcel van. All this under normal circumstances would have been good reason for leaning out of the window and taking in all the activity. However I now had something else to think about and I must admit that we were getting later and later for our honeymoon bed!

We had ordered a taxi to drive us from Barnstable the ten miles to Bideford but as we were almost an hour late I began to imagine our first night stretched out on a railway station seat. God bless the taxi driver – he said that our train was always late but he was always prepared to honour his fare.

We had a wonderful two weeks in north Devon, visiting many well-known beauty spots and taking lots of pictures with my box-brownie camera. Perhaps our first two weeks as husband and wife can be summed up by the words I printed in our wedding photograph album, ‘and the moon came up like honey’.

Scene Two

Marriage and Family Life

And so married life started in earnest. Marian's parents were absolutely wonderful. They made over their front room for our living room so we could eat and relax on our own. They did likewise in the back room. Marian did her own cooking and housework and we lived by agreement as separately as possible from her parents. During the two and a half years we lived in the Burford house I cannot remember a single argument or time of tension.

What were our expectations as we set out on our married life together? We both came from what would be described as middle class, home-owning families. The norm for young people from this sort of background – and very often for working class families too – wishing to live together, was to marry, set up home hopefully in a house that you owned, but almost invariably bought with a building society mortgage. This arrangement was considered the duty of the husband to provide for his wife and for starting a family. That may sound paternalistic and a male-orientated scenario and perhaps against today's political correctness it was, but I can say that with us it was a true partnership in everything we planned and did. There was, however, a fairly clear understanding and agreement about each partner's contribution to the new family's life. The husband went out and earned the money and the wife kept the home and did the lion's share of bringing up the children. These were the roles that society had worked out for the best environment in which to bring up children. Living with in-laws was not ideal, regardless of how well everyone got on together, and as we had no savings the prospects for living in our home were somewhat bleak. Many were the times we walked round the district looking for houses that might have a flat to rent. Then Marian became pregnant. We were of course overjoyed but the need for a home of our own became even more pressing.

A baby girl was born to us at 7pm on November 26th 1951 in Kingston General Hospital. Fathers were not expected to attend at such occasions but I had let my presence be known before the event by several anxious phone calls to the ward. Marian had gone into hospital three weeks early but once in I hoped for things to happen immediately. The word immediately isn't part of the vocabulary of a baby still in the womb and so I became frustrated at the delay and almost demanded some action! A hot bath finally did the trick and soon afterwards MY waiting was over! The choice of names for the new arrival had been discussed by parents – now grandparents – and us for some time. My mother's suggestion of Sandra was agreed as well as our choice of Claire. So Sandra Claire she was baptised – in Union Church Heathfield – but as no one really liked the name Sandra (including my mother, she later admitted) she became known as Claire and has remained so ever since. There is little doubt that the birth of a child – especially the first – is a ground shaking experience for the mother and father and it certainly was for me. We were now responsible for a new life and there were times when it weighed heavily on our young and inexperienced shoulders. Fortunately we had Marian's mother close at hand and she helped in so many ways to put our worries in perspective and assure us that little babies are tougher than we imagined.

At this time I was earning eight pounds a week so with the arrival of Claire my father-in-law reduced our rent to one pound a week. Even so we had a hard struggle financially and Marian's budgeting skills were sorely tested. Milk was something – a few pennies – and three farthings a pint. The milkman tried rounding up Marian's weekly bill to the nearest penny but she wasn't having any of that – several farthings over the weeks added up to a whole penny! It seems quite impossible today living on so little money but inflation had not had its wicked ways then, as we shall find out later in a very dramatic way. Financially it was unfortunate that I wasn't paid for overtime, as some extra income would have been greatly appreciated at this time. Long hours at work and broken nights with a crying wet baby taxed our stamina but we survived and cherished our new child.

It was in September 1952 that a large envelope landed on our front door mat. This delivery was the result of something going on over the other side of the world. The two versions of Korea, North and South, had been scrapping across the 38th parallel for about two years with the aid of China, and America and Britain respectively. For some strange reason the high-ups at the Air Ministry in London had a vision of Korean aircraft – presumably the North variety – appearing over the English Channel and therefore the RAF radar chain needed galvanising into a more operational state. As I had been in limbo, since 1948, on what was called the G Reserve, the Air Marshals decided I could help in this venture and consequently the letter requesting my attendance at RAF Cardington for two weeks training. Two things happened on my arrival at what used to be a famous airship station; I was issued a full compliment of 'kit airman for the use of' including, for two weeks in a lovely September, a greatcoat and thick woollen underwear; I was offered a choice of station to which I could be posted. Having an intimate knowledge of the geography of Sussex, I chose RAF Wartling – that being the nearest to Heathfield. So I was posted to Wartling and Marian and baby Claire were posted to Mudros –not the one off Greece – but the one where my parents lived. On arrival at Wartling I immediately applied for, and was granted, a living-out pass. The two weeks turned out a very nice free break from work and I didn't have to endure the hardships of living in an RAF hut. As I had never worked before on the particular equipment at Wartling, my contribution to the enhanced defence of the realm was absolutely nil! All this at the taxpayer's expense. At the end of this temporary call to the colours, I was instructed to keep all my free-issue kit in good order as it would be required if those Koreans ever did venture towards our shores. The greatcoat will appear again many years hence in my story.

Work at Decca continued with the construction of more transmitting stations to increase the operational coverage of the system. The company had a small factory in Maidenhead to which I was seconded to carry out the special aerial coil work at which I had become expert. Still basking in the delights of marriage and parenthood, the thought of separation, even for a week, was not to be contemplated.

Near the delightful village of Cookham beside the river Thames, I found a caravan for hire that was to be our home – and nightmare – for several weeks. We had no car and any public transport cost money. But there were compensations that we do not enjoy today such as ordinary passenger trains taking on board bicycles and prams. And so we loaded into the guard's van at Malden Manor station one bicycle (to transport me from Cookham to work in Maidenhead); one pram (large coach built variety), not just to carry Claire, but large quantities of foods, including several big glass containers of home bottled peas, and cooked chicken and bacon. Either end of the pram hung wicker baskets full of the needs of daily family living. Then there were two big suitcases and ourselves of course. Struggling up Reynolds Road to the station would have delighted the heart of any film director shooting the scene of refugees escaping from the ravages of war. The Southern Railway in planning its route layout and train schedule had not closely considered the likes of us wanting to travel from Malden to Maidenhead. If my memory serves me correctly, we had to change twice including walking some distance from one station to another in Windsor. When we arrived in Maidenhead we trudged all the way to Cookham via a muddy lane to the caravan in a field. Young love is very strong and/or totally mad. Marian was completely isolated as the lane was so muddy, added to which I worked long hours in Maidenhead. We stored the chicken and bacon under the van for two days until, during the night, the farm chickens made a raid and destroyed the lot! On another night we heard a loud bang only to discover the peas had fermented and blown the tops off the bottles. Finally to finish this tale of woe, the dampness in the van gave Marian severe sciatica. After three or four weeks, the work was completed and none too soon we returned home to sanity.

Soon after our foray into the gypsy life, there were two important good developments in our lives. Decca, in the form of my departmental manager, came to recognise that I had two talents that should be exploited for the good of the company and for myself. Electronics, as I have said before, is a combination of science and art – or design. The real boffins applied science to research and develop new systems and the 'not-quite-boffins' – like me – applied art and design to package and wire up these new products so that they didn't fall to bits or seize up when put into harsh operational environments. Of course that is a simplification of the division of labour – the whole process from first thoughts to final production was an overlapping effort of many skills and expertise. As the company was producing very small quantities of a large range of different electronic units, this meant that the usual processes of production didn't always apply. Apart from my skills of 'engineering packaging' I was developing some skills of man-management. And so I found myself, with a small team of men, and later women, in a department working directly with the boffins producing various electronic navigational equipments.

The other good news at this time was in the form of Marian's uncle Percy and my mother and father. Between them they provided sufficient money – call it very long term loans – for us to set about buying a house in which to live and bring up our family. Building societies, mortgages, interest rates, estate agents, deposits, contracts, completion dates; all these and much more came to fill our young and inexperienced thoughts and attention. It was all new to us and full of pitfalls.

After several false starts a friend of Marian's, who worked in an estate agents office, gave us information about three houses being built in West Moseley. This was in 1952 at a time when building societies wouldn't lend more than three times the man's annual salary and at least ten percent of the cost was required as a deposit. As I was earning only ten pounds a week and the cost of the house was two thousand five hundred pounds and we had no savings, you can work out how much our kind benefactors provided.

26 Monks Avenue, West Molesey wasn't the most salubrious of addresses. When we first visited the site the house was still under construction. It was surrounded by some rough ground; a row of factories; a rather tatty pre-war housing estate and the high banks of west London reservoirs. There were some more upmarket addresses just down the road, including Hampton Court and Hampton Park Race Course. When the wind was in the wrong direction we were either assaulted by the sickly smell coming from the nearby Elizabeth Arden factory or the disgusting smell of the pigs kept by our builder living four doors away! However, it was a three bedroom detached house, reasonably well built and something we could afford. It would belong to us – well, so long as we were able to keep up the mortgage repayments. This was at a time when the country still hadn't recovered from wartime restrictions, including restrictions of materials and design. It was very much a basic, four-wall, square house; no cavity walls or insulation. The kitchen best illustrated how basic – no fitted cupboard; a sink and draining board; a small grey solid fuel boiler for heating the water; red quarry tiles for the floor. There was a fireplace in the two living rooms and all bedrooms – no central heating but there was a garage and small garden.

At the end of the day that we moved in, we shut the front door, we were in our own home, we owed nothing to anybody (except over two thousand pound to the Woolwich). We had thirteen shillings in the whole world! By careful financial management and some good luck no doubt, ever since that day we have owned our own house and never been in debt.

On January 22nd 1955 our second child was born in the Bearsted Nursing Home near the front door of Hampton Court. This time there was no kicking my heels fuming for something to happen. Things were definitely stirring so the ambulance was called just at the same time that London was experiencing one of its 'pea-soup' fogs, a phenomenon caused by the lack of wind to blow away the smoke from millions of coal fires. On these occasions the air became thick and foul TASTING beyond imagination. With the visibility down to two yards, the only way to arrive safely at the nursing home was by my walking the two miles in front of the ambulance with a torch shining on to the curb. Fortunately I knew the route like the back of my hand as I cycled it everyday to work. Our new daughter was born soon after a very fraught journey and we named her Fiona Vayla – names that had nothing to do with fog. Fiona always was a favourite of Marian and Vayla is a Shetland name – suggested by Dorothy who was living with Teddy in those northern islands.

The couple who bought the new house next door to us turned out to be good neighbours and soon Claire was running in and out of 'Uncle Ron's and Auntie Phyllis' at all times, more especially when there was a children's programme showing on the black and white television – a luxury we would have to wait many years to acquire. Our life was taken up with long hours for me at Decca and hard work for Marian looking after two young children. She made all their clothing and her own, even trousers and an overcoat for me. Home baking and a variety of culinary skills were the order of the day, as money was 'tight' and many convenience foods were still a thing for the future. Our laundry facilities were primitive to say the least – each Monday Marian set up a large round galvanised bath on bricks on the red quarry tiled kitchen floor with a portable gas ring underneath. This was our 'washing machine' of the day. The clothes were stirred by hand with a wooden paddle. On one occasion, this lethal conglomerate of low technology decided to strike and so the bath tipped over and poured boiling water down the front of Marian's legs. It all ended up with the whole family going back to Reynolds Road until the huge blisters had healed. This painful experience together with our thoughts about schools for the children put in train the idea that we should move – but where to?

Schools in the area were not the best one could have wished for. The quality and way of life in this outer suburb of London didn't come up to the standard we set for our children and for ourselves. We were looking for a cleaner and more country-style life – perhaps a small market town with good schools and open spaces and a large garden for the children to play in and I could be like my mother and grow lots of vegetables. My boyhood days in the country were beginning to sprout shoots out of our married life. But my work and future were by now firmly established with the Decca Navigator at New Malden.

I have always said that if I were to be the Desert Island castaway and asked what book I would choose, it would have to be an atlas of the British Isles. Think of all the journeys and routes you could plan – what would be the best way to get from A to B? In those days the Bartholomew atlas maps included different colours for different heights, starting with green for the lowlands and ending with dark brown for the mountains. With a little imagination you could have a 3-D picture of the land – what places 'looked' attractive, what places to avoid. So out came the atlas. Here was Motspur Park railway station, the closest to Decca Navigator. Here were the railways. Roads didn't come into it as we had no car. How far south could we go in, say, about an hours commuting train journey? It didn't need any navigational aid to tell us we had landed up at Horsham in West Sussex.

A visit to Horsham to check out schools and housing and train timetables and the nature of the town, confirmed our choice that this was the place to bring up our family. Horsham, in those days, was a medium sized market town of about thirteen thousand souls. There was no smoky or smelly industry – the air was clean from the surrounding countryside. It had modern schools for all ages, a small hospital, and perhaps the most beautiful street anywhere to be seen – not that we could afford a Tudor house in the tree-lined Causeway leading down to the parish church of St Mary. The town shared with Oxford the distinction of having a Carfax – the meeting, into a square, of four roads from north, south, east and west. In those days the routes from Dorking, Brighton, Haywards Heath and Guildford met in the Carfax. Even so the whole town had an atmosphere of calm and gentility – and there was a 7.50am train from the station to Motspur Park in time to start work at 9am. So here was the place that was to be our home for seventeen years and where our children would plant their roots and school days – where we would make life-long friends and enjoy a great deal of happiness and fulfilment. It was also to be the springboard from which the second half of my career was to be launch.

An added bonus to living in Horsham was that we would be nearer to my brother and his family now in nearby Crawley. After four years in the Meteorological Office served on the wilds of the Shetland Islands, they were posted south and were now living in the calmer climes of West Sussex. We would also be closer to my parents in Heathfield, although the train journey from Horsham was somewhat convoluted, involving changes at Three Bridges, East Grinstead and Groombridge and even, sometimes, Eridge for good measure. Still I mustn't say anything against my favourite mode of travel and East Grinstead was one of those interestingly quirky stations built on two levels – before the Dark Age of Doctor Beeching.

But before we could start our version of the Good Life there was the small matter of selling our house in Molesey and buying a new one in Sussex. Fortunately our first experiences with builders and solicitors and building societies had successfully rubbed off and we were now far more aware of the traps and pitfalls of house purchase. We decided to sell 26 Monks Avenue, move back to Marian's parents and then when we had the money in our sticky little hands buy a house in Horsham. This arrangement would protect us from the financial possibility of having two mortgages at the same time or overspending on the new house. During the spring, summer and autumn of 1956 our plans came to a successful fruition. We sold our house for three thousand pounds, making a profit of five hundred pounds, and purchased a newly built two bedroom semi-detached bungalow for two thousand three hundred pounds. In November 1956 the British and French armies marched into the Suez Canal fiasco and Marian, Bryan, Claire and Fiona Strange marched into 92 Cootes Avenue, Horsham. This time we had money to spare. My parents waived the outstanding payments of the money they had lent us for our first house and Uncle Percy gave us a belated wedding present of a hundred pounds after he waived our last repayment.

The bungalow we were about to purchase was smaller than the accommodation of Monks Avenue and not to Marian's liking! I had chosen our new home without her being present! It was, as a building, a bit down market but with Horsham and all it had to offer in the way of life-style, it made an attractive move – so I thought! Fortunately as there was some surplus money from the sale and because the building was hardly started when we signed the contract, we were able to incorporate certain improvements and changes that just prevented a divorce! The building practice of covering the bare inside walls with only wet plaster – no dry lining – meant that a great deal of water suspended throughout the building took several months to dry out. Consequently when we first moved in, only a week after the builders had left, everything became damp and covered in moisture. The bungalow was one on a large new estate and the builder's intention was to get the people in as fast as possible, with as little outside work completed as he could get away with. We had in fact moved into a building with no paths – just a sea of mud and rubble between the road and the front door. We were damp inside and out, physically, and not a little spiritually as well. This was the first time Marian had lived any distance away from her parents and, with all the other difficulties and trauma of moving, made it a hard time for her. But hope and encouragement was at hand!

Still surrounded with packing cases, mud and damp walls, a few days after we had arrived there was a knock on the front door. "I have come to welcome you to Horsham and to your new home – may I come in for a few minutes?" announced the man standing there. He was the vicar of Horsham, the Reverend Ronnie Goodchild. His twenty minute visit was to have a very profound impact on all our lives and especially on mine. His visit became far more than just a welcome – as important and delightful as that was – he started us thinking about the religious upbringing of our girls, our own faith, and what we should be doing in that direction. He made the connection that can link starting a new life in a new place with a new start to the deeper aspects of life. Part of the reason why we hadn't given this subject its due attention was that Marian was an Anglo-Catholic and I was 'Chapel'. We knew that in all things concerning the bringing up of children it was vital to present common ground between mother and father. Anyway we did get our shoes cleaned the next Sunday and attended the parish church of St Mary at the far end of The Causeway. That was the start of my conversion to Anglicanism and the start of a long and happy – and busy – membership of the church in Horsham.

By 1956 I had worked eight years for Decca Navigator, during which time I was paid as a member of staff by a weekly salary. All pay for factory shop floor workers was calculated on an hourly basis whilst the 'staff' was paid either weekly or monthly, depending on your seniority. This hierarchical system of employment and payment was the norm for the engineering industry in those days and produced a great deal of discontent and expenditure of energy by the unions representing the 'hourly paid' who had to clock-on and clock-off, while the two grades of salary staff kept good time 'on trust'. On Friday afternoons the wages lady came round with the weekly pay packets. Those on an hourly rate immediately ceased all work and meticulously checked their cash against the times they had clocked on and off – including overtime. There was always much coming and going with foremen and department managers trying to sort out those who reckoned they had been done out of ten minutes pay. We of the salary-types had no such hassle because over-time wasn't paid, even though we nearly always worked many extra hours each week.

At the time of our move to Horsham I was earning about twelve pounds each week, but then as a reward for my labours the management decided I should be transferred to monthly staff at a salary of £800 per annum. I really began to think I was going places, even if it meant long hours away from the family. Six days each week I left home at 7.30am to peddle to the station to catch the 7.50 train. Hardly time to say 'time to get up' to Claire and Fiona before I was away. For many years I didn't arrive home until 7.30 pm, by which time the girls' eyes were more shut than open, but later, with the reduction in working hours, it was 6.30pm and sometimes I didn't have to work on Saturday morning. Weekends usually started at 2.30pm on Saturday afternoon when I arrived home after completing a five and a half day week. Was it worth all the travelling time and long hours at work? Yes, it was! I had a stable job with just about enough money to live on and bring up the family. Having a home in Horsham was so different from living in London. There was a far greater sense of identity and we came to know people and be involved in a life far outside work. And then there was the countryside. I shall always remember Dorking tunnel – it was the great divide between work and home. Sitting in the train travelling south through the North Downs and coming out of that hole in the ground was like passing into a new world. I was leaving built-up London and arriving in a green and pleasant land. I know that beauty spots like Box Hill were north of the Downs, but to me such places were 'London country'.

Not all was lovely with the trains. My commuting (nearly one hundred miles every day) was up and down on the Horsham to Waterloo line. The coach sets were old, badly heated, and non-corridor; they stopped at every station. They compared poorly with the express service that ran from Horsham to Victoria via Dorking. This comparison was brought home to me in the evening as we stopped at Epsom station. We, being the slow train, had to wait for the Victoria train to speed through. How frustrating it was to see the city gents sitting in their posh train as it passed us lesser mortals and knowing they would arrive home into the bosom of their families twenty minutes earlier than me. But not all was lost! Continuing my schoolboy interest in railway workings, I would watch the exit signal at the end of the other side of our platform. If it remained at red as the Victoria train came into the station, a smart bit of footwork got me across the platform ready to jump into the nearest carriage before the signal turned green. This didn't happen very often, but when it did I was more than pleased. My transference from slow to fast was not condoned by marauding station staff and always produced much shouting of "stand clear; stand clear", flag waving and whistle blowing.

At home we bought from my father a Hoover washing machine – the very latest in appliance technology. It was not very big; a top loader with a hand operated wringer; an electrically driven impeller which did a marvellous job of winding all the clothes into a sodden mass; the water heated by electricity. Of course it was not 'plumbed in' but had rubber pipes that were draped across the sink to fill and empty the machine. More often than not the system filled the kitchen as well with water! We also became the proud owners of a refrigerator.

The plot at the back of the bungalow called out for my gardening expertise to be exercised, such as it was. There were two fundamental gardening principles that somehow had taken root in my brain. Straight edges and level playing fields were out. Not for me the square flat patches that I saw behind London's rows of terraced houses as I travelled home. Different levels of flower beds and lawns required the construction of low dry walls – at which I became quite proficient. Garden building was one thing, but I never really got to grips with the names of all those plants unless they were of the edible variety. The garden had to be attractive but also serve as a playground for the girls as they were never allowed to play out in the street.

So what were these two little daughters like that we had brought to live in the pleasant town of Horsham? Claire was five and started straight away at Trafalgar Infants School. Fiona was two. Neither ever attended a nursery school as Marian was always at home for them – and what better place and person to have as preparation for school life? Claire was extravert, full of bounce, perhaps a little wilful and always ready to 'go for it'. Everything was for her, but not necessarily at the expense of others. She always had to be at the 'front of the queue' and she was quite happy to go off to some activity without us. Fiona was just the opposite. She was far more pragmatic, laid back and a little introverted. She didn't like being separated from us, although she wouldn't admit it. When they were both Brownies, Fiona only agreed to attend 'camp' if Claire went as well – but she wasn't to speak to her! Their characters were exactly demonstrated by the way they responded to one of our house rules. If you had hurt someone in any way, then everything stopped until you said "sorry" – and not just a grudging "sorry" but an honest "sorry mummy," or whoever. Claire found this very hard, especially the added "mummy." A confrontation with her could go on for quite a long time and on one occasion Fiona became fed-up with it all, and said to her sister "Why don't you just say 'sorry mummy' – you don't have to mean it and then we can have our tea"!! Marian spent a lot of time reading to them – such books as 'Anne of Green Gables' became part of their young lives. Marian was always at home when they arrived back from school – perhaps that hour 'letting off' together between four and five was the most important part of the day.

During those years in Horsham, three strands of activity and experience became interwoven to be the way of life for me – strands that had a bearing on all our lives. First there was the family life – Fiona soon followed Claire to Trafalgar Infants School and both advanced up the education ladder to Greenway Junior School. These institutions fully realised our hopes for good schooling away from London. The whole gambit of getting two little girls off to school and collecting them again; after-school activities; Brownies and Guides and ballet dancing lessons; birthday parties with frilly new frocks – all this fell heavily on Marian to arrange and to sort out the tantrums that inevitably resulted when little children come together. She was the one who took Claire to a London hospital when she, Claire, kept running a slightly high temperature. A rather zealous young GP had suggested this course of action that ended up with a little girl standing on a table surrounded by a consultant and several medical students. The doctor collected this group together – along with Marian – to explain the symptoms that the under-training doctors might come across in future times. The doctor observed that here they had a perfectly healthy little girl with a slight temperature that wouldn't go down – and an over worried mother!! If only the floor below that worried mother could have opened up! A week's holiday by the sea soon restored equilibrium to the family.

I escaped much of this sort of activity, being more than fully occupied with things electronic far away in New Malden. But there was something else going on in New Malden that was to cast a shadow on the family. During our pre-Horsham stay at Reynolds Road Marian's mother often retired to bed in the afternoon suffering from quite severe stomach pains. She said she wouldn't go to the doctor until we had moved, but now we were established in our new home, advice was sort – she had developed cancer of the pancreas. In the spring of 1957 she came to stay with us for several months until we couldn't cope any longer and on returning to New Malden she went into a nursing home, for her last few days, before dying on July 20th. A few months later the Reynolds Road home was sold and my father-in-law moved into a bungalow in the next road but one to us. He became a city-gent commuting to Victoria. The death of my mother-in-law was the first major tragedy we had to experience and her loss to Marian came as a very great blow. Marian, a long time ago, had cut the apron-strings, but that hadn't prevented their deep relationship from continuing.

The electronic strand of my life once again changed when I was transferred to a small department specially set-up to develop a new piece of navigational equipment. Roy Swale was the engineer-in-charge and for several years I was to be his second-in-charge. I must now interest the scientists amongst my readers, probably to the bewilderment of the artists. There already was a development of a Decca navigational aid called a Flight Log (Omnitrack). You will remember that the radio wave information picked up by the Decca receiver was displayed by three dials giving numbered grid readings. This dial information had to be transferred on to special maps with the grid lines overprinted – resulting in a plotting process that was not suitable work in the cockpit of modern aircraft, especially of the domestic passenger carrying type. So a moving map and pen recorder presentation of the information had been developed. The track and position of the aircraft was drawn automatically. Technically this was a success but the equipment turned out to be heavy, expensive and bulky – it being an electro-mechanical analogue computer system. It had a poor reliability record. What was needed was a simpler machine and this is where Roy Swale and a mechanical engineer by the name of Tim Holden came in. Between them, they developed a system that took the analogue information from the receiver and converted it into digital information. Today everything is 'digital'; today computers have almost no moving parts; today the wizardry of integrated circuits and other miniaturised components gives us computing facilities beyond the wildest dreams of my sixties days with Decca. And yet it was the concept of digitising analogue information that made the Swale-Holden version of the Flight Log a success. Again it was an electro-mechanical system, but much smaller, simpler, and reliable. Over the years we slowly designed in new solid-state components that produced smaller and even more reliable equipment. By the time I left Decca in the early seventies nearly all the 'mechanical' had disappeared. Working with computers was so new that we couldn't even spell the word correctly – we had equipment labels engraved computors (!) I remember a discussion in which it was agreed that computors was the spelling for a piece of hardware and computers was reserved for people who computed.

It is interesting to philosophise on the nature of the digital condition. To digitize is to brake up continuously changing (analogue) electronic information into discrete, or individual, parts. The greater the number of bits produced (pixels, digits and all that), the more precise is the digital representation to the continuously changing information. Each individual bit or part of information is completely separate from all the others that go to make up the whole. Each bit stands isolated from the rest. And yet all are dependant on the rest. Take away any individual bit and the whole is that much less whole. Life and society today can be described as digital in that we live lives that are broken up into isolated bits; we sit as separated individuals in front of our computer and television screens; our business is carried out using isolating Information Technology systems, e.g. 'the hole in the wall' money dispenser; families live in smaller units (nuclear) rather than as a community (extended); 'congregations' (not just church ones) become smaller and smaller as we drape ourselves in front of the 'telly' and don't want to go out and socialize in the evening. Society has become differentiated (digital) instead of being integrated (analogue) – to use mathematical jargon. Life today is not writ cursive but print. All this is a great pity as life is best when it is joined up with other people, when we live in community; when we live holding hands and not separated like soldiers standing to attention in a line.

But back to the early 60's and that 'computor' we designed. It was at this time that I came nearest to being a scientist and not an artist. I really understood how that machine worked because it was based on a technology that I was familiar with. We were still – just – in the age of thermionic valves and mechanical relays but I did become involved in the development of some of the first printed circuits to replace conventional wiring techniques. Today printed circuits appear in just about every piece of electrical and electronic equipment we buy.

Our department was a classic example of how the company worked. A team of six did everything from the original circuit design to producing half a dozen prototypes. We had to call on other departments, such as machine and sheet metal shops and drawing office, but the design, assembly and testing was carried out in our department. Even so, I learnt and practiced the rudiments of metal work and technical drawing required for the very first models put together to prove our circuit designs. All these skills still come in useful today in our age of DIY. We also drew up the test specifications and operating instructions. The testing of our equipment including flying it in the Company's aircraft – an old Avro Anson – at Croydon Airport and at several other civil and military airfields. The flying bit always put me in a dilemma, as I hated being off the ground and Marian wasn't keen on the idea either. Fortunately other members of the team fell over themselves to get airborne. The scope of the work increased over the years and we ended up with a department of over thirty people. It was at this stage (late 60's) that things began to change in my working life and job expectation – but first to the third strand of my life.

That visit by the vicar of Horsham began to have repercussions, as we became regular worshippers at St Mary's church. My translation – that word is usually reserved for times when bishops are moved from one diocese to another but never mind – from 'chapel' to C. of E. was fairly straightforward, as long ago I had not become too depressed by that sign over the Sussex wayside chapel informing me that the wages of sin was death. The Union Church in Heathfield didn't preach or practice the darker side of exclusivity of some sects and St Mary's Horsham was far from High Church. Another plus point was that the vicar's preaching was short, like his visit, which was refreshing after the long and tedious sermons of Unionism. After a time of preparation I gladly accepted an invitation to be confirmed and so entered fully into the liturgical and sacramental life of Anglicanism. The Bishop of Chichester went sick the day of the confirmation service and so a ninety-year-old retired episcopal authority was dragged from his fireside to perform the act of confirmation with the Holy Spirit. Being young in this new brand of the faith, and perhaps somewhat naive, I was a little disappointed when the old hands laid on my head did not produce tongues of fire, nor the sound of a mighty rushing wind – not even a white dove. Still it was a start – a start that quickly progressed into commitment and a lot of hard work. It also meant that all four of us could attend church together and we parents could present a common front to our children concerning the important ramifications of the Christian faith.

This was at the time when the church became very conscious of its need for more money. The traditional methods of collection were enshrined in such activities as summer fetes, Christmas bazaars, plates in church, jumble sales (very popular), coffee mornings and various other fund raising efforts – even raffles. Unseen behind this activity, were the Church Commissioners beavering away at investing the legacies of the dead to pay for the livings of the clergy. All this activity was deemed to be inadequate and contrary to

Biblical teaching. It was all too random and how could the church treasurers budget on unknown quantities? No, what was needed was a long term regular financial commitment by every member of the congregation and, if possible, even from those outside the church door. So was invented Planned Giving, or as it later became known, Christian Stewardship. But how much to give – what was expected of each of us? Well the Bible had the answer – a tenth of all our money!! Work that out for yourself and you will soon realise how far most (all?) fall short of contributing the Biblical tithe. To educate good traditional Christian folk in deciding just what was the amount of money each was expected to give, the Church employed professional staff to come into a parish and run 'a campaign'. I can tell you it was a pretty hard sell and a hard time for the likes of me when about a hundred of us laymen were trained to become 'visitors'. Lists of people from regular to highly irregular church attenders were shared out amongst the visitors who then knocked on doors and expounded the principles and administration of Planned Giving. Now money, and how much we have and how we spend it, is something we very much keep close to our chest – it's our business and nobody has any right to question us about it. So, it is obvious with what trepidation I set out to fulfil my Christian duty as a newly fledged Anglican! In all I visited over seventy different families and, believe it or not, I mostly got a kind and understanding hearing. Unbeknown to me, at this time a seed had been sown that over the next few years was slowly to germinate and change my life forever. There were the lighter sides of my Church visiting activity. One night I knocked on a door and was invited in by the lady of the house. Having introduced myself and explained the purpose of my visit, she said that money matters were the concern of her husband and would I please come through to the living room at the back of the house. There in front of the fire I saw the back of a man's head, shrouded in swirling steam, sticking up over the brim of a tin bath. Hubby was having his weekly bath! I never saw his face. Although we never knew what a person's response was – how much they finally decided to give, or not to give – in this case I didn't even have the satisfaction of seeing what sort of reaction my little homily had. I said my piece and left! Over the years I became more and more involved in the work of Christian Stewardship and by 1970 I became chairman of the whole movement in Horsham. I am not sure if my enthusiasm for the work was shared by Marian who spent many a long evening alone at home – after a long day with me away at Decca – while I was about the 'Lord's business'. And it didn't stop there. I was elected to be a member of the Parochial Church Council, a lesson reader and an administrator of the chalice at the Eucharist. Towards the end of the 60's I became a Pathfinder leader – a combination of Sunday school teacher and youth leader. Working with any children in those days didn't carry the scrutiny of the law and police records. Only the traditional jokes about scout and choirmasters linked grave impropriety between the old and young. However, it was a great responsibility to be given charge of young people as I found to my distress one Saturday night. A large group of Pathfinders and leaders had taken part in a rally in Worthing and a count of heads on arrival back in Horsham revealed one child from our group was missing. As I was in charge of the outing, it fell to me to go to the family and report the loss. By the time I arrived at the child's home, the little girl had rung mum and dad saying she had missed her lift and "please come and pick me up." What a relief, but I was responsible.

My participation with conducting public worship threw-up something that was to dog me for the rest of my life. I was extremely nervous of standing in front of people and talking in public. It was bad enough reading from a prepared script or from the Bible, but anything off-the-cuff was a nightmare. I felt sick beforehand and would come home from church and literally ache all over from the tension. This reaction might have been a warning or signal that I just wasn't cut out for this kind of activity, but somehow I ignored these signs, believing that God would always see me through. He never let me down but it was a mighty (Almighty?) near thing on many occasions!

In 1960 my brother was posted for one year to the tiny island of Gan in the Indian Ocean. This sea level strategic island was a staging post for RAF transport planes flying to the Far East and Australia and needed the skills of those expert in matters meteorological. This left Dorothy and three children somewhat isolated in Crawley, so Marian made a weekly visit to them.

Another regular activity for the family was cycling. Each of us, including my father-in-law, had a bicycle – well Fiona only had a saddle that was attached to the crossbar on my machine. Claire's stead wasn't much more than a large fairy cycle and she had to peddle like mad to keep up with the grow-ups. She was never one to be beaten in her determination not to lag behind but it was always accompanied by screams of "it's not fair, it's not fair" because Fiona had to make no effort at all. This statement about the vagaries and unfairness of life was to become a family hallmark, but particularly associated with Claire – not that she ever had time to waste bemoaning the fact! Cycling with country picnics was very popular with our daughters and a favourite spot was Denne Hill just south of Horsham off the Worthing Road. From its summit (all two hundred feet or less) could be seen a panoramic view over Horsham and on a clear day the North Downs beyond. One memorable Easter all my brother's family were with us and a picnic was organised for Denne Hill. Unfortunately, even with Teddy's meteorological influence, nothing could stop the snow falling and the trip was called off. The children weren't to be outdone and so the picnic was eaten in the sitting room – wearing Wellingtons and scarves!

By the early sixties Claire and Fiona were beginning to grow out of their shared bedroom and so the prospect of another move loomed on the horizon. After Christmas 1963 we found a larger house on the other side of the town and nearer to the station. Unfortunately that wasn't the only thing happening at that time – no sooner had we put our bungalow on the market than it started snowing. The ensuing freeze-up for three months prevented any but the most hardy and urgent traveller to come to Horsham, let alone down Cootes Avenue to look at houses. Ultimately all the business of selling and buying was completed and by late spring we had moved into 1 Potters Croft, Horsham.

Scene Three

A Square Peg in a Round Hole

Potters Croft was so named because in times gone by earthenware goods were produced here. The house deeds included a clause prohibiting the current owner from participating in such activity, so there was no chance of me making a penny or two as a sideline. Still it was a good-sized three bedroom semi-detached dwelling and provided extra space for the girls to spread their wings and have separate rooms. Downstairs there were only two rooms. A large through living-room included what was all the latest in architectural fashion – two very large picture windows, one at each end. These panes of glass acted as unwanted radiators in summer and unwanted refrigerators in winter, as double glazing was still a bit 'new fangled'. Still, we had a panoramic view of the houses close all around! The kitchen was also large and included a modern white solid fuel boiler and, at the rear end, an area for eating. It was in this kitchen that I decided to exercise my talents for the first time with a major do-it-yourself (DIY) project. I built more cupboards and also what was a new innovation for those days, a peninsular unit across the kitchen to separate the eating area from the food preparation. Burnt orange was the colour theme. Next came wardrobe cupboards in our bedroom. We had come a long way since the frugal and bare days of Monks Avenue.

Claire had successfully negotiated the eleven-plus examination and started the next stage of her education at Horsham High School for Girls. Three years after moving to Potters Croft Fiona followed suit and they both advanced through a busy and happy traditional sort of life with Girl

Guides, ballet dancing classes, church youth club and of course finally BOYS! Fortunately we were still in the age when it was relatively safe for young people to be out in the streets without fear of certain mugging or worse – I say fortunately not just because it was safer but at the beginning of the sixties we still had no car.

1963 was a moving year for The Strange family. My brother had returned two years previously from the Island of Gan. The rejoicing at his return resulted in the birth of their fourth child; first was Gregory in Salisbury, Peta in Shetland, Warwick in Crawley and then, Mark, again in Crawley. Now, promotion prospects were not high in the Met. Office but Teddy had some considerable artistic and draughtsmanship skills and this, together with his passion for fishing, encouraged him to apply for a post in the Scottish Civil Service Marine Laboratory in Aberdeen, and so later in the sea-fishing world he was to become a well-known expert on all kinds of commercial fishing nets. His successful application resulted in two other things; for him and his family, moving to Aberdeen; for our family, a future lifelong love affair with Scotland.

This was to be Teddy's first experience of house purchase that appeared at one stage to be ending in disaster. He started work in Aberdeen before the family moved and so he was responsible for the house hunting. One evening he rung Dorothy and said he had bought a bungalow – a two bedroom bungalow. By this time, not only did they have four children, but also Dorothy's mother living with them. Dorothy thought her husband had taken an early liking to the Scottish national drink, but the Scots are cannier in many things than the English. They were building bungalows with space reserved to add, later, a staircase up to a large open-area loft. This ploy kept down the initial cost of the building and gave the purchaser his individual choice of how and when the loft was partitioned off to make extra bedrooms. It was a brilliant scheme and ultimately turned Dorothy's nightmare into a six-bedroom home. Also, the Scots do not depend just on concrete for foundations – bedrock, like for the sensible Biblical man, was the base on which dwellings were built. This requirement gave Teddy a massive honeycomb of unfloored cellars (rates free) under his bungalow in which all sorts of hobbies and activities took place.

Scotland became home for my brother and all his family and now, two generations on, they are more Scottish than English. For my family, Aberdeen became a place giving us a six hundred miles journey to see my brother. But help was at hand – Marian's uncle Percy sold his car to us, well Marian's father paid for it and I learnt to drive. My male pride was very much dented when I was required to take the driving test twice before passing – a dent that was further deepened when later Marian passed first time! The car was an interesting piece of automobile engineering. It was a Vauxhall Vanguard-Vignale (Italian styled by a man named Vignale, I think); it had a full width front bench seat, a steering column three-gear change, an overdrive (fourth gear) operated by a switch located next to the gear lever. It was built as strong as an army tank. The overdrive arrangement was a wonderful idea and very useful for accelerating when overtaking – that is when it worked. The joker in the pack was a solenoid that I discovered was housed under the gearbox beneath the car. When operating correctly this electro-mechanical device moved the gears to a higher ratio without any clutch work. Unfortunately it didn't always agree to work and so one could be left in an awkward and dangerous predicament when hoping to pass another car in grand style. I discovered that the solenoid 'stuck' and so didn't change the gears. The immediate answer to the problem was to stop the car as safely as possible, and armed with a hammer, crawl under the car and give the offending mechanism a sharp tap on its bottom – not the ideal activity when dressed in Sunday best. The registration letters of the vehicle were VOY and so she became known to us as Auntie Voy – Vi being wife to Uncle Percy who sold us the car.

It was in this monster of a car that in August 1964 we first set out on the long journey north to the land of purple heather and multi-coloured kilts:- of yellow gorse and broom, of black and white mountains, of blue lochs, of green valleys and grey cities. Unfortunately long before we reached the border into this Technicolor country, even before we were north of the Watford Gap, we had to negotiate the dreary forty miles of London streets from one side of the conurbation to the other. Motorways were few and far between and the North Circular Road as a bypass had already become a joke. To get to the Lake District in one day meant some pretty hard driving and then we had to find a campsite and pitch our borrowed frame tent. To add to the joys of this first-time experience, Fiona sat in the back of the car clutching a plastic bowl in which to catch the contents of her last meal. Unbeknown to us, this was probably the start of a grumbling appendix that two years later was removed. Our first night under canvas was wet and rough and not being familiar with the requirements for putting up a frame tent, I obstinately insisted that the guy-ropes should be slack, resulting in the tent barely standing up in the wind and rain. Despite Fiona's discomfort, there were great shouts of exaltation as we passed over the border – we were in foreign parts for the first time. It was a Sunday morning when we passed through the grim outskirts of Glasgow and the place was almost deserted except for the ladies – all wearing hats – walking down the streets going to the Kirk – funny the things you remember!

We were given the luxury of sleeping in one of the original downstairs bedrooms at 10 Deeside Drive, Aberdeen, as Teddy hadn't completed the loft conversion. But what had been completed for many years was the royal railway, just below the back garden wall, that carried kings and queen up Royal Deeside to Ballater and so to Balmoral. The royal train passed Teddy's window at breakfast time on several occasions when we too were visitors to Scotland. Unfortunately the carriage blinds were always drawn so we never discovered whether they ate Scott's porridge oats for breakfast – and did they eat in their dressing gowns?

Over the years we must have visited Scotland at least twenty times. It started by camping en route, then having the comfort of a caravan and finally becoming really soft and 'going B and B'. Motorways later shortened the distance and reduced the energy required to drive hundreds of miles. During these visits to Aberdeen, and then after Teddy retired to Inverness, we have enjoyed nearly all the varying beauty of Scotland:- the rugged wet and windy west coast, the grandeur of the Highlands, the softness of the east coast and the Moray Firth, lots of castles. We have camped by beautiful lochs and climbed many hills and on one memorable occasion a mountain.

Lochnagar is nearly four thousand feet above sea level at its summit. It sits more or less in the middle of the Cairngorms National Park a few miles south of the road between Ballater and Braemar. To get closest to it by car you take the little road over the bridge, south out of Ballater and drive up the beautiful Glen Muick to the Spittal of Glenmuick, a drive of about ten miles. In front of you at the end of the road is the fabulous stretch of Loch Muick with Lochnagar climbing above as a backdrop to the water. Words cannot describe it – its beauty, its expanse and its silence. We have visited this place on many occasions, two of which are especially memorable. Once we had a rare sighting of a pine martin sitting up in the sun showing off his yellowish chest. These weasel-like mammals are arboreal – tree living – and rarely seen in open country. The other time of note could have ended in disaster if it had not been for Gregory, my eldest nephew, who is now a well-known climber in Scotland. Teddy and I decided we would climb to the top of Lochnagar, although climb is not exactly the correct term for this journey – it is just a long stiff walk and school parties are taken to the top. The evening before we were to set out, Gregory insisted we carried a compass and map just in case the cloud suddenly descended and placed a shroud over us.

Now a compass and map are not much good unless one knows how to co-ordinate them and to this end Gregory attempted to instruct us. My brother and I considered this quite unnecessary and we didn't really pay much attention. The following day we all went by car to Loch Muick (but not Gregory) and Teddy and I walked to the top of the mountain leaving the rest of the party to go round the loch below. Fine. Well, not fine, when the cloud and rain rapidly came down and within a few minutes we could see only a few yards around us. We were totally disorientated – Teddy said we had come from one direction and I was just as sure we had come from the opposite way! Two rather sheepish-looking walkers could be seen crouching down behind a large boulder trying desperately to remember what had been said the night before. Without the map and compass, and finally sorting out how to use them, we could easily have been candidates for the mountain rescue team or even another kind of shroud. As it was, all we got was the sharp edge of Dorothy's and Marian's tongue when we got down far later than we had promised!

Our visit to Scotland in August 1967 is remembered by a special meal. My father-in-law had been ill in Dorking hospital for several weeks but we had planned that if he was well enough, he would come to Scotland with us, as his first visit there. Unfortunately he was diagnosed suffering from lung cancer and his holiday with us didn't materialised. He was very disappointed, but gave us money with which to buy a family meal for us all. It was this meal (I think I remember correctly) that was eaten in a wooden shack of a cafe at the Falls of Shin, costing half a crown (twelve and a half p) each for a huge plate of home-cooked nosh.

On January 5th 1968 Frederick Burford died. So both of Marian's parents were carried away by cancer before either of them reached old age. Hard for us all, but especially for Marian. He left her sufficient money, after the sale of his bungalow, to do something quite substantial if we didn't just want to invest it. In the spring of the same year I was having a hard time at work. On one or two occasions I found the responsibility of my work got the better of me – stress I suppose we would call it today. I cannot recall if this particular occurrence happened at the same time that Roy Swale (head of our department) developed a brain tumour and after a short illness died. His death was a great blow to me as we had been close colleagues for many years and together had been responsible for the development and production of several navigational aids. By this time we had introduced many new types of components into the equipment – first transistors and then integrated circuits. All this new technology was OK for scientist but not so easy for artists like me. I could still engineer and package the new innovations without understanding exactly how they worked, or being able to manipulate them into new and wonderful pieces of avionics technology. Now, although I was second-in-charge of the department, there was little doubt that the head had to be a scientist. So at this time there was a lot of tension as to who should take charge. Some people advised me to accept the position of head of department, but I knew my limitations. Whether it was this particular situation that caused me to go sick, I cannot remember, but sick I went and the doctor prescribed something rather unexpected. He said that Marian and I should go out each day and enjoy ourselves! In other words forget about the stresses of work and find some other interest in the fresh air. This we did and during one of our daily trips we passed a large caravan sales lot and in a flash of inspiration we drove in and before you could say tow-bar we were the proud owners of a tiny home on two wheels. That quickly got rid of some of Marian's inheritance and I was soon back at work where the question of the next head of department was resolved by my suggesting to the management that Roger Bangay, the very competent, and chartered, senior engineer should be given the post. Roger became head and I remained second, to the satisfaction of all, but it was about this time I had the first rumblings of the idea perhaps I was a square peg in a round hole. But first back to that caravan.

Prior to my spell off work we had sold 'Auntie Voy' and bought a smaller Triumph car with which it would be easier for Marian to learn to drive. Being completely naive about the technicalities of towing caravans, we didn't realise that we had been ill-informed about the capability of the Triumph to pull the caravan we had purchased, even if it was only small and light in weight. We planned a grand progress from Horsham to Dornoch, far up in the north east coast of Scotland, via Essex to collect a special awning to fit against the side of the caravan and give extra covered space. Our very first night, ever, in a caravan turned out to be almost unbearable. We had selected a site, from the Caravan Club book, where the individual pitches were approached up a short sharp incline. Our car took serious objection to this task and immediately the clutch started to slip and there was a strong smell of burning. We finally made it to the top, just hoping that we hadn't done too much damage. But more aggro was to follow. British Rail operated very large shunting yards at various places throughout the country. At these sites grown men, instead of being tucked up in bed at night with their wives, practice their skills at making up long trains by changing the position of individual wagons until satisfied they are all in the right order. They carry out these exercises, not by gentle persuasion, but by brute force and banging and clanging the wagons together – all night long! As luck would have it, one such yard happened to be right alongside our chosen caravan site. We were a pretty fraught family by daybreak and without even staying for breakfast, we were out of there before you could say Dr. Beeching. Fortunately the clutch held for the long journey right up to Dornoch, where we joined Teddy and Dorothy and family for one of our many happy holidays exploring the Scottish scenery. On the return journey we got as far south as Consett, west of Newcastle, and again our inexperience in caravanning almost brought serious disaster. The seasoned tower will always carefully check his intended route to avoid steep ascents. We didn't. Halfway up a sharp gradient we stalled and started to slip backwards. I shouted to the family to get out immediately and applying the brakes managed to stop the downward drift. A gang of men on a nearby building site came to the rescue – I unhitched the van and they pushed it up to the top of the hill. One lives and learns. I think it was on this trip home that we stopped in Cambridge late in the afternoon. We had exactly a pound left of our holiday money, after filling up with petrol. We trawled the city and found a cafe where curries were on offer for five shillings (25p) each. With four free glasses of water with the meal, we arrived home stony broke – but happy and owing nobody anything.

By this time we had been proud house owners for over fifteen years and had learnt the wisdom that bricks and mortar are the best commodities in which to invest any available assets. Even in those days it was obvious that house prices were rising and likely to continue so. Little did we know how much they would increase in the years to come. We agreed that the money still unspent that my father-in-law left Marian should be invested in either moving to a larger house or building an extension on the side of 1 Potters Croft. We opted for the latter and increased our accommodation by adding a hobbies room, a utility room and a loo. The old prefabricated garage was dumped and a double garage built with a larger hard standing for the caravan. Another axiom of house ownership is to be sure that the costs of any major improvement can be fully reflected in an increase in the selling price of the property. A few years later we realised we had failed to keep this rule, but for now life went on happily.

We all became lovers of weekend caravanning – but not every weekend. On a Friday afternoon Marian would load up the caravan – the little van and Triumph car having been replaced by a delightful Thompson model and a more powerful Reynault. Within the hour of arriving home, we would be hitched up and on the road heading east to the Caravan Club site at East Hoathly, near the Decca transmitting station and only four mile south of Heathfield. There is something about caravanning that is difficult to explain if it hasn't been experienced for oneself. It's all so 'laidback', relaxed and beyond the reach of the telephone and sudden calls to the front office. The site at East Hoathly was set in beautiful quiet countryside with my lovely South Downs rolling across the background. Caravan Club sites never provide anything other than basic toilets and water – never any noisy entertainment attractions – and so we enjoyed a haven of peace and tranquillity. To lower the caravan stays, boil the kettle on the Calor gas stove, stretch out on the bench beds, was absolutely heaven on earth. We became great friends of the site owner, Joan Chidson, who encouraged Fiona with her guitar playing and later became instrumental in another way when she introduced us to the delights of Labrador dogs. Being only a few miles from Mudros, we had many happy times entertaining my mother and father with baked beans on toast and Club chocolate biscuits. Come Sunday evening we would head home again thoroughly refreshed and ready for the fray on Monday morning.

Boys came and went as friends of Claire and Fiona. Fortunately by this time I owned a car so was able to take on the role of taxi-driver and ensure the safe return of my daughters from the clutches of late-night marauding young men!

1970 saw Claire fly the nest to Durham University where she had applied for a place to read botany and geography. Unfortunately she didn't pass the necessary A-levels to be accepted but, as always, not to be outdone, she persuaded the authorities to give her a place for an alternative course. After the first year she changed tack and in the end collected a second class honours degree – in botany – well who couldn't with David Bellamy as your tutor? That wasn't the only thing she collected – she collected a boy friend who became her husband.

Meanwhile Fiona became very involved with a church folk music group in which she played the guitar. This was at a time when the church had begun to dabble in alternative language from the Book of Common Prayer. Young people, especially, found it hard to relate to the old English words and phraseology that had been used since the current Prayer Book authorised way back in 1662. With the introduction of modern language services, came a desire to match the new words with music that fitted the day. So was born a rash of musical settings for the Eucharist (Holy Communion) in the idiom of folk music. The older 'Prayer Book diehards' were horrified, but it worked – by far the largest congregations assembled when the 'folk' parish communion was on the menu. Fiona also became a lover of sailing, through the church youth group, led by our young boat-owning curate Peter Crick. Church life for us all was full of activity under the guidance and leadership of the dynamic vicar at this time, the Reverent Peter Gillingham. He had a wonderful understanding and vision of the community of the church embracing all facets of life, social and educational, as well as religious. He loved a good party as well as a large responsive congregation in church. It could have been Peter Gillingham who first coined the adage: 'Children and young people are not the church of the future but are part of the church today'. The church in Horsham was vibrant and it was having a deep effect on my thinking.

With Claire's departure to university came the need for extra money. Although in those days there were no tuition fees and student grants were allotted, extra costs fell on the family budget including petrol for the six hundred mile round trip to Durham that we completed several times. To boost our income, Marian landed a job at a local meat factory – no, not as a butcher, but to set up a quality control department. The management there consider that as Marian could extract blood from people to see what condition they were in, she shouldn't have any difficulty to bore into dead animal flesh to find out if it was fit for human consumption. The company required a new inspection department since they had recently contracted to supply Findus with meat for their delectable pies. To this end Marian spent four weeks commuting to

West London to learn the details of Findus's requirements and then had the pleasure of spending thousands of pounds equipping a new test laboratory at the factory. It was a pretty lethal place in which to work with dozens of strong men wielding carving knives as they slashed away at the carcases. As Marian had worked in a hospital, she actively acquired responsibility for first aid! It soon became evident to her that the poorer the quality of the meat the more likely it would land up in a pie on someone's dinner plate and this created something of a strain between the management and Marian's scruples – and put me off meat pies for life. After about two years she left and returned to blood-taking work at Crawley hospital. I was a little apprehensive about this move – would she remember that she wasn't still in the meat factory?

Marian for some time had become expert at using another kind of needle – the knitting needle, or rows of them as assembled into a knitting machine. Her mother had been the family knitter but when she died father-in-law bought Marian her first machine, since when designing and producing knitwear has become a passion for her. Her skills haven't made any money commercially but her garments have saved us many a pound over the years and we always have model designs. Her expertise became even more productive and money saving as pullovers and not jackets became a fashion for men.

I wore a suit to work and always with a collar and tie. Well that was after I had worn out the blue battledress with which I started work at Decca when a very junior technician. Now I had even more need to look 'managerial' as I was given the job of head of the pre-production department of Decca Navigator. The company had decided to concentrate all the prototype and small-run production in one department and as there was a general feeling that I had missed out on promotion in Roy Swale's old department, I was offered the position of running the new set-up. This agreed with me very well as I became more involved, and interested with, the management of people and not just 'making things'. Prior to my promotion I had attended a part-time management course that culminated in two weeks residing in Churchill College Cambridge. Here we were subjected to some pretty high-powered indoctrination of management techniques as developed and exported by our American friends. The course ended with a grand soiree for us all with our wives – perhaps to train us in the correct protocol at future company social functions when lowly managers' wives came in contact with, or were cornered by, managing directors and the like!

At this time, there was an increasing demand for professional personnel management in the recruiting, training and welfare of company staff. This brought me into conflict with our Personnel Department as I wanted to be responsible for the well-being, training and advancement of the people in MY department. I felt this was a major part of a departmental manager's job – but 'Personnel' thought differently. I even had the idea of joining the enemy but other things were stirring in my brain that were far more radical than a change to another department or company.

"What made you decide to go into the Church?" I would love to have a pound for every time I have been asked that question; I probably have given a different answer to every questioner because there really isn't a fixed single reason. And it is a non-question in the first place. I didn't suddenly make the decision to apply – it was more a case of bowing to the inevitable because for two or three years I resisted any 'call' as being purely imaginary. Each time I think about it different events and different experiences – and excuses – come to mind all of which were drawing me to have to do something about it.

My involvement with the church in Horsham was the general platform on which my religious understanding was founded and began to develop. But in a way not even that is true. We have to go back to the red brick Union Church on the street corner in Heathfield. No doubt the ministers there taught the fundamental Christian truth of God's love for us and "that whosoever believes in him (God) shall have everlasting life." And "It was not to judge the world that God sent his Son into the world, but that through him the world might be saved." To a small boy itching to get out and play, yes on Sundays as well, these words would have had little meaning. My parents, not being over talkative on such subjects as sex, health and religion failed to enlighten me, even when I was at an age of some discernment. So my understanding of any deep theological concepts was based on how I lived and what was expected of me. To be a Christian I had to be GOOD. It was in being good and in doing good, but above all else in being seen to be good, that I became a Christian and remained a Christian. The very worst and recent manifestation of this long standing misconception was for me to sit in the train going to work reading the Bible and hoping my fellow passengers would notice!! I cringe to recall it now. This fundamentally flawed idea hadn't even been swept away as a result of my confirmation preparation some years before. Then in 1970 the vicar's son, Bruce Gillingham, and several other Oxford undergraduates, including one Nick Sagovsky, descended on the parish to run a traditional parish mission. Special meetings and services were held for a week that culminated in the grand finale in St Mary's Parish Church one Saturday evening. It wasn't quite like a Billy Graham mission – it was more a teaching experience than an immediate commitment-demanding rally. The centrepiece of this concluding service was a sermon by The Reverend Dick Lucas, rector of St Helen's Bishopsgate in London. It was this cleric who put me straight after all those years. A Christian isn't someone who is 'good' but someone who believes that what Christ did on Good Friday and Easter Day opens the way to how we should live today. It isn't what I DO now, but what God DID then. Any 'good' that I do now only comes as my response to what God has already done for me. This is the way to salvation – and certainly saved me from an awful lot of role-playing and artificial effort to appear good. It was like a heavy weight being lifted from my shoulders. There was still the same amount of work to do in the church and for others, but now the basis and reason for that work was seen in a completely different light. I do things for the glory of God and not to make me look good. It may be difficult to understand the effect it had on me, but if I hadn't experienced this change, then I feel sure nobody would have had the opportunity to ask me that recurring question. I call it the night that the penny – or the pearl of great wisdom – dropped.

At Decca Navigator my new responsibilities failed to change my mind that I was perhaps in the wrong sort of work. Then there was the prospect that I wouldn't get much further up the promotion ladder and I would be stuck in the same wrong rut for another twenty years. Claire and Fiona were now more 'off our hands' and so there wasn't the pressure to maintain a stable and reliable financial and home base as when they were much younger. Marian's father no more required our attention and company. Perhaps I could branch out and perhaps spread my wings. As I said, for some time I had felt that God was calling me to a full-time ministry but I had been resisting such a radical step, even if my present work wasn't right. I suppose you could say I was a very mixed up kid. There were so many things pulling me this way and that – so many things in the melting pot.

What I needed was something definite that would give me the answer to my predicament. How about a blinding flash on the road down to work one morning or a voice in the night, calling "Bryan, Bryan?" No such luck. It finally came in the form of Nick Sagovsky, one of the students from the Oxford mission. He encouraged me by saying that I was the right sort of person for the church's full time ordained ministry, but it would be my decision whether to apply or not – well not quite – it would be my decision only if Marian was totally agreeable to this possible change in our lives; without her on board, it wouldn't work and I would remain in the electronic world.

We arranged a caravan holiday in South Wales, not just to help make up our minds about the future. We knew that

Taffy Evans of St Eval days lived in one of those Welsh places with names mostly made up of double L. We also knew that his father was, or had been, a schoolmaster. Trying to find our particular Taffy with only this information was a tall order, even if we were in Wales, but after a certain amount of detective work we did track him down in Abergavenny. But would I be able to track down the answer to my greater problem about the future? Yes I did. After a long walk by myself up to the highest point of the Brecon Beacons I came down – not quite like Moses with his tablets of stone – knowing that I should apply for ordination into the priesthood of the Church of England. How did I know? The nearest I can get is to say it was like the knowing when you want to ask someone to marry you – it just seemed right and inevitable. In both cases it is a step out into the great unknown! I also decided that there wouldn't be any half measures – I would go for full-time residential theological college training – none of this home studying course. I had suffered from no formal qualifications for too long and now was the chance for all that to be changed. I would ensure that I would be best qualified for the work to be done and the equal of anyone else.

Little did I know what a long and torturous path my application would be. First I had to persuade my vicar that he thought I was a suitable and upright person to become a priest. That hurdle wasn't too difficult and so my name was passed up the line of authority to the Bishop of Chichester, who in turn passed it on to his DDO – the Diocesan Director of Ordinands – who also was the Archdeacon of Hastings. After a long Sunday afternoon drive over to the other side of the county, we arrived at a large rambling house in the village of Ninfield in which the venerable archdeacon lived. My only recollection of that interview is that Marian remained sitting outside in the car, not even being offered a cup of tea. There was no mention of travelling expenses and I regret to say that this was a foretaste of things to come.

Several weeks later I received a letter from the bishop

saying that he required me to attend a selection conference run by the Advisory Council for the Church's Ministry (ACCM). Talking to another man from our parish, who was already in training, I gleaned a few useful tips about these selection processes. They were held at various establishments across the country, usually at some Christian community such as a retreat house or conference centre. My interrogation was held at a West London convent run by nuns who were experts at cooking and providing a comfortable and relaxed environment for the three-day examination. A group of about twenty aspiring priests gathered together and were put through a series of questions and discussions by six inquisitors. The standard joke about these affairs was that we were to be checked out to ensure we didn't eat our peas with a fork turned up the wrong way and we didn't belch at the table! Armed with the advanced advice to 'be myself' and to enjoy myself, I suppose that the five learned clerics, and one mathematician, had to decide that I wouldn't preach heresy and could lead a congregation into the ways of Godliness as espoused by the Church of England. Fortunately I didn't have to wait long for a letter from the bishop, to whom the board reported their findings, and to whom the police had reported no misdoings on my part, saying that he would be pleased to sponsor me as a Chichester diocesan ordinand. I was in and the die was cast – but with a proviso. The Right Reverend Lord Bishop of Chichester, Roger Wilson, only had one thing on his mind, as far as he was prepared to disclose to me – could I assure him that I was able to support my wife and family during the two years of training at theological college? And so the question of money and how the C. of E. views it, reared its ugly head. If you become a police cadet or a student nurse you are paid during training but if you become an Anglican ordinand you are not paid. There were various sources of help that could be tapped but the whole system of financing theological students is a complicated and messy business and for me was to become extra daunting as life unfolded during 1973.

Not a squeak of this impending change of my life was disclosed to the management at Decca Navigator. Even when I had time off to attend a church medical board, I said it was for some new insurance I wanted to take out. Once the doctors had agreed that I was fit and strong enough to withstand the rigours of life in the church, the next hurdle was to find a theological college who would agree to train me. The Diocesan Director of Ordinands provided me with a short list of establishments that he thought would suit my training requirements. The church at that time ran about fifteen colleges throughout England, most of them located next to cathedrals or within the universities of Oxford and Cambridge. Each college was known to have an evangelical or Anglo-Catholic or liberal (theologically) foundation. Now I would have thought that as I was from a low church – even chapel – background, my list of colleges to choose from would reflect my preferences. Not so, there were places suggested right across the spectrum and I was to discover that this policy did have great merit.

The first college that we chose to visit was, as you would expect, an evangelical establishment. We were shown round, joined in a college meal and church service. We met the principle and several tutors and students and we viewed some flats for married students. After we had left, Marian said nothing to me, but I decided it wasn't for me – it was all rather 'cold' and unattractive. This was a great relief to her as she then confessed it was awful! The next port of call was to the Anglo-Catholic Salisbury and Wells Theological College, located in the most beautiful of all cathedral closes, Salisbury, of that wonderful slender spire fame. My hopes were not high or enthusiastic at the prospects of training in such a foundation but again we went through a similar process as before but with one difference – here we were allocated one particular student whose task it was to be our guide and friend for the day. His name was Dinis Sengulane. He was a black African. A more attractive and warm soul you couldn't wish to meet and he somehow reflected the whole ambience of the college. Our visit was a most enjoyable day and what I saw and heard gave me a wonderful sense of expectation for the future. Once more as we left, Marian said nothing. I said I didn't need to visit any further colleges – this was the place for me and she wholeheartedly agreed. I was offered a place at Salisbury and from that day my theological understanding was to take yet another different direction.

So, in spring 1973 all the pieces of the puzzle were in place, except for matters financial. My parents were somewhat shocked, especially my father who found it all very disturbing. On June 24th I handed in my notice twenty-five years, exactly to the day, after starting at Decca Navigator – you see I was determined to receive my twenty-five year service watch! My ego was greatly boosted when Bill O'Brien, the technical director, walked into my office and asked me how much more money I would need to stay on! It's good to feel wanted, but I am afraid God had the upper hand and nice as Bill was, he didn't stand a chance.

The following months were a time of great activity, most of which was welcome but some not so welcome. Things had been moving apace for Claire as she came close to her finals at Durham. Her time at university hadn't all been taken up with books. She found time to develop a friendship and then courtship with William (Bill) Birdwood who was reading theology, some of the time. Bill's proposal of marriage took place at traffic lights in Princes Street, Edinburgh, after they had been potato grading to earn money that came in useful to buy a ring. I am told the lights went from red to green. Bill's great uncle was Field Marshal Lord Birdwood of Totnes; his father a vicar in Hertfordshire. 'Churchyness' was beginning to gang up on The Strange family.

Claire and Bill had strong leanings towards the evangelical and charismatic manifestations of Christianity. The worship at a charismatic church is centred on the recognition and presence of what is known as the 'gifts of the (Holy) Spirit' – the gifts of healing, prophecy and speaking in tongues being prominent. One night Claire rang and said she wanted to speak to me – usually it was her mother who was in demand – so I immediately knew that something was up. With much excitement and enthusiasm, as was her way in most things, she blurted out that she could now speak in tongues. This information, to her, was as natural as saying she could now ride a motorbike, but to me it sounded like something that required the attention of a doctor or psychiatrist or speech therapist and I told her so. I was really concerned about her as she could be over enthusiastic and sometimes prone to action before thinking. The next morning I unburdened my worries on my two travelling companions whom I knew attended the Baptist church in Horsham. Before we got out of the train, the mysteries of the gifts of the Spirit had been explained to me and I began to think that things weren't as bad as I had imagined. From all this came yet another aspect of religious perspective for me, some of which over time I have taken on board and some I have not. Any and all spiritual experience and different forms of worship can come in useful in a priest's life if he is to be able to relate to everyone who needs his time and attention.

As I said, these months were times of great activity and the future sequence of events from May 1973 onwards now looked something like:- finding a new home in Salisbury, Claire and Bill's graduation in Durham, my leaving work, Claire and Bill's wedding, selling Potters Croft, moving to Salisbury, starting training at college at the beginning of October. What a jigsaw puzzle with no picture on the box to help us. Then there was Fiona. She was sitting A-levels and making decisions about her further education. She was also making noises about not wanting to leave Horsham and all the activities that took up her time. Why couldn't just I go to Salisbury and she and her mother remain in Horsham? It was the great East Anglian mystic Julian of Norwich who centuries ago wrote: 'but all shall be well, and all shall be well, and all manner of things shall be well'. To believe and understand those words and to ask God to make them come true was constantly in our thoughts!

A visit to Salisbury was arranged for one Sunday in May, after receiving details from several estate agents of properties for sale. We knew the selling valuation of Potters Croft and already had it on the market. In the delightful village of Winterbourne Gunner, just north of Salisbury, we found Glebe Cottage. House buying isn't just about checking if there is room to get all the furniture in and enough bed spaces and if there is rising damp or death-watch beetle in the roof – it's about 'feel' and 'atmosphere' and 'invitation'. As we were shown over Glebe Cottage, we immediately knew this was the place for us and not because the name sounded appropriate for someone connected with the church. It was a small modern detached house but with a cottage character. The three rooms downstairs circled a central stone fireplace and there was even an oak beam in the sitting room. Looking out through the window over the kitchen sink you saw a small garden with open countryside beyond. We discovered later that if you placed a marble on the wood floor just inside the front door, it would roll unaided right through to the kitchen at the back of the house. Fortunately this feature hasn't prevented the house from standing upright for some years. Down one side of the house was a drive and space for the caravan, but more attractively, a white painted brick and flint wall of the house next door. It was just perfect and totally different from our previous homes. It kind of fitted with the changed life that was coming to us.

The mortgage arrangements for the purchase posed an interesting situation that was overcome by the Woolwich having their wool pulled over their eyes. The application form required me to state my annual salary but, fortunately, as based on my previous year's income, that being three thousand pounds. My actual income when I started paying the mortgage was going to be something very different – in fact I was to have no salary at all – and as I was still at Decca Navigator when I filled out the form I could say that they were my employer! Why the Woolwich thought I wanted a house in Wiltshire and still work in New Malden, I cannot imagine!

'Put your trust in the Lord and he will provide', is a text often quoted when money is short and hard to come by. My final salary at Decca Navigator was three thousand pounds a year but at one stage in the transition from electronics to theology we had no projected income, on paper, with which to face the future. A trip to the Brighton offices of those in charge of finances in the Chichester diocese ended by being told that the last available money had already been allocated to a more deserving ordinand. Afterwards Marian and I sat on a seafront bench and almost burst into tears, but instead started laughing. Good old Julian of Norwich! Things did improve when I was granted a Local Education Authority living grant and help towards college fees. Fiona finally agreed to make the break and come with us as a student at Salisbury College of Art and as such she also received LEA grants to study photography.

There was also a thirteen hundred pounds refund – all I had paid in over the years, less income tax – from the Decca pension fund, which sounded all very nice at the time, but meant that I would receive no Decca pension for my twenty five years service when I came to retirement age. The Tuesday before Claire's wedding I was summoned to Decca headquarters on the London Embankment. This was the day I was to receive my gold watch from Ted Lewis, the company chairman. He, being a rather shy man, preferred to hand out the company largess individually in his office – no gathering of colleagues or cups of tea in the director's suite. I had been primed that if I talked about cricket things would proceed smoothly as Lords was his second home. Having received my suitably engraved gold watch, he then said he had something else to give me – and handed me a cheque for a thousand pounds from his personal funds with his best wishes for my future. My trip to headquarters from New Malden had been accompanied with a slight discomfort in my lower stomach – nerves no doubt, I thought. By the time I got on the train to return to Burlington Road I felt quite poorly and decided to go straight home. At seven o'clock that evening I was lying flat-out in Crawley hospital's operating theatre having my appendix removed. Not only was this a physical operation, but therapeutic as well. It all happened so rapidly I had no time to dwell on what certain white-coated people were going to do to me and I actually discovered that these people were very much like myself! Ted Lewis sent a message that he knew he had funny effects on people, but nothing like this! Having one's appendix out only five days before your daughter is to be married certainly did have some funny effects in all sorts of serious ways. We had a full house with Teddy and Dorothy arriving for the wedding. The reception was a 'do-it-yourself' affair, Marian having spent a month off work to fill a very large freezer with home-cooked food. There were a myriad of last minute things to organise and collect and in the midst of it all I was on my back in hospital. Friends and family rallied round and the great day arrived, but who was going to give the bride away? I think my father was rather disappointed when it was agreed by the surgeon that, if great care was taken, I would be able to walk Claire up the aisle of St Mary's Church. Tightly strapped up around my middle, our friend Roy Davidson drove me from Crawley hospital to the gate of the church where a wheelchair and attendant were waiting. I was wheeled to the back of the church, stood upright – or as near upright as I could tolerate – by the side of Claire, and we walked up the aisle. In the meantime the wheelchair was quickly taken up a side aisle ready to catch me at the other end! One of the guests, who hadn't heard of my predicament, said afterwards that he thought I didn't look very well! After about half an hour at the reception, held in the church barn (hall), I returned to my hospital bed – satisfied but very weary.

The following day was our wedding anniversary. As it was a Sunday the hospital main entrance hall was almost empty and it was here that we had an indoor celebratory picnic of food left over from the day before.

By this time my employment at Decca Navigator had

ended but as soon as I was fit enough Marian and I returned to receive several leaving presents, including a complete record playing system. So finished my twenty-five years with Decca Navigator. Looking back on those years what can I say? They had provided me with uninterrupted employment and a stable environment in which to enjoy a happy family life. Of course there were ups and downs and like everyone else more money would have been useful, but we had more than survived. The Decca experience also provided me with one fundamental truth; people are worth something, and given the right environment and opportunity to express themselves, then many hidden talents will bear fruit for the good of the individual and the company. I was about to endeavour to practice this truth in a different world.

Before leaving, several middle management friends came to me and said how they envied me and what I was preparing to do. Not that they wanted to follow my madness and 'go into the Church', but that I was going to do something different. Different it most certainly was going to be!

Recovering from a major operation – no keyhole in those days – wasn't exactly the bodily condition for undertaking moving house. But what are friends for? Ron and Phyllis of Monks Avenue vintage came to the rescue and did sterling work emptying our loft and helping install us in Glebe Cottage.

Act Three

Scene One

Theological College

Whoosh! Whoosh! Whoosh! And so it went on and on. The Bishops Move van had finally driven off, leaving us deposited in an unfamiliar village in Wiltshire where we knew nobody. Now was the time to sit down and use what always should be the last thing to put on a removals van – the teapot – and contemplate exactly what we had done. Our revelry was soon interrupted by this strange whooshing noise. Remember I said never buy a house on a Sunday afternoon? It wasn't Sunday anymore and cars and lorries were finding their way – whooshing – past our front door. We had bought a house cheek by jowl with one of the routes from Southampton, with its docks, to the industrial heartland of the Midlands. Within a week I had rapidly extended my DIY skills to include fitting secondary double-glazing to keep out the noise. The traffic on the road was the only downside feature of the place we had moved to, but before we were to leave Winterbourne Gunner, two years later, that road was to make amends in one small but maybe unique way.

So, what was this place really like? It was no more than a collection of houses of all ages and sizes with a village shop, a garage, a Methodist chapel and two Church of England places of worship with a shared vicar whose name was Gideon. Gideon was as unlike the traditional image of a country parson as you could image. He was quite mad but the most loveable person you could hope to meet. We came to know him and his family very well and he was a haven of support and comfort to me in my more difficult times at college. He also frequently rushed into Glebe Cottage as there was no public lavatory at our end of the village. There were trains, however, travelling from Waterloo to Salisbury, but unfortunately as the track across the field opposite passed us in a cutting, I couldn't sit at the bedroom window and watch them as in my childhood.

Winterbourne Gunner was quiet and tranquil – mostly – apart from the road and sometimes the roar of aero engines at the Air Ministry Experimental Establishment at Boscombe Down. There was also Porton Down, the secret government establishment playing with deadly germs, no more than three hundred yards down the road from Glebe Cottage. Porton Down was so secret that we barely knew it was there and we never caught any mysterious ailments or glowed in the night. The village was set on the edge of rolling Wiltshire countryside and as I was coming home from college one evening I saw on the smooth curved skyline several large hares cavorting in the sunshine. That was the sort of place it was, happy, unsophisticated and a bit carefree. The immediate neighbours were delightful and soon became our friends. It was, most importantly, to be a place to which I could escape. Although my college experience would be stimulating and exciting, it was also to be pretty stressful and demanding. I was to live, mainly, within a religious community, to which Marian and Fiona would also take part to some degree, but Glebe Cottage gave me a respite. You must remember that I wasn't a young student living on a university campus, but a forty seven year old father being a bit erratic.

What of Salisbury and the college itself? A beautiful city with a beautiful cathedral, built in the thirteenth and fourteenth centuries, set in perhaps the most famous close in England. The cathedral spire soars gracefully and slenderly for 404 feet into the sky to make it the tallest in the land. The college, built in the close, shares this wonderful atmosphere of an ancient Christian past but with a vibrant present. Dozens of coaches come every day from all over Europe bringing visitors to this place so what better setting to come and discover how God and people should live together?

The college, address 19 The Close, Salisbury, is thought to have been designed by Christopher Wren but there are no known plans to prove this. Built about 1677, on what is said to be the site of a medieval school of theology, it was purchased for its present use in 1860 and received its first theological students a year later. A few years after opening, the well-known architect of Keble College Oxford and many other churches, Herbert Butterfield, built a college chapel. When another modern chapel was added in 1970, Butterfield's contribution became known as the Old Chapel and it was in this place of great solemnity that one of the funniest things happens during my time at Salisbury. There have been further modern extensions and additions (library, refectory and bedroom-studies) but these have been secreted at the back of the original building, leaving the front looking the same over the centuries. For me Salisbury, the cathedral, the college were all the ancient bricks and mortar of a new and exciting life and so different from anything that I had experienced before. It was about as remote from the electronic world that had been my lot for the last twenty-five years as you could imagine. And the amazing thing was that for all its newness and not knowing really what was in store for me, it didn't hold any great fear – the kind of fear that I had experienced before when confronted with something new and unknown. From the very first day in Salisbury I just felt that I was a square peg in a square hole.

Having arrived in Wiltshire in August 1973 we had six weeks to settle in, so all was in place to start actually being a theological student. The college had just lost Principal Canon Harold Wilson, who had taken me on, and so we were welcomed by the stand-in principal, The Revd Tony Barnard. On that first day in college, as he entered the room to greet us, I noticed he was carrying a bottle of sherry to share with his eight new students – a good start I thought! I want to record something about each of those students because they and their wives were to have a very great influence on me, my training and my ministry. We were a motley looking lot:-

starting with a fresh-faced young Welsh newspaper reporter Martin Reynolds who was gay in both senses of the word, a huge hulk of a man with a big black beard, an ex-army Intelligence Corps sergeant, Bob Vernon (Jynnie), a young man with a lovely broad Dorset accent who had earned his living by looking after cows, Alan Gill (Margery), a slightly rotund computer expert, Noel Baker (Brenda), a thin young man with a bright red beard who was a school teacher, Ian Coomber (Jill), yet another red beard and insurance inspector, Greville Cross (Pauline), a company chairman, Paul Macarty (Betty), two others of whom I cannot remember any details as they soon became detached from the rest and me – clean shaven and the oldest by a good few years. I have included after each name the wife – all were to play an important part in our present and future life as friends and supporters. Together we represented the very broadest spectrum of churchmanship, some of which was totally new to me. What was about to begin was in some measure a rubbing-off on to me parts of their experience and way of expressing the Christian faith and worship. Together with the Anglo-Catholic foundation of the college, I was in for an exhilarating, painful and rewarding two years.

The college had six ordained staff to guide us into the mysteries of the Old Testament, the New Testament, Church History, Ethics, Liturgy and Doctrine. There was also a lady to help us concoct good English for essays, and later sermons, and another lady to help us deliver those sermons clearly. This latter lady acquired an imaginary 'reputation' by making the students lie down on the floor with her – but only something to do with practising proper breathing.

There was a constant flow of well-known clerics and other members of the ecclesiastical establishment who visited the college and delivered highly erudite lectures to further our preparation to run a parish – or even a diocese maybe.

In 1971 the college had expanded in student numbers due to the closure of Wells Theological College and combining two establishments in Salisbury. There were about one hundred and twenty ordinands and not enough study/bedrooms for everybody. As I had a bed out of college, for the first year I had to make do with a study desk in the library. Although I never formally signed up to the National Union of Students, which was quite militant in its activities, there was some attempt, made by the union, to get a reduction in my fees due to 'lack of facilities'. Efforts were made for further reductions as I ate some meals out of college that had to be paid for out of the meagre family budget. All this came to nothing – yet another example of the nature of church attitudes to money. The financial burden was lightened a little by Marian receiving two or three free meals in the refectory each term.

Now for the work itself. Perhaps the best way to describe it would be to come with me through a typical day. Up at 6.30am to catch the 7.15am bus into Salisbury. Run from the bus station to be in chapel by 7.45am for Morning Prayer. 8.30am breakfast. 9.00-10.30am lecture. Break. 11.00-12.30pm lecture/group tutorial/ private study, Eucharist (Holy Communion). 1.00pm lunch. 1.30pm group meeting/coffee to discuss the service we are conducting on Friday evening. Afternoon free/games/catch up on essays still to be finished. No tea provided. 5.15pm Evensong either in the college chapel or in the cathedral. 6.00pm dinner. 6.45pm bus home and several hours reading and writing essays/remain in college for visiting speaker. Saturdays were usually a free day but for me it was again work, trying to keep up with the everlasting demand from six tutors for essays.

Sundays varied, perhaps in the morning helping with the children's service in chapel and/or visiting a local church to take part in their evening service. But every unallocated hour was always needed for studying and writing. For me, this bookwork reminded me so much of my days at Stockport Technical College, just hard graft. There is not much doubt that I have never been an academic – in fact I suspect something quite solid between my ears! Not even the fact that at Decca Navigator I had spent most of my time 'using my brains' was any preparation for my current work activity. My first attempts at writing essays were received by the tutors with a certain amount of disdain, reflected in very low marks. They weren't really interested in what I thought, but what I had discovered by reading what other people thought. This was the way to broaden ones understanding of what the Church of England had come to practice.

Monday's Evensong was always conducted in college when one of the tutors would preach a special sermon to impress the students and make them shudder at the thought of having to preach themselves! One Monday Gian Tellini, the doctrine tutor, was detailed to preach. Unfortunately the flu' bug caught up with him and so Richard Buxton, the liturgy tutor, was drafted in at short notice to replace him. This preaching slot was supposed to be a theological high point of the week, given only by the ordained and vastly experienced. Just after 5.30pm Richard got up to deliver. By way of explanation he said that it was very short notice that he had been given to prepare his sermon, and then went on, "so I stand here before you – I stand naked before you – I hope you will bear with me!!" He took off his glasses – he was very short-sighted and a little shy – and buried his head in his hands, not able to believe what he had said. The congregation of uncouth ordinands – well, we roared our heads off!

Friday evenings were always special when friends, wives and families came together for the big weekly college Eucharistic Celebration. The students were put into 'worship groups' of about eight bodies. Each group was made up of first, second and third year men, to help the newcomers and allow the old hands to blossom. The groups took it in turns to conduct the Eucharist (apart from the consecration of the bread and wine) on Friday evening in the New Chapel. Now you may be forgiven for thinking that little variation can be introduced into the Prayer Book service of Holy Communion. Well, first of all you would be hard pressed even to find a Book of Common Prayer in Salisbury Theological College – only the new 'Series 3' services were used because the college was very enthusiastic about experimentation and innovation regarding worship. The Church out in the parishes was largely considered to be moribund and had forgotten that all the senses should be used to worship God. Colour and movement had been laid aside for too long. We needed to recapture the glory of the old Tractarian Tradition when ritual was the way to lift up the populous from the greyness of everyday life to a higher plain. Smells (incense) and bells and lots of candles were definitely 'in'. Worship also needed to be in a language and idiom that suited today. The message was the same but the messenger had to be different. So each college worship group would try to be more dramatic (outrageous?) than the previous Friday's offering. The consecration of the bread and wine of course was conducted by one of the ordained staff, but the rest was in the hands of students bursting with energy and ideas. We were going to change things and fill every church to its very last available seat when we got into our parishes!

Just to give one example of the sort of thing that happened – picture the chapel – it was a large square room and all services were conducted 'in the round'. The service started with everyone sitting facing outwards and through the windows you could see the lights of the city streets. The sermon was about 'conversion' and the centrality of the Cross. Conversion was about 'changing direction'. At the appropriate point the assembled company was invited to turn their chairs round and about-face as all the chapel lights went out and a spotlight focused on a large wooden cross in front of the altar. This was followed by a long silence before the liturgy continued. After these services we always had a party that, in my early days at college, I found somewhat distasteful and incongruous until I dawned on me that through the liturgy we had received the greatest gift that God has to offer us – the gift of forgiveness and a new start. We really did have something to celebrate!

I had been warned by previous ordinands that because the college was Anglo-Catholic and I having an Evangelical upbringing, the first term would find me being torn apart – theologically – which would be a difficult testing time. It wasn't the fundamental message that was to change but in the way it was expressed particularly in worship. If I could withstand and accept this reorientation, then in the subsequent terms I would be put together again with a far broader understanding of the church's teaching and worship. In a nutshell, this is what happened and I shall forever be grateful for those two years at Salisbury Theological College; Christianity became far more concerned about living with others in community and not just a personal commitment to Christ; Christianity became objective and not merely subjective; College life was about sharing stresses and pleasures together in love for each other. So deep did that love grow that the members of my group have remained in contact and friendship now for over thirty years. And in all this the wives and children have taken an equal share. None of this would have been my experience if I hadn't been led to full-time training at Salisbury. Christianity isn't only about believing, its about sharing and living and to this end numerous visits were arranged for us to visit different kinds of establishments – schools, a crematorium, an army base, a borstal, hospitals – all to widen our understanding of how people lived and worked and how we could bring the Christian way to their lives.

Around the time of the saints' days of Petertide and Michaelmas, students would 'go forth' from college at the end of their training to their various dioceses to be ordained. These occasions (with others!) were good excuses for holding a party. A dance had been arranged but it was agreed that we would dress informally. As the proceedings got underway, on the arm of one of the students in swept a most beautiful blond girl, and dressed 'up to the eyeballs', including a full-length gown and long sleeved gloves. On closer examination we discovered that she was none other than David Saint, a male student, but dressed in drag!! Here was a statement about a subject that hadn't really had much of an airing in my life –

sexuality. I am not saying that just because someone dressed in drag they had to be gay but obviously here was something for me that wasn't quite straight. During the time I was at Salisbury, out of the one hundred and twenty students, about thirty were homosexuals. As far as I knew I had never knowingly met a homosexual person until this time. It was a great cultural shock to many of us but after some lengthy discussions with the rest of my group we all came to totally accept gay people – including our own group member Martin Reynolds. I can honestly say that I haven't found more dedicated and loving people who have made some of the finest priests in the Church of England in recent years. My contact with gay people not only gave me insights into their difficulties and the general prejudice against them, but also how important it was to be accepting of all people who are different from me.

Starting, I think, in my second term, came an added activity. Each student was allocated to a department of the local Social Services for what was called 'pastoral training'. My lot, once a week, was to visit and inspect playgroups around Salisbury. Fortunately it didn't take too much technical or administrative information to check that there were enough loos and towels etc. etc. for the number of little darlings enjoying getting covered with paint and Plasticine. The point of the exercise was to meet and relate to people in completely different situations – something one was going to encounter in parish life. For another term I was sent to the local hospital for mentally handicapped elderly people. We worked as very basic assistants on the wards and day rooms, just talking with the patients and administering cups of tea. One dear old lady took me on a long journey to a castle in Germany where we were to share a huge pile of gold coins she had hoarded there. Sometimes at the end of a shift I wasn't sure of my own sanity but it worked wonders for me – it was to be the final piece in the jigsaw that purged me of my phobia of all things medical, even if I wasn't given one of those dreaded white coats – just a brown one like the porters wear!

At the beginning of the second term our new principal arrived, the Revd Reginald Askew. In some ways he wasn't an easy man to understand but he continued the general ethos of the college particularly concerning worship and the attitude to the gay students. We did ask him what we should call him but we never got an answer, so everyone called him Reggie.

By this time on the home front, Claire and Bill were living not far away first in Poole and then Wool where they bought their first house. Bill had a job with Social Services and they both attended a Bible College that spawned the charismatic version of Christianity, whilst Fiona settled into learning the mysteries of photography at Salisbury College of Art. She also settled into visiting the theological college, apparently to see me, but in fact to sample certain of the younger students, one of whom was to become her husband. Financially we just about kept our head above water. Marian did wonders with her culinary skills taking full advantage of the good prices in Salisbury market and we wangled a card to shop wholesale at the local cash and carry. The food served up by the college kitchen was absolutely awful, not due to the lack of the chef's skills, but because of lack of money and there was a running battle with the bursar to improve the quality and quantity. I would get home after college supper and attempt to dig into Marian's evening meal, but they got wary of this tactic and I found they had finished and cleared away before I arrived! One 'trick' that we were appraised of by more experience students, was that we could sign-on at the local Labour Exchange during holiday times. This was possible because grants were not earnings and were given to cover for term times only. During vocations we lawfully classified ourselves as unemployed. One had to be available for work at any time but you could only be offered a job of a similar nature and standard as your previous employment. As I knew there were no electronic companies around wanting managers for a few weeks, I was on a very good bet that no employment could be offered me and so I could sit at home studying and receiving benefit at the same time.

During the previous nine months Marian had suffered 'womanly problems' which resulted in her landing up in Odstock Hospital, just outside Salisbury, for Holy Week and for a hysterectomy. This wasn't a happy experience as the Nissen hut wards fell well below the standards she had known in her working days – she told the sister in no uncertain terms what she thought of the hygiene – and the surgeon hadn't a clue how to sew. She was discharged fairly rapidly because there were people to help at home. However things initially didn't quite work out as hoped. When she was discharged, I was flat on my bed with a painful back problem; Claire and Bill arrived but Claire went straight to bed with the flu; Fiona disappeared sailing, which left Marian in the tender care of an undomesticated Bill. Still, the college was a caring community in which we all lived as one family and shared the ups and downs of life. We were well loved and helped during this awkward time – even the principal came out with Holy communion on Easter Day. Later we were able to reciprocate when Bob Vernon had an almost fatal accident and one of his young daughters stayed with us.

We were now coming towards the end of my first year at college. Yes I had been torn apart in many ways by what I had learnt and experienced but the putting together again had been successful and I felt that all we had planned and gone through was going to be all right in the final run-up to ordination. We enjoyed a happy holiday, caravanning in the beautiful Exmoor village of Dulverton – without DHSS benefit as I wasn't available for work!

In my second year at Salisbury I opted for one day each week travelling to Poole Technical College with the express purpose of broadening my sociological understanding of life. To say that it was an indoctrination of 'red' ideas might be a step too far, but it came across that a Conservative government might not have all the answers to the problems of the nation and its poor. It was an attempt to make sure that when we arrived in our parishes we didn't just take afternoon tea with the elite using their best china but could enjoy a chipped mug of coffee in some worker's small and grubby kitchen. The alternative to Poole Tec. was to spend six weeks in a South London vicarage sharing life with the dispossessed. With Marian still not fully recovered from her operation, I took the easier option.

We were slowly getting used to participating in acts of worship until finally we came to a major hurdle in our training – to preach to the whole college. It was a nightmare! All students are very unforgiving of the weaknesses of fellow students and professionally ordinands are no different. I preached on something about those who have ears to hear, let them hear – how much they heard I am not sure. Fortunately for my second year I could vacate my seat in the library and enjoy the luxury of a study, the bed of which often had my body to contend with in the afternoon.

Perhaps the funniest and cruellest thing I ever saw, when students were conducting services, happened at Evensong in the old chapel. To appreciate this sheer piece of pantomime – for this is what it turned out to be – you have to visualise the layout of the chapel. It was long and with the sanctuary going up about eight shallow steps, stretching right across the width of the building, from the front seats of the naive to the high altar under the east window. It was just a wide-open space rising up with nothing to hide all the splendour of a typically Anglo-catholic altar with candles and lamps in all sorts of places. Noel Baker and Paul MacCarty were detailed to conduct the service. There was a small vestry either side, each with a door opening out half way up the sanctuary steps. Now the procedure was for the two student officiants, fully robed in cassock and surplice, to walk out of their respective doors, walk a pace or two towards the middle of the steps, turn, bow deeply to the altar, about turn and sit down in chairs provided. All this they started to do with great solemnity under the full gaze of the rest of the college. However, when they had entered and turned to face the high altar, Noel saw that he was standing one step higher than Paul and Paul saw that he was one step lower than Noel. This was a serious situation that both realised needed to be rectified. So Noel stepped down one step as Paul stepped up one step! This was repeated three times much to the delight of all the student congregation. It was a hard way to learn one of the cardinal rules of conducting services – NEVER try to correct a mistake because nobody will ever notice unless you do!

Easter 1975 came. We had conducted the whole canopy of the Holy Week services that culminated with the Easter morning sunrise service to celebrate the empty tomb of Christ and the Resurrection. This we did under the magnificent vaulting of Salisbury Cathedral, starting at five o'clock and watching the light of the sun slowly rise through the east window. The service finished as we processed outside and across The Close back to college singing 'Thine be the Glory'. It was a memorable and moving occasion and to this day I never sing that hymn without that morning coming vividly to mind. What was almost as memorable was the breakfast the kitchen put on for everyone – it was sumptuous – but as was generally agreed we had suffered short rations days before to pay for it! Never mind, it was a wonderful occasion to start the Easter holiday and then the final preparations for ordination.

On returning to college for the summer term, I was assigned perhaps my worst task during training. Sixth form boys from the local grammar school came to me for 'religious' discussion. I was given no brief to define exactly what we should discuss but as this occurred for the last school period on a Friday afternoon, the boy's minds no doubt were more on what they were doing over the weekend and which girl was the likeliest bet. Most arrived late and most had good reasons to leave early – which for me was no bad thing. It did teach me one thing –only those who want to hear will hear!

There are several hurdles to be negotiated before any bishop is willing to lay his apostolic hands on new raw recruits for ordination to the order of deacon. The most stressful for the likes of me was the five essays that had to be written after two years training. Fortunately as I was over the age of thirty the final testing was by the essay scheme – those under thirty trained for three years and, even worse, were required to sit examination papers. The writing, which started before Easter and was completed by the end of June, took place alongside all the usual lectures and other activities so life was extremely hard and tempers became somewhat strained. Each essay was submitted to the appropriate tutor for initial comment before being despatched to some distant panel of learned clerics. I remember in particular the subject for the doctrine essay – 'Is salvation universal?' The whole question of salvation had vexed me for some time and in the end I came to the belief that, because of the unrelenting loving nature of God, nobody would ultimately finish 'down there' rather than 'up there'. This was totally contrary to my chapel upbringing, and the evangelical teaching that if you didn't become Christian in this world, your time was really up when death overtook you. Another belief I had embraced in the last two years was that by taking odd sentences from the Bible out of context, you could prove that black was white. Although my tutor agreed with my conclusions, he said my explanation was so poor I should rewrite the whole of the dissertation. I didn't take his advice and I received my highest marks for the doctrine essay!

We didn't fall out over this matter but he did get a real earful from me on another occasion. Each student had to preach a sermon in a local church during our last term. The poor unsuspecting folk of the large parish church of St Thomas in Salisbury were to be burdened with my efforts one Sunday evening. My knees were knocking with fear and nerves as I mounted the steps of the stone pulpit. As I opened my mouth to deliver my words of encouragement and hope to the congregation, I saw John, my doctrine tutor, take out a writing-pad and pencil and start to take notes. Nothing could have been more off-putting and I told him afterwards in no uncertain terms, adding that next time please sit behind a pillar where the preacher couldn't see him.

Then before ordination, there was the question of which part of God's vineyard would I be called to serve. With the help of the Holy Spirit and the creaking wheels of the Church of England, the college Principal surveys the annual list of vacancies and pairs off ordinands to parishes as he felt would be to the greatest advantage of both parties. Everyone was supposed to go to what was termed a 'training parish' where the vicar or rector was particularly endowed with the skills of continuing the training of the newly ordained and keeping them on the straight and narrow path. Some parish vacancies were advertised in the Church Times, but these were not really for first-time appointments. One such opening for a deacon was at Headbourne Worthy and Kings Worthy, the adjacent parishes just outside the northern walls of the City of Winchester. With my parents still living in Heathfield and not getting any younger, it seemed sensible to hope for a parish not too far from the Home Counties. It was on returning from a visit to Sussex that we decided to stop and take a look at these two Winchester parishes – just drive round and get the feel on the place. We liked what we felt. Well, let's see if the rector is at home, I thought. He was. Within twenty minutes of meeting we had decided that we could get on well together and that I would fit in with the brand of worship expected at the two churches, and so the Reverend Matthew Lynn offered me the job. Talk about the slow grinding wheels of the Church of England – not where this southern Irish protestant priest was concerned! More about Matthew later, but for now I was faced with the task of telling the Principal what had been agreed. I sat opposite Reggie in his study and explained what had happened. I had no qualms about what I had to disclose because I truly felt that I had found the place the Good Lord had lined up for me. Fortunately, and as a good start to this encounter with the Principal, I was older than him! There was complete silence for about five minutes – as was usual when questions were being discussed with Reggie – after which he looked up and said, "Well, we will have to see about this" to which I replied "Yes we will, won't we." We did, and so I got my first parish arranged for the following September. I am not sure if Matthew could be described as a traditional training incumbent but he turned out to be just what was needed when I started work as his deacon.

The last hurdle before ordination was to prove that I had no financial debts – the church had no money to bail out impecunious clergymen and then there would be the scandal. I don't remember being asked to produce bank statements or any other written evidence of solvency – perhaps the church wasn't so paranoid about money after all. Anyway we had come through owing nothing to anybody but it was a near thing especially with another wedding to pay for.

By July 1974 Fiona's visits to my college had paid off with an invitation to go to Canterbury for the ordination of one of my fellow students – Graeme Martin Elmore. Graeme, for a short time, was a novice monk but had decided that ordination to the priesthood was far enough in foregoing the secular joys of life. This trip to the home of Anglicanism seemed to us to be a little out of character for Fiona because she would not only attend the service but also meet a boyfriend's parents – a step too far for her, up to now. Within a month of Graeme putting on a dog-collar they were engaged. Graeme's first parish was Norbury in South London so Fiona's old Triumph car travelled a good few miles in the following year. The wedding was arranged for the end of July 1975 just at the height of my preparations for ordination and moving to Kings Worthy. So here we were again. Marian, being the mother of the bride, had all the usual arrangements to make – but what could be usual with virtually no money? The wedding service was to take place in St Thomas's Church in Salisbury – the one of my unpleasant preaching experience – and the college gave us use of the refectory for the reception. Marian was to make the wedding and bridesmaids dresses, the cake, all the food and wine – we still had that enormous freezer. The college chef offered to ice the cake and all my fellow students volunteered to serve at the reception so long as they could finish-off the leftovers from the feast. The church music was to be provided by Fiona's old Horsham guitar group and an organist friend of Graeme. An art college friend of Fiona would take photographs of the happy couple. All-in-all it was to be a pretty cut-price and home-made affair because so many people were prepared to give and work for no money.

You will remember that I said the road outside Glebe Cottage would make amends for all the hassle it had initially given us. Fiona had seen a wedding dress for seventy pounds that she very much liked but which was out of the question to buy. Now Wiltshire County Council had grand ideas to widen the road through Winterbourne Gunner to let the traffic make even more noise but, unbeknown to us, we owned the narrow margin of land between the front garden wall and the highway. The Council came to us with an offer of fifteen pounds to purchase this important strip of rough old grass. Marian, who had experience of haggling with the stall-holders in various town markets, said "no thank you." The Council then said, well, how much did she want? She said "seventy pounds." Fiona got her wedding dress!

Everything went according to plan for the wedding except that the night before nearly all the corks of the sherry Marian had made popped and we discovered it was undrinkable. Teddy, my brother, kindly bought replacements. The service itself was a mixture of many strands of churchmanship; the traditional organ bits alongside the rhythm of modern guitar music; the order of service was written by Graeme taking most of it from the Roman missal; there were 'smells (incense) and bells' much to the amazement of my mother and father. We were never sure if Fiona and Graeme were ever legally married – certainly not according to any authorised Anglican order of service – but it was a wonderful ceremony followed by a wonderful reception in the place that had brought us all together. Fiona was the first clergy-wife in the family but was soon to be joined by others.

Following the wedding, we enjoyed a caravanning holiday on a farm in Axminster and returned for the final few weeks before my ordination on September 29th – the feast day of St Michael and all Angels. Matthew Lynn, my new boss-to-be, arranged for me to preach in his church on several occasions before we moved in but I am not sure if these attempts to spread the Good News of Jesus Christ helped to overcome my nerves when standing in a pulpit, or strengthened my belief that preaching was always going to be a hard act for me. At the very least they saved Matthew having to prepare a sermon!

And so everything was in place for the great day. All my final essays had been good enough – just – and my bank balance was in the black – just. Now I had a recognised and necessary qualification that gave me the authority and standing to carry out the task that was set for me. Some may say that that is not the real requirement for a profession that is a 'calling'. Of course there were other matters of belief and conviction that were necessary to become a Clerk in Holy Orders, as was my official job description, but I can honestly say that not once was I ever to experience again that feeling of inadequacy that bugged me for so long in my electronics life. My Decca Navigator years were not to be wasted, however, as all life's experiences prepare someone for the job of being a priest. Unless I could relate to people in their diversity, then my new qualification wouldn't be enough. The Bishop of Winchester, the Right Reverend John Taylor, who had approved my appointment at Kings Worthy, sent me a questionnaire in which he asked what I thought would be the most important thing I had done in my life to prepare me for the priesthood? My reply wasn't that I had been this or that in the church but that I had twenty-five years experience working alongside many people in an industrial concern.

The final act before leaving Salisbury Theological College was the Forth Going service in the cathedral. This was a very grand affair in which we ordinands processed right down the long naive garbed in cassock and surplice to receive our college hoods, although we were still not arrayed in dog-collars. Like most great college occasions there had to be a moment of dramatic humour. The organ was played by ordinand Myles Davies who was a brilliant exponent of the instrument and who came from Wigan of pier fame. The preacher, the Reverend Barry Rogerson (later Bishop of Bristol), extolled the virtues of some of the ordinands including mention of the organist's abilities despite his connection with Wigan and it protrusion. Myles responded by playing the deepest note possible on the consol which must have been the loudest fart ever heard in that holy place. We responded to this instant piece of comedy with our usual outburst of laughter but the dean of the cathedral was not impressed and the next morning Myles was summoned to the Deanery study to receive an ecclesiastical rocket.

The physical move of nearly all our worldly goods from Winterbourne Gunner to Kings Worthy took place about a month before my ordination. There would be little opportunity to settle in once my dog-collar was in place so as we had the caravan we had a delightful few weeks living by the side of an empty Glebe Cottage but still with its hot water and loo.

The last piece of business finally to be settled before leaving was the question what should we do with Glebe Cottage? The church would provide us with free accommodation for the foreseeable future but we knew the day would come when a home would have to be found for retirement and there was the old adage 'once on the property ladder never get off'. In the end we arranged to let the house to incoming theological students. For fifteen years a series of college families were our tenants during which time no written contract was ever signed, just a gentleman's agreement and handshake. Some kept the place far cleaner than others, but the rent paid for the mortgage and that was all that mattered.

Unbeknown to me, arrangements for my ordination were

going somewhat awry – the right hand certainly wasn't communicating with the left. The service for several ordinands, who were going to various parishes in the diocese, was being arranged to take place in Winchester Cathedral (of Beatles Fame), to be conducted by the suffragan bishop of Southampton on September 29th. At the same time Matthew Lynn was organising with the suffragan bishop of Basingstoke to ordain me in Kings Worthy parish church. How much episcopal bartering went on for the honour of laying holy hands on my head I shall never know, but Basingstoke won and did the honours a few days after Michaelmas. I cannot remember very much about the service itself, except that the church was packed with parishioners and well-wishers, including my mother and father who I think found it all rather unreal and perplexing. The most difficult part for me was not to feel self-conscious with a strange stiff white collar round my neck with the collar stud at the back. I also wore a new grey suit that mainly was to hang dejected in my wardrobe for most of the next thirty years, as I was to find that trousers and a pullover better suited my image of a priest.

September 1975 saw important changes in our lives, not only had I become a cleric and Marian a member of that strange breed of women known as 'clergy wives' but we also became grandparents. Lisa Claire Birdwood was born in Poole to Claire and Bill on the 25th September.

So had come to an end our two years sojourn in Salisbury. It was perhaps the most exciting and enjoyable period of my life; a time of theological and liturgical reorientation; a time in which we made many good friends including those half dozen men and wives in my college group who were to continue being a support and delight for many years to come; a time in which I came to understand more about myself and what I could properly contribute to society and that mystical place called the Kingdom of Heaven. And it was a time when I discovered a fundamental flaw in my understanding of the meaning of right and wrong in connection with the accepted understanding of morality.

The question of morals had been thoroughly worked through at college and I came to the conclusion that in the realms of personal and corporate behaviour it isn't a case of this is right and this is wrong, simply because this or that is 'moral' or 'immoral'. Something is right if it is good and something is wrong if it is bad. Morality has its foundation in the old laws of the tribes of Israel at the time when Moses staggered down the mountain carrying his tablets engraved with the commandments and when all the other subsequent hundreds of little laws about behaviour were promulgated. It wasn't because these things ensured the people were moral but to ensure they were healthy. Morality was – and still should be – about health and safety. As with so many aspects of what I had learnt in the past two years, Christianity was something to be lived corporately and in community, so the laws were laid down to ensure the health and the stability of the community and, later in Jewish history, the nation. Of course in those far off days people had no scientific or medical knowledge, as we have, which is the reason why today much of that law seems trivial and ridiculous. Moreover, morality in the near past, especially as espoused by the Victorians, has been hijacked and used for all sorts of systems of prohibition and restrictions of life. For instance, adultery isn't immoral because someone says so – it is bad because it breaks up family life and the stability of the nation. Sex outside marriage is bad because it increases the chances of widespread disease and not just because it is 'immoral'. Fundamentalist interpretation of the Biblical teaching on homosexuality only appeared correct in those times when human knowledge knew nothing about the complex genetic workings of the body. Taking this more open or liberal view of morality was to help me immensely not to be judgemental in dealing with people but to be loving and only wanting the best for them.

For Marian it was the start of a difficult change in life – all said and done she had married a kind of boffin and landed up with a parson.

Scene Two

A Dog-Collar and New Life

As a deacon and assistant curate I was entitled to free accommodation in the parish. In years past the main source of curates was from young men just out of university, still wet behind the ears, and so there lingered among the church hierarchy the idea that all curates didn't really require a full family home with a study in which to work and to talk to and share life with concerned parishioners. Before agreeing to serve in Kings Worthy and Headbourne Worthy I had turned down two other parishes, to which the college Principal had sent me, because the accommodation provided was totally impracticable for a married man with a family coming to stay at various times. The chalet-type house at Kings Worthy wasn't any palace or large multi-bedroom vicarage but it did have a study and very large kitchen and an even larger garden with a huge vegetable patch. This 1930's house was to be our home for two and a half years.

Kings Worthy was a patchwork of private houses, council estates and the odd shop dotted around, with farmland still clinging on around the edges, except where it virtually joined on to Winchester. The nearest thing to a village centre was just the church and an excellent pub, the Cart and Horses, to which Matthew and I often retreated to hold meetings about the needs of the parish. Most people worked in Winchester but we were to find that there was plenty of agricultural activity going on around. Headbourne Worthy was a scattered collection of houses and a little gem of an ancient church with a detached graveyard two fields away. As a deacon, my stipend was £1300 per annum, plus the free house, help with the telephone and car bills and a small allowance for such expenses as providing coffee and biscuits for parishioners who came knocking at my door. Two years previously my salary was £3000 per annum so it is plain to see that life wasn't easy, although Marian's part-time job at the SPCK bookshop in Winchester provided some relief. Further help was at hand due to the agricultural activities in the neighbourhood. Our diet wasn't entirely made up of watercress, kale, eggs, chicken, tomatoes, marrows, beans and peas but they often appeared on the table due to their local production. The watercress grew in beds just down the road where there was beautiful clear running water as often to be found in that part of Hampshire; the kale was provided by the kindness of a local farmer who gave me permission to help myself from his field; eggs with cracked shells were cheap from a chicken farm; beans and peas were bought by the bucketful, cut or shelled, from a food processing plant and frozen by us. The chicken weren't quite so straightforward – they were rather tough old birds after egg-laying had ceased and came complete with feathers and everything inside. Neither of us were knowledgeable or experienced in plucking or cleaning chickens and a first assault in the kitchen resulted in feathers covering the whole room and ourselves, so we retreated to the bathroom with twenty dead chicken, having first stripped ourselves naked. After several hours we emerged triumphant, with the chickens naked as well. Summer 1976, being one of the hottest on record, we ate a bumper crop of home-grown tomatoes with every meal and lots of marrows stuffed with minced meat.

The decision to come to work with Matthew Lynn soon became evident as the right one. We were almost the same age, although he had a completely different background from me. He was a Southern Irish Protestant and history graduate from Trinity College Dublin who had been a headmaster at a school in Ireland and after a short Irish curacy was appointed rector of Kings Worthy and Headbourne Worthy. Talk about chalk and cheese! However he was exactly what was needed to ground me firmly on my feet at the start of my ministry. In a nutshell, he was just a super, loving, loveable family man and always prepared to share a glass of whisky – never to be called Scotch! I was treated as an equal and given pastoral responsibility for a particular part of the parish, mainly consisting of council house tenants. Perhaps he was the most laid-back person I have ever met, as became evident in some of the things he taught me – well, taught isn't quite the right word – that rubbed off on to me. First I had to find my way around the old Book of Common Prayer as Matthew and his churches were traditionalist. This was balanced, in a small way, by him telling me that it was the privilege of the priest to be the first to kiss the bride when taking a wedding service! His whole attitude to life was that everything would be all right – don't worry. His Irishness suggested that this could be assured by kissing the Blarney Stone although in reality I am sure it was really the Holy Spirit who was the source of his strength and his calmness. He told me never to worry about the actual conducting of services because, he claimed, once an Anglican service had started nothing on earth could stop it – only divine intervention from heaven could but then there would be a good reason!

If there was any weakness in Matthew's ministry it would have to be his inability to keep a tight diary. He was a bit like Frost on the television – pieces of paper in pockets recording important information. There had been for some time in the parish a Prayer Group for Healing that held a prayer and teaching service once a month. As a deacon I was expected to attend every event held in the parish and so I turned up for my first attendance at the healing meeting. Matthew also arrived with the news that he had double booked himself and so would I (or was it, I would?) lead the proceedings. Healing – amongst many other topics I was soon to discover – had barely a place on the college theological agenda, so here I was thrown in at the deep end and learning very rapidly. From that first meeting I never looked back on my interest and belief in the healing ministry of the church. With input from people like Claire and Bill and their charismatic teaching about the Gifts of the Spirit my understanding and exercising a healing ministry has always been an important part of my parish work.

So how did I spend my time day by day in my first parish? Getting to know people was the very top priority and there is only one way to achieve that – visiting, visiting and more visiting. First the regular congregations, then the sick and dying and then as much just knocking on doors as was humanly possible. All this, thankfully, came quite naturally to me – but then my mother always said I was a 'poke-nose'! I am interested in people, and what makes them tick, and it is in the knowledge that the clergy are interested in them that the scene is set for them to be invited to come and worship God. My job was to 'stand alongside' where people 'were' in life and the best place to achieve that was over a cuppa sitting around the kitchen table. For the uninitiated, most churches and services are daunting places and occasions, but to have met the man in the dog-collar before can be a great help. Visiting also threw up all sorts of needs and problems in the various neighbourhoods in the parish. One dear old lady living in a council bungalow showed me a large patch of black gunge all over her larder wall. She said "look at all that compensation (!) on the wall" – and could I do anything about it? Well, a letter to the council was the least I could do. Another lady I visited asked if I could go into the roof and stop the water tank making a funny noise – you don't get to know people by watching them sitting in a pew – and we weren't taught plumbing at Salisbury but I climbed into the loft and found a bird's nest on the water-valve.

Service preparation – sermons, prayers, talks – all took a lot of time at first but the trick was to prepare them as soon as you knew they were going to be required. Get them out of your mind and get out and meet more people. All parish clergy are asked to carry out extra-parochial duties and it fell to my lot to be appointed as the Scouts chaplain in the district. The duties were not at all onerous, although I had never been a Scout in my life. My main task was to prepare and conduct the annual St George's Day service in the cathedral. Preaching always has been extremely hard and bad on the nerves and so the thought of standing high up in that cathedral pulpit was as daunting as it comes. Still, there aren't many deacons who can say they have preached in a cathedral! Matthew gave me the task of running a young peoples' weekly club in a council estate church hall. This was time-consuming, as each week needed some different activity and talk to prepare. Even so it was enjoyable and rewarding – perhaps my main contribution to the youngsters was just 'to be there' for them. Then there was Potty Training! Post Ordination Training continued for three years and took the form of lectures and seminars at the diocesan centre at Old Alresford Place, the birthplace of the Mothers Union. All the recently ordained in the diocese gathered, sometimes for residential periods and with wives, to be instructed in many different facets of parish ministry. It was also a time in which to share experiences, to let off steam about difficult parishioners and generally moan about the shortcomings of the church, but the best bit was the hospitality and cooking of the community of lovely nuns which gave us a break from the rigours of parish life.

The church at Kings Worthy was dedicated to the Blessed Virgin Mary, but she wasn't the only saint associated with my parish. There was Mrs Morton. Mrs Morton for many years held the position of sacristan and she epitomized every detail of that calling – she lived for the work of keeping everything in the sanctuary and the priest's vestry in exact order. She was devout and meticulous through and through – and woe betide anybody else who wasn't, especially the clergy! She ruled Matthew and me with a rod of iron, but she was lovely and helped me to get things right with Saints Days and special liturgical occasions. At my first Maundy Thursday evening celebration of the Last Supper and Washing of Feet, the time came for the sanctuary to be stripped, as was custom in many churches, in readiness for the following day, Good Friday. Everything in the sanctuary is removed, leaving just a bare altar. Matthew, with the aid of Mrs Morton and me, did all this with appropriate solemnity and then returned for the final prayers. But this wasn't good enough for Mrs Morton –the long carpet in front of the altar was to be rolled up and removed as well! During the following year Mrs Morton became ill and I had the privilege of being at her bedside as she lay dying. She sat up and recited the Nunc Dimittis ('Lord now lettest thou thy servant depart in peace…') and very soon afterwards she died. When it came to the next Maundy Thursday service Matthew and I stripped the altar and returned for the prayers. He was standing at one side of the sanctuary and I at the other. He caught my eye and looked down at the carpet. Without a word or hesitation we both bent down and rolled up the carpet! The spirits of the dead live on and Mrs Morton certainly was still on duty.

During my first year at Kings Worthy we had an addition to the family. Through our friend Joan Chidson of caravanning days at East Hoathly, we heard of a litter of golden Labradors for sale. We already had Jake, a black cat from a litter of one of Fiona's cats. Marian has always been a person having as much time for animals as for humans – well, almost as much – and her delight in our furry friends wasn't diminished with the arrival of Lucy. After Jake and Lucy had been playing happily in the garden one evening, the cat was put out for his last attention to nature before coming in for the night. Unfortunately he didn't return and was found the next morning dead in the road. For days Lucy looked for him in the garden but she did get a companion soon after with the arrival of another black cat from Matthew who we named Heidi. She too got run over but despite some terrible injuries survived and lived to a ripe old age.

My ministry soon included baptisms and funerals and later, when ordained priest, weddings. When still a deacon I assisted Matthew at wedding services and claimed my share of bridal kisses. Weddings, I found, were quite stressful as it was a service in which absolutely nothing should go wrong. I always wrote the names of the bride and groom at the top of each page of the service sheets! Incorrect names could make the ceremony illegal as well as being highly embarrassing. Then there was the problem of the bride's dress. The happy couple, at the end of the service, kneel down in front of the priest to receive The Blessing. Standing directly over them, one got an unimpeded view down an off-the-shoulder dress – all very nice but one had to keep ones eyes on the script regardless of any interesting distractions!

Funerals, I found, were not difficult although there was an awful lot of work of preparation with the next-of-kin. With my newly found belief that in the end everybody would finally find a place in heaven, non churchgoers presented no difficulty and I soon realised that mourners were entitled to have what they wanted in the service so long as I included a Christian commendation for their soul to God. However slushy and sentimental requests seemed to me, that was no reason for not allowing them. I suppose the 'trick' for getting through a funeral was to carefully prepare the service and then at the ceremony become very professional i.e. outwardly to be involved but inwardly standing back a little. A weeping parson did no good for anybody. One occasion, however, did get me in a stew, not for any emotional reasons, but because I hadn't given the correct instruction to the gravedigger. It was after the cremation of the mother of one of our close neighbours and the urn was to be placed in an area specifically reserved for ashes. The small plots were allocated in lines. The first plot of the current line was already occupied with a wife and next to her was her husband. Now he had taken a second wife after the death of his first and reserved the next plot to him for her so finally he would lie peacefully, without any favours, between the two. Unfortunately, for me, the second wife was still in the land of the living. Also unfortunately, I had forgotten this and placed my neighbour's mother in the reserved plot, which was not what the already buried man had had in mind! I realised my mistake as soon as I had covered the ashes and the mourners had left the graveyard. Clear thinking and decision making are necessary at times of difficulty but I knew that once an interment had taken place a Home Office Order was required for exhumation which was just what I was contemplating carrying out. Within a few moments I had seriously broken the law and moved mother one plot up the line. I then had the task of going to the bereaved family to explain that mother was no longer where they thought she was, but my good fortune returned as they saw the funny side of what had happened.

On visiting a family to arrange another funeral, I discovered that the deceased was still reclining somewhere in the West Country, so I asked Matthew if he could arrange for the Winchester undertaker to have the body brought to their chapel-of-rest in readiness for the service in our church. On the morning of the funeral I had a phone call from the rector saying he hoped everything was going to be OK but there had been a slight hitch in the arrangements. He then went on to explain that just after last midnight he was getting into bed when he suddenly remembered he hadn't asked the undertaker to collect the body from distant parts. Now Matthew was a most super person and everybody just loved him and would go to the ends of the earth for him. Well, in the middle of the night the undertaker did drive down the A303 on a mission on some urgency. To cut a long story short, there were no two clergymen waiting at a church gate more relieved than us, as we saw a large black hearse slowly draw up with a flower bedecked coffin – and exactly on time. The family and mourners all gathered at the church had no idea of what had happened and we certainly had no reason to tell them.

Funeral directors staff, I was soon to find out, were a jolly lot and many is the time I have sat in the front of a big black car with the driver, but separated from the mourners behind by a glass screen. They would all be sitting tight-lipped in the back while in the front the driver would be telling me jokes or funny stories of his funeral experiences.

As long as I only listened without a hint of a smile or turn of the head, everything would be OK!

By September 1976 I was considered sufficiently trained and a safe pair of hands to be ordained to the order of the priesthood. This took place in Winchester cathedral by the Bishop of Southampton. Now a bishop is a bishop is a bishop, but I did feel a little second-class as both my ordaining clergy were Suffragan (kind of assistant) Bishops and not Diocesans. Anyway, during the service I was to experience something that was to dog me for many years until I finally gave up conducting services. Part of the ceremony required me to stand alone and physically unsupported on stone steps facing out to the congregation. The wide empty open space in front gave me little close at hand on which to focus. This had the effect of upsetting my perceived balance and I began to feel that I was going to keel over – and what a disaster that would have been! What made it worse was that the more I thought I might go over, the more I tensed myself which is just what I shouldn't have done.

Once priested I could conduct all varieties of church service, including the all-important Eucharist. Four years had now elapsed since I decided I wanted to become a priest and at last I was able to offer people the whole range of all that the church practiced for the well-being of Christians. I could now fulfil my calling. The first time any priest celebrates the Eucharist is very special but also daunting, as it is amongst other things, a public ritual – a public performance – and I was to stand at the altar in the full view, and facing, the congregation. Theologically I was standing in place of Christ at the Last Supper. No wonder my knees were far from still! In most parishes – those that are officially known as training parishes which thank goodness mine wasn't – the vicar or rector will be present to see the new boy doesn't make a total mess of his first celebration. Matthew, however, said he thought I would do better on my own and in any case he had another appointment. How perceptive and understanding of people that man was.

As Bill, our son-in-law, had decided to go into the church – he said he never would but in the end God usually wins – he had been going through a similar process as I had endured with interviews and ACCM. He was advised to go to Salisbury Theological College as he too needed to be stretched from a very evangelical and charismatic background. In the same month as I was priested, Bill and Claire and baby Lisa moved to a small terraced house they bought in Quidhampton, just outside of Salisbury. The Strange family were becoming a bit nomadic and a bit ecclesiastical.

Further duties came my way now I was able to celebrate the Eucharist. I filled a chaplain's vacancy at the maternity unit of Winchester Hospital that meant visiting the wards of those involved in bringing new babies into the world. One afternoon a week I would go and chat up all the young mums and, if requested, bless the newly arrived. It was also a chance to offer the church's sacrament of baptism when the mums got back to their homes and to invite them to Holy Communion in hospital the following Sunday. One very young mum said she would like to take Communion and I explained where and when it was to be celebrated. She then said she wasn't married – to which I replied that that made no difference to me. Next she said she wasn't confirmed and finally admitted she wasn't even baptised, let alone ever went to church. I talked to her some more and it was obvious she just wanted to do this thing for herself and for the sake of her new baby. So again I broke all the rules the next Sunday morning and gave her Communion, after which I suggested she should go and see her parish priest. Whether she ever did I never knew but I was sure I had done the right thing. I was beginning to learn that religion cannot be bounded by rules; I was beginning to learn what a privilege it was to be involved with families and those vitally important events in their lives. I was beginning to learn that a priest's life wasn't a nine to five job – more like sixty to seventy hours in a six day week.

During my time in the church's ministry I have been fairly strict about taking my one day off each week – not to do so is to court disaster and would be unfair on Marian and our family. There were very few evenings when I was at home which gave me lots of interesting things to do, but was pretty lonely for Marian. The importance of getting out of the parish for my weekly day off soon became apparent – staying at home and resting never stopped the phone or the front door bell from ringing.

Towards the end of my second year at Kings Worthy I began thinking about the future and the next step in my ministry. For a curate of my age and experience, about five years was the minimum time required before a priest could expect to be appointed to the incumbency of a parish. In those five years it was usual to serve in two different parishes, the second one in a more senior role. Now to explain how Church of England clergy are promoted or moved on or changed job would be like trying to describe nuclear fission to a baby. There is no set pattern – it is a combination of all sorts of requirements, of wheels within wheels and the Old Boy system and who would fit where and when. Junior clergy like myself were not expected to start searching for pastures-new on their own – they should seek the advice of others, especially of their vicar and their bishop. They could make noises in certain directions, but actively to find a new parish wasn't done. So I began to look again in the Church Times and came across a vacancy for a senior curacy in Taunton in Somerset. The Church Crimes, as we called it, had served me well in getting my first post – I would try it again and see what happened! I wrote a long letter to the vicar of Wilton, a town parish in Taunton, for the post of curate-in-charge of his daughter church at Galmington. I waited and waited for a reply and in desperation one evening I rang the Revd Roland Clark to find out what was happening and did I have any chance of the job. His reaction was immediate, asking Marian and me to come to Taunton that week for an interview. At this point I told Matthew what was afoot and I asked him if the bishop should be informed – to which he replied "no not yet." So off to Taunton we went and after a long chat with the Revd Clark and the churchwardens and a guided tour round the parish, I was offered the job. My response was I would think about it and then write my reply. "Oh no!" I was told, "I want to know today." We were given the time to go away and drive around for an hour, after I had waited six weeks for my initial letter to produce any response and now the man wanted an answer immediately!

Fortunately we had no hesitation in accepting, which was an indication of what we really thought of the vicar. He was super, despite his obvious difficulties with keeping to some sort of schedule – an observation to be confirmed many times in the future! The very next day I had a telephone call from the Bishop of Southampton requesting me to go and see him as he wished to talk to me about two parishes that he thought I should consider moving to. Accepting a new parish is like getting engaged or married – you just know it is right and you go and get on with it, I thought. That was how I felt about Kings Worthy and now again with Taunton and so I told the bishop that I had already accepted a post in the diocese of Bath and Wells. He could barely control his disfavour of what I had done!! Of course if Roland Clark had allowed me days to consider, then I couldn't have told my bishop that everything was sewn up. The strange way the Church of England works is like a double-edged sword, there are few rules laid down in stone, which can be extremely frustrating, but then it is difficult to take action against those who are rebels like me.

Again, the die was cast and after giving three months notice we were once more to be on the move – and with every encouragement and kindness of Matthew and the parishioners. Other changes in the family were also happening.

Graeme and Fiona were moving to the Truro diocese and the parishes of St Erme and St Allen just to the north of the cathedral city. Visiting them would be a far longer journey but much nicer to stay in Cornwall than South London. Claire and Bill in Salisbury found time to produce another daughter, Hannah Jane, born on 5th April 1977.

Our departure from Kings Worthy was marked by a marvellous farewell party and most generous leaving presents. Friendships we had made, remained so for many years. The only sadness that had befallen us there, apart from the death of Jake the cat, was the loss of our caravan. We found we just couldn't find the time to use it, and as we had an excellent offer, we sold it and our caravanning days came to an end. Happy memories!

The move to Taunton wasn't without difficulty. The curate's house, three bedrooms, detached, and a stone's throw from the church, was pleasant enough with a good garden and fruit trees. However there was one drawback – no study. This meant that the dining room had to double up as a place to eat and a place to work and interview parishioners. The third bedroom could have served as a study but inviting some parishioners, young and female especially, upstairs could be fraught with unthinkable situations. The other problem that faced us was that, apart from the kitchen, every room required redecorating. Fortunately there were two weeks before starting my duties, so when the removal men unloaded our belongings into their respective places, it was all piled in the middle of the rooms until I had finished with the paintbrush.

For the day of my licensing and first appearance (not induction, as I wasn't the incumbent) the church was packed to the last seat – everybody wants to see what this new man is going to be like! Such occasions are extremely hard work, especially the meeting of new people after the service, and trying to remember their names. Which reminds me of an instance when the vicar of Horsham asked a lady what her name was, he got the reply "Mrs Brown – the same as last week and the week before that." After Marian and I arrived home we were so tired we were asleep on the bed when the phone rang. It was my brother to say our father had died. This news came through to Teddy in the morning, but he had the good sense and understanding to delay ringing until after my first service in Taunton was completed.

Bryan Strange in priest's robes. Taunton 1978

The death of my father, on May 7th 1978, at the age of seventy-eight, was a terrible blow for my mother after well over fifty years of married life together. It also meant the end of any Strange as a presence and influence in Strange Electrical Co. Ltd. and it wasn't long before the old firm as I had known it, was splitting apart and never to be the same again. Short-term, for me, it meant delaying my starting work in the parish for ten days as we had to travel to Heathfield for his funeral and to spend some time with my mother.

On July 2nd 1978 Martin William Frederick Elmore was born in Trelisk Hospital, Truro, becoming our third grandchild and as it turned out our only grandson. In September of 1978, Bill was ordained in St Albans Cathedral by Bishop Runcie who was to become Archbishop of Canterbury (no small fry for him!) and the family moved to their first parish in Royston Hertfordshire – a long and tedious journey from the middle of Somerset.

St Michael and all Angels, Galmington, was a church very different from anything I had previously experienced. It was a daughter church of St George's in the Wilton area of Taunton and as such did not have parochial status. That is why I was officially labelled 'assistant curate' but in practice I was in charge of the day-to-day running and worship of St Michael's. Roland Clark was 'The Vicar' and in many ways he kept a pretty tight reign on what went on and what I got up to. Some of my duties including conducting, or just attending, services at St George's – what we called 'the big time' – and that at times I found a rather irksome discipline, as there were several active retired clergy around, as well as Roland running the show like a team ministry. The core foundation of St Michael's centred on a large and active Church Lads' and Church Girls' Brigade which, with parents, was extremely supportive and the monthly Brigade church parade could muster up to two hundred souls. After each parade service, the uniformed boys and girls formed up and with the brass band sounding off, we would march around the district and housing estates as an act of witness – yes, and I was expected to march as well wearing my cassock. In a way I found it all rather bizarre and yet underneath I knew it did a tremendous amount of good. Captain Bill Walker, the Commanding Officer, was the driving power and example to us all, especially for the youngsters. He was a dedicated leader, not only as an upholder of Christian principles but one who believed in the place of worship in our lives and all officers were required to be communicant members of the Church of England. Anyone who missed church parade had to answer to Bill. During the week there were numerous social and recreational activities and a camp every summer. All this made St Michael's a lively, active and witnessing church –and I didn't have to do any organising of it! Well, that isn't quite right – I was expected to support everything the Brigade did and stood for and that I was certainly prepared to do.

The church at Galmington started as a little mission church, at the time when Taunton began to expand and build large housing estates across the south-west corner of the town. The original building was a small 'tin tabernacle' which by my time had been replaced by a prefabricated square structure with a local council temporary building permit. Its sanctuary, along one side of the building, had folding doors behind it, the other side of which was a lengthwise-on prefabricated hall. This arrangement more than doubled the seating capacity of the church and was always required for parade and family services. As the hall was in constant use for other activities during the week, Saturday evenings were always reserved for setting out chairs and preparing the place for Sunday worship. Standing side-on in the sanctuary to conduct services and facing alternatively left and then right had the same effect, for me, as watching a tennis match at Wimbledon. Family services were held twice a month with the aid of an active group of Readers and other folk who were prepared to stand up and proclaim the gospel. With a large, vibrant, and talented young choir tutored by Chris White, all the services were highly stimulating and an example of what can be achieved when dedicated leaders are prepared to put in time for young people.

Although it was a lively and active church I had inherited, I was able to add something to its ministry during the two and a half years we were there, starting a Bible study group and a healing group. But again I made visiting my priority, ever more sure that that was the only way to maintain and expand the local commitment to corporate worship and to let it be known that the church cared about people. A door I knocked on one day was opened by an old lady who told me how pleased she was to see a priest as she had things on her mind that needed the attention of God and a mediator. After a long talk, prayer, and a cup of tea, we got things sorted out. The next day I was told she had died. Why did I knock on that particular door? Only the Holy Spirit can answer that.

In May 1979 Graeme and Fiona moved to Newlyn – almost off the end of Cornwall and still further for us to visit them – having been offered and accepted the living of St Peter's Church. This lovely Cornish fishing town increased its population with the birth of Peta Mary Elmore on the 25th of October 1979.

Towards the end of my second year at Galmington, the Archdeacon of Taunton, who was my immediate superior after Roland Clark, began to make noises with me about having my own patch – about becoming the incumbent of a parish. Archdeacons are traditionally associated with 'drains and gutters', being responsible for the fabric of church buildings, but more importantly they are concerned with 'brains and gaiters' – not that we wear gaiters any more – parsons and where they should minister.

As I have said before, the system for appointments in the church is no system, just a strange collection of different strands often working in isolation but somehow coming together and keeping parishes staffed as well as possible. Each parish in England has a living patron who, with the diocesan bishop, is responsible for the final selection and appointment of incumbents. Nearly all patrons have received their privilege and responsibilities as a hand-down from years, often centuries, ago. Due to the quirks of ownership, some private estates having passed into public ownership, producing such patrons as the biscuit makers Huntley and Palmer. The tying together of the State and law of the land to include the Established Church doesn't always make much sense. In England the Queen is the patron of about seven hundred livings, as the parishes are called, and it was towards one of these jobs that the archdeacon had me in mind. Now, obviously, the monarch cannot find the time to interview every cleric who might be considering applying for one of the parishes of which she is patron, so she delegates this task to the Lord Chancellor. Now, obviously, the Lord Chancellor cannot find the time to interview every cleric who might be considering of one of the monarch's parishes, so he delegates this task to his Ecclesiastical Secretary who arranged for me to be interviewed in his office at 10 Downing Street; yes, at none other than the Prime Minister's London home. The holy grapevine had whispered to me that, possibly, the archdeacon had a particular royal patronage parish in mind to send me to – well four little parishes way up in the wilds of Exmoor. Marian and I spent an interesting day sussing out these beautiful but remote parishes with the thatched roofed vicarage in the largest of the villages. Marian was smitten but I was not! If I were looking for a parish prior to retirement, I might have been interested, but I was just about to start out on the most important part of my ordained ministry and I wanted something more challenging than a few farmers and their sheep. In other words rural ministry wasn't for me. When the great day came for me to knock on the front door of 10 Downing Street, I was prepared not to present myself as being a possible country parson. Sure enough, the interview centred very much on how I would run a rural parish to which I made it plain I wouldn't have a clue.

Meanwhile in Royston our next granddaughter was born on April 5th 1980 and named Alice Sarah Birdwood.

It was a few months after my Downing Street visit that I had a telephone call from the Archdeacon of Bath. The following day we were to set off on one of our bi-annual trips to visit my brother and family in Aberdeen, when I got the call from the Venerable John Burgess. I was being offered the chance to go and see the living of Kewstoke with Wick St Lawrence – patron, The Queen. After asking the obvious question; "where is Kewstoke never 'eard of it", and being informed it was on the outskirts of Weston-super-Mare, I told the archdeacon that I would speak to him in two weeks time after returning from Scotland. Unfortunately the archdeacon was in a hurry and said he wanted an answer immediately – please get over to Kewstoke now and see what I thought of the place. As my next appointment was going to be very important, we had little option but to delay our long journey north and instead make our way the short distance up the motorway to Weston-super-Mare.

This visit was to be incognito. Nobody in all the world was to know – except the archdeacon and us – that anything was afoot. We were to go and take a surreptitious look at the church, the vicarage and the area in general. We were to speak to nobody and to appear nothing more than any other holiday visitor just having a day out. The object of the visit was to decide if we were interested in being considered to fill the vacancy at Kewstoke with Wick St Lawrence. That sounds all quite simple and unthreatening, but there is a sting in the tail. When an archdeacon, with the patron and finally the bishop, have made an offer, and perhaps more than one offer, to a priest for some particular post, they become somewhat agitated if the offer is rejected. Unless there are very good reasons that the priest can substantiate to reject the proposal, relationships between master and servant can become rather strained. Of course no decision is made without the acceptance of the priest and the Parochial Church Council in question, but church hierarchy does not like being messed around. Unfortunately the Church of England hasn't embraced either the normal interviewing of several candidates and selection system used by employers, nor the military's arrangement of simply posting a person to their next appointment. The church authorities, with the patron, pick a person they think would be suitable, present him or her to the Parochial Church Council and they 'take it or leave it' – and as I have said, bishops don't like PCC's or parsons 'leaving it' because the whole system then has to be started all over again with another candidate. No wonder the archdeacon was in a hurry!

So, what did we find as we drove through the woods around the hill north of Weston-super-Mare? That area is dominated by two features – the Bristol Channel, with its muddy sand, and a toll road. Yes, to get into Kewstoke, we had to pay! Kewstoke village sits under the lea of Worlebury Hill, facing north-west over the grey waters that flow strongly up and down between England and Wales. We saw three things. A beautiful ancient church next to a large Georgian vicarage and a sunset. With the land sloping away steeply to the shoreline, the church and vicarage had been built on a levelled plot and so commanded a magnificent view of the water bordered on the far side by the distant hills of South Wales. We stood in the back garden of the vicarage and watched a glorious sunset dropping far over the western edge of the Channel. The archdeacon knew just what he was doing when he said to go and have a look. We went, we saw, he conquered! Some may want to say that that isn't the way to decide if God was calling me to minister to the people in that part of his vineyard – maybe, but it was a good start! The archdeacon got the telephone call he wanted and the next day we set off north again but this time with contented hearts and for Aberdeen. On our return from Scotland, arrangements were made to meet the churchwardens and have a closer look at everything in the two parishes.

Kewstoke parish is a conglomeration of differing kinds of areas. Along the sea front of Sand Bay can be found traditional seaside bungalows and houses with hundreds of holiday caravans on several large sites, all strung out facing the briny and in the middle of this rather untidy and unplanned area a large holiday camp. I say sea front, but one isn't to conjure up a picture of Brighton or Eastbourne, for here is just a concrete wall built to hold back the tide of muddy water and the tide of sand. It isn't for nothing that it is called Sand Bay. Due to the seabed topography and the powerful Bristol Channel tides, the distance between low and high waterlines can be nearly a mile. Across this twice daily open expanse of flat sand and mud can be heard the plaintive call of a variety of sea birds. In winter it's a bit of a desolate place – wonderful to walk along with the dog to blow away the stresses and strain of a hard day – and in summer full of the sound of Brummie voices. Sand Bay has no pretensions of grandeur but thousands of people from the Midlands visit it for their annual holiday, as I was later to discover. A quarter of a mile back from the shoreline is the north-west facing escarpment of Worlebury Hill and the old village of Kewstoke, with its church, vicarage, chapel, pub, a few shops and the homes of a few hundred souls, tucked in under the lee of the hill. Driving up the corkscrew one-in-four hill from the village we come to the outskirts of Weston-super-Mare and the slightly middle-class residential area of Worlebury. Here is no monochrome setting for an English parish but a variety of landscape, and a variety of people – again as I was soon to find out. And that wasn't all. To the east, connected to Kewstoke parish by a narrow strip of un-inhabited shoreline, is the other part of my patch to be, Wick St Lawrence. Wick consists of the church, village hall, farmers – nearly all of whom seem to be related – animals, grass and nothing else. It was to this disparate collection of souls that my meeting with the churchwardens resulted in my appointment to the living of Kewstoke with Wick St Lawrence.

Once again we were to say farewell to many people we had come to know and love and for the fourth time in seven years the removal van pulled up outside our home. My two and a half years ministry in Galmington was a spirited experience and once again I had been fortunate in having a really super vicar, with his wife Norma, who have remained close friends ever since.

The van that was to carry our home to the seaside, still rather inappropriately, had written on its side ‘Bishops Move’ – well there is no harm in continuing to hope!

Scene Three

People and Parish

Marian was buying carpet in the Weston-super-Mare Co-op store a few weeks before we moved and as she was completing the deal with the salesman, a woman came up and said she wanted some of the same roll. Marian said sorry but she required the whole roll. The other lady was quite indignant but little did she know that Marian had already bought yet another complete roll of carpet. All this goes to show two things, that the PCC had kindly given us £500 to help carpet the vicarage and that the vicarage was enormous.

The building started life around the end of the eighteenth century and was a substantial three storey house with a narrow Victorian single story extension across the side that included the front door. Downstairs was a dining room, sitting room, study, kitchen, washroom (possibly used to be the butler's pantry) and loo. All these rooms, off a grand hall, were at least double the size of any in our previous homes. The first floor was in two parts, front and back, divided by the main staircase, near the top, splitting left and right. To the right were two huge bedrooms, one including a dressing room, with windows giving beautiful views over the Channel and the church, and a bathroom with airing cupboard. To the left were two more bedrooms, a boxroom, and a washroom. On the second floor were two semi-derelict bedrooms. At the rear on the first floor was a self-contained flat with its own front door but also with entry from the main part of the building – that we immediately had boarded up. Every room had a fireplace and sash windows with shutters – it was a fine Georgian house built for a fine Georgian family with lots of money and servants. Outside were brick coal and garden storage buildings and a garage that had been the stables. Records show that at one time the vicar had a household of nineteen people – now the vicar was going to rattle round with only his wife. Lisa, our oldest granddaughter, on her first visit, said how nice it was for grandpa to buy such a big house because there was so much room to hide and play in! One of the back bedrooms was big enough to easily take four single beds and a large table, making a wonderful room for the time when Claire had four children. It was the sort of building that would have made a good example for one of those TV DIY programmes where the new owner, with pots of money, comes and retains many of the original features but all the facilities are updated. Although there was some central heating we just didn't have the money to keep the place anywhere like warm, even with a £200 grant from the diocese.

For a large portion of the seven years we were in the vicarage we had the company of builders trying to keep the place dry and habitable and replacing worn out bits. Twice the roof leaked dirty water in the airing cupboard and death-watch beetle caused havoc at one time in the kitchen. The outside sewage drains several times showed serious signs of decrepitude – as the smell forewarned us. The final attempt to bring things up to scratch was to shroud the building in scaffolding to replace the whole of the roof. There was over an acre of garden and orchards, the larger part of which sloped down the hill towards the sea. I made no attempt to tame this patch and so it mostly reverted to an untidy natural habitat. As the Kewstoke Story unfolds, it will be revealed that after almost two centuries of vicars this one persuaded the diocese that enough was enough and the time had come to move out to a new vicarage. It belonged to a different age, unsuitable for a modern vicar who wasn't the traditional country gentleman of a past era with a private income. To mitigate the effects of the cold, we made one of the bedrooms into our sitting and knitting room, with the dressing room becoming the dining room, and leaving the huge high ceiling rooms downstairs unused except for special parish and family occasions. Of course the study had to remain downstairs – it could easily seat twenty people for a meeting. The outside was rendered and finished with a white coating, completing a building with which we came to have a love-hate relationship.

On the first morning after moving in, I was standing at the front door looking up at the church tower, only a few yards away beyond the gate into the churchyard, when I saw a man and woman leaning over the church wall at the top of the drive. Every now and then they would move over and look down the drive towards the vicarage. I was soon to discover that one was Henry Cole, the local builder/handyman and the other Betty Longdon, the church verger. The best way to describe them would be by calling them, independently, Mr Kewstoke and Mrs Kewstoke. They knew everything and everybody in the village – if you wanted any information just ask Henry or Betty. Similarly if you wanted any information to reach the local population just talk to Henry or Betty. As loyal servants to the church and good friends to us, they became indispensable in getting things done!

There was something else I noticed on that November day as I finally went and introduced myself to the interesting couple at the top of the drive – which is what they were really hoping for. It was a lovely sunny day, well it was down the hill and over the sea, but there was no sun to be seen around where I stood. Henry explained that after about the middle of October the sun never climbed over the top of Worlebury Hill and its rays never graced the vicarage and all the other buildings nestling up against the north facing hill until the end of the following March. Never buy a house on a Sunday and never in the winter! I found this solar phenomena rather depressing and many of the village houses smelt damp. The church tower became a huge summer calendar because as the sun rose higher in the sky over the hill, so its rays fell lower and lower down its side.

There was the 1:4 road that climbed up the north side of the hill ending in a double S-bent at the top. This short stretch of ridged tarmac was the well-known Monk's Hill and connected Kewstoke at the bottom with Worlebury at the top. I say connected, but that was conditional on the thermometer not dropping below zero. As the road was nearly always damp in winter – no sun – the slightest hint of low temperature turned the hill in a sheet of ice. Snow would lie on its sheltered surface way after the sun had got to work elsewhere. For long periods of midwinter, the top half of parish was cut off from the church – unless you travelled several miles round the hill – and the council would never grit the road, even after my many irate letters. Monk's Hill – so-called because there was supposed to be a onetime hermit's hovel in its side – was not my favourite geographical feature of Somerset.

The new vicar is supposed to keep a very low profile until the day of his induction – the day when the Church of England pulls out all the stops and puts on a show calling up as much ancient ceremony and flummery as possible. A bishop and an archdeacon or rural dean descend from on high to conduct the service and encourage the congregation not to give the new man too hard a time before he is settled in. There is a saying that for the first year everyone thinks the new vicar is lovely; the second year he can do nothing right; all subsequent years they couldn't care less. Fortunately I was to find this wasn't entirely true.

So one evening the week before Advent 1980, a large crowd of people crammed into St Paul's Church to join with the Bishop of Taunton (still no diocesan bishop for me) who duly handed to me the cure of the souls of everyone living in Kewstoke and Wick St Lawrence. To announce my arrival to the surrounding countryside I tolled the belfry bell ten times, which unbeknown to me, was saying I intended to stay for ten years. I was to be proved wrong – but only just! I was also handed on a red velvet cushion the huge old key with which to lock and unlock St Paul's Church. To me that key symbolised the whole ethos of the two churches I was now in charge of. That key had stood the test of time and done its duty, but really wasn't what was wanted in this modern age.

I had already decided that things were going to change and tomorrow I would make a start.

But first I must explain a little of the relationship between the Kewstoke and Wick St Lawrence churches. Several years previously Wick, only having a population of about one hundred and twenty, became part of a new church parish called Kewstoke with Wick St Lawrence and its church status changed to a chapel-of-ease within that parish. There was only one PCC with representatives from each church but Wick had a church committee to run its own local affairs. There was no real social or generic connection between the two places, and Wick being a fiercely independent farming community, much resented any suggestion of subservience to Kewstoke. The arrangement was the result of some downsizing exercise by people far away at the top of the authority pyramid and that led me to a lot of work duplication. Because I could understand how the people at Wick felt, I knew that it was required of me to treat both churches the same –particularly in the acts of worship I arranged for them and any attempts to have combined services always ended in failure. However, it was natural that because of the size of Kewstoke and its congregation, I should concentrate my efforts in bringing St Paul's into a more modern world.

My first priority was, as always, to visit as many people as possible. You cannot know people unless you have had a cuppa with them in their home.

These visits were first to the active members of the churches and later to hundreds of those who rarely or never came to a service. By the end of my ministry in Kewstoke and Wick I knew far more non-churchgoers than worshippers, and there was goodwill generally towards the church that manifested itself in many ways as we shall see.

My next priority was to sort out the worship. At both

churches there was a mixture of Prayer Book and 'home-spun' services – all pretty uninspiring in my estimation – and which would have to go. Everything was a far cry from those Friday night services at Salisbury Theological College! After a period of time and a certain amount of hot discussion at various meetings, it was agreed that St Paul's each Sunday would have an 8 a.m. said Prayer Book communion and a 10 a.m. sung modern Parish Communion. Wick services were timed differently as I couldn't be in two places at once and farmers anyway were busy, seven days a week, until evening time. Later I added a Family Service at both churches once a month as a response to popular demand from an increasing young congregation. The hymn-books were changed to include modern hymns and songs. During this slightly turbulent time of re-orientation one of my churchwardens came to me and suggested it would be a good thing if I slowed down all this modernisation. This 'dour Scotsman,' Harry Mellor, said people needed time to get used to my radical thinking and scheming but in principle he wasn't against me and my ideas – just calm it down a bit! Harry, over the years, became a true friend and supported me through many difficult times and decisions. I did give my parishioners a hard time but I have often wondered if I would have achieved the necessary changes if I had pussy-footed around? Remember that old saying 'the first year you are lovely – the second year you can do nothing right' and a new broom is to sweep clean!

Marian was automatically expected to run the Mothers Union and even perhaps the Sunday school. Marian, however, had other ideas and priorities that she soon made known. The only responsibility she had was to ensure the health and welfare of the vicar and that was all. Of course she welcomed the callers and answered the phone and joined in with many parish activities – but running things, oh no! She found herself a part-time job in a Weston- super-Mare sewing and knitting machine shop – the money helped to keep us warm and clean in that massive and decaying vicarage.

Before we moved to Kewstoke we brought my mother to view the vicarage, with the idea that perhaps she could take up residence in the flat. We would reconnect it to the rest of the vicarage so she could have easy access to us and our activities. She had been intensely unhappy since Buller died over two years ago and so we thought moving next to us, but not in with us, might make life for her a little more bearable. The visit was a disaster – nothing was right – 'oh I couldn't live with that' was the only flavour of the day. Now I am approaching something of her age I am beginning to understand what she was saying! Just two months after we had moved in a telephone call from a neighbour in Heathfield told us that mother had been found dead on her bed. That was on January 3rd 1981. She had just returned from a happy Christmas spent in Seaford with her much loved niece Janet and husband Peter. We made the long trek to Sussex and over a period of four days held her funeral service in her beloved Union Church, cleared the bungalow, and arranged the despatch of nearly all the furniture to Kewstoke where it soon melted into the many rooms of the vicarage.

One day when I had collected Marian from work in the car she turned to me and said I had my 'smug look' on and why was I grinning to myself? Well, you may remember that in 1950 I had been instructed to keep all that government-issue clothing ready for the day when an enemy would appear crossing the English Channel skies. Being a good citizen, I had kept that order, to some degree anyway, until the moths finally won the day, but the RAF greatcoat had been my constant companion on many a cold night ever since – it just would not wear out and I was as slim as ever. Marian for years had said it should be thrown away and get myself dressed like a proper parson.

Now there is a fraternity of men who have inside information about the sighting of vicarages and the nature of their incumbents – by some secret coding they pass information amongst their members as to which establishments will offer comfort and sustenance – I refer of course to gentlemen of the road, or more commonly, tramps. These men spend their time criss-crossing the country on foot, in all weathers and seasons. They come to know where to find free food and even more importantly, I discovered, hot drinks. Many such gentlemen had knocked on my front door ever since I turned my collar round – all said and done the Bible says we should welcome the stranger, they know. There is a sure method of knowing that a tramp is genuine, and not a local yobbo 'on the make', by the smell. The kosher tramp exudes a strong aroma, derived from lack of washing water for some considerable time, which I am afraid would leave them in the porch to down my food and drink. One such tramp was Robin. Now he was a real gentleman – even if very smelly – and on the visits he made to our vicarage he always offered to pay for his victuals, not in cash, but by sweeping up leaves or weeding the garden. Another sign of a real tramp is that his coat is always long, black, and extremely greasy – it hangs on him in all seasons, hot or cold. Robin had no such coat, and that did set him apart, but in this winter I thought he would be very cold and exposed and so I offered him my RAF greatcoat. I could feel the wings sprouting out of my back and a ring of light appearing over my head as he put it on. Marian couldn't believe her ears when I told her what had happened. A few weeks later I came home to find a plastic bag parcel in the front door porch and discovered it was my greatcoat! With it was a scruffy little piece of paper on which was written "I regret I cannot after all accept your overcoat as I feel the Queen would not approve my wearing her armed services uniform". Also regrettably, I felt unable to wear my coat again, so after thirty years it finished its life in the dustbin but fortunately those bombers still haven't arrived over the south coast.

During my first few months at Kewstoke I began to understand the size of the task I had been given. As vicar I had the spiritual care of two churches and their congregations, a church hall, a hundred-bed convalescent home, a holiday camp, a church school – of which I was chairman of governors – and within a year the chaplaincy of the Royal Hospital in Weston. Then there was the vicarage with all its building problems. Later I was appointed a governor of the local LEA primary school and a Victims Support councillor. The churches, being listed buildings took up an inordinately large amount of time keeping them in good order. The Wick church tower was registered as unsafe and about to fall down due to a large horizontal crack near the base of the stonework. You cannot imagine the amount of work this one problem caused me until finally after some considerable time and countless meetings the crack was stitched up by cementing in layers of flat roof tiles across the split. Sometimes I wandered if I wasn't also being stitched up by the amount of administration work to be got through.

The vicar can do nothing but minor repairs to his church buildings without what is called a faculty, granted by the diocesan hierarchy, giving authority for the work to be carried out and this could be a long drawn out procedure. Any permanent change of furniture or fixings layout inside the church also requires a faculty and it was a matter of some seriousness to flout the rules. My Salisbury friend Noel Baker tells the story of how he was appointed to two country parishes in Gloucestershire. Before his induction he visited his churches and in one saw a very beautiful oak chest of some great antiquity and value. Later, after he was officially the vicar, he was in the church and noticed that the chest had been removed. Noel questioned the churchwarden, who was an elderly farm worker, about its removal and asked if a faculty had been obtained for its removal. The reply was "Oh No! Sir, we got a horse and cart."

On 1st October 1982 our sixth and final grandchild was born to Claire and Bill in Harlow and named Naomi Laura. I say named, and not baptised or christened, as none of the four girls had been through the waters of baptism – that for them was to come when they could 'decide for themselves'. I had the great pleasure some years later of baptising all four together in Bill's church in Bishop's Stortford where he was then team vicar – a job lot one might say!

The financial health of my two churches was not brilliant but not desperate. From the beginning I had informed the PCC that I had no intention of becoming a fund-raiser – that was the responsibility of the lay people – but of course I would support any legitimate moneymaking activity that was necessary to keep the show on the road. Now Kewstoke's ministry to the visitors at Pontins Holiday Camp had for some time taken the form of putting on a Songs of Praise every Sunday evening in the camp ballroom. This had been arranged in a most crafty way. The evening schedule at the camp ran something like this; 6.45p.m. supper in the dining hall; 7.45p.m. bingo in the adjoining ballroom. Holiday camp meals are not known for being long drawn-out affairs and so by about 7.15p.m. the replete visitors were flocking into the ballroom to get the best seats for the bingo. What better opportunity to fill the waiting time by allowing them to sing praises to our heavenly Father? The singing I discovered, after a few weeks, was desultory and largely ignored but the collection at the end, from several hundred people, provided the church with a fair proportion of its weekly takings! My displeasure of this arrangement brought a mixed reaction at the next PCC meeting but agreement was reached that in future the service would be held at 5p.m. when only genuine worshippers would come and praise God. An increase in the church congregation helped to compensate for the reduction in holiday camp giving but later we did organise a full-blown Christian Stewardship campaign. However there were other things about to happen that transformed the finances at Kewstoke and at Wick St Lawrence.

During my visiting I had come across one Mrs Daisy Oldfield. Mrs Oldfield was what I call a permanent refugee from Birmingham and owned a rather posh lady's dress shop in the more up-market part of Weston-super-Mare. Mrs Oldfield – never Daisy – called me to her home in Worlebury one evening and sought answers from me regarding some quite deep theological uncertainties that had been concerning her for a long time. We parted good friends and I felt she was relaxed and satisfied about the answers I gave her. She was just another person I had met, making a connection between the church and one of the souls I had charge of. But she never came to church. Not too long afterwards she died.

One morning one of those substantial long brown envelopes dropped on to the porch floor – one of those envelopes that you know can only come from a solicitor's office. I was being informed that Mrs Oldfield had left some money to St Paul's Church Kewstoke and some personally to me. Over the next weeks it emerged that she had bequeathed £120,000 for the maintenance and work of the church in Kewstoke. Her person never darkened the door of the church, as they say, but her generosity brought light that was to shine for many years in the most unlikely places. Some time later, my dour Scots churchwarden friend, Harry Mellor, wrote to me saying "it was God's gift brought about by the power of the Holy Spirit." How true he was, but like all God's gifts, they come with a tag attached marked 'use responsibly'. Such gifts present all sorts of opportunities, but can also result in a subversive reaction, because part of the Christian response for all God's blessings is to maintain and increase his church, by its members giving financial support – what we have come to know as Christian Stewardship. When a local church receives a very large windfall, there is a danger that the congregation imagine they can relinquish their individual financial responsibilities. This is a common misconception and has lead many a church to slowly die of apathy. So I immediately called a special meeting of the PCC and put before them what I thought was the way forward.

When big decisions have to be made, I have learnt that to present the assembly with pre thought-out positive ideas has the best chance of things not going pear-shaped! Here was my plan for the use of the money; one tenth to be given away, outright, as per the Biblical command to tithe; a sum of money to be immediately used for several 'capital' projects to improve the church facilities and carry out longstanding repairs; the remainder – £92,000 it turned out – to be placed in a legally drawn up arrangement, to be called The Oldfield Trust.

The recipients of the initial tithing included the local evangelical chapel, our next door church at Worle and Wick St Lawrence church, as well as many Kewstoke village organisations and overseas missionary societies. The capital projects included refurbishing the church hall and making safe our sloping car park that had for a long time threatened to slip silently one night into the adjoining garden or even worse land on someone's head. We replaced the rather old-fashioned sanctuary candlesticks and crucifix and commissioned a local seamstress, with the design help of Marian, to produce new modern altar-frontals. The choir-stall desks were lowered so that the view from the naive to the altar was improved. Other small improvements were included so that whilst the church building retained its ancient beauty, the inside took on a livelier and lighter aura. A piece of very fine oak that had been under my brother's bed for a long time and waiting to be shaped by him into something worthwhile, became a beautiful new lectern from which to read the Holy Scriptures.

The setting-up of the trust fund brought all the weight of ecclesiastical and legal jargon poring into my in-tray. Fortunately the diocesan solicitor was sympathetic to what we were trying to achieve and rather than get legal help locally to decipher the documents, I acted dumb and so we finally got something that most laymen could understand. The meat of the document held three clauses that laid down just what we wanted; three fifths of the income from the investment was for the maintenance of the fabric of St Paul's Church Kewstoke; one fifth for 'the advancement of religion and other purposes beneficial to the community of Kewstoke'; one fifth for 'the advancement of religion in the promotion of missionary and evangelical work in the UK and abroad'. The local qualification was far more open than that for overseas with very good reason – locally we could keep an eye exactly on how the money was being spent while further afield this would be more difficult.

What might be considered an inordinately large portion of Mrs Oldfield's bequest for the fabric of the church building was agreed. St Paul's church was a Grade 1 Listed Building and its maintenance and good repair had been a heavy burden on the parish for many years. There is little doubt that it was a gem of a building with its Norman entrance archway and unusual high clerestory naive windows. It had ancient connections with the nearby Woodspring Priory that in past times had provided monks to administer the sacraments and preach the Gospel in Kewstoke. It was open to the insidious work of salt and sand, blowing off the Bristol Channel and twenty years ago it cost £150 to replace just a single outside corner stone. We had a responsibility to keep faith with those who had maintained it in the past and to hand it on in good repair for the generations to come.

Amongst the local projects we arranged was a weekly bus from Kewstoke for shoppers to Sainsbury's in Worle and a paid leader to run a youth club set-up in the church hall. For the overseas distribution we wanted something that could become more than just a charity hand-out – we wanted something in which the congregation could become involved. I came to hear that an engineering son of one of the parishioners was going to help expand the work of the hospital at Lakhnaden near Nagpur in Central India that specialised in the treatment of eye diseases. Through this contact the Lakhnaden Group was formed and for several years we received letters and information about the work that our money was helping, until the Indian authorities became bolshie and spurned charity giving from the UK. Apart from helping restore sight to many poor people in India, Mrs Oldfield's money made a contact between the Church and non-churchgoing folk in the village. The engineering son married an Indian girl and when the couple returned home we had a grand 'Lakhnaden evening' with them in the church hall.

During the twenty years since that fateful brown envelope came through the vicarage letter-box over £130,000 income has been allocated and the capital value of the trust is now £150,000. I think there is a good chance that Daisy Oldfield rests in peace and is on her way to eternal life.

And that wasn't the end of my not having to worry about fund raising. Shortly after the Oldfield Trust had been set-up a retired schoolmaster by the name of Routlidge left £29,000 for the maintenance of Kewstoke church. He too never came to church, not in my time at least, and his legacy came right out of the blue. Having just gone through so much legal hassle, it was agreed that this money should be spent as and when required. Then there was Jack Crease. Jack had been a lay reader and friend of Wick St Lawrence for many years and he certainly left his mark on his beloved church, in life and in death, in at least two different ways. In his will, he left over £32,000 for the maintenance and work of St Lawrence Church. Money in the end comes to an end but Jack ensured that the memory of his life would last far longer. Wick church is surrounded on all four sides by a graveyard, but the area at the rear away from the road remains empty, after centuries of parish burials, apart from the grave of Jack's late housekeeper. The good lady lies in the middle of this open space and Jack left instructions that he would like to keep her company. They now lie there side-by-side, not just to be close to each other, but as a mark of defiance against a local belief and fear. During the time of the Black Death plague in the fourteenth century, the corpses were buried in this part of the graveyard and to this day the received wisdom is that any disturbance of the ground would release the deadly plague germs. I am pleased to report that the health of the village is still very robust! A more pleasing and beautiful memorial to Jack is a stained glass east window in which his lifelong passion for cricket is remembered, by the figure of a cricketer leaning on his bat. His love of children – he was a much respected probation officer – and flowers are also remembered, by a girl holding a bouquet. The initial design for the window was drawn up through the talents of a local artist and some ideas of a small committee of church members. When this was presented to the diocesan authorities for one of those faculties, I think they had difficulty in coping with a modern pastoral setting of people and village dwellings. The final design now includes some rather strange minaret type buildings as a background to the country scene. Even so, it is a pleasing memorial to a good man.

Meanwhile family life went on and occasionally the vicarage resounded to the noise of grandchildren. As both Claire and Fiona were married to vicars and living in Bishop's Stortford and Newlyn respectively, the number of times we saw the families were somewhat limited. Clergy only have one day a week free, so such things as a 'long weekend' never occurred. The best we could achieve was in winter when Pontins was closed and there were no afternoon baptisms and only a morning service at Wick, then Marian would load up the car and as soon as I had said the final Amen and shaken the last hand, we would drive straight off along the motorway and be in Hertfordshire or Cornwall in time for a late Sunday tea. Then a night and day away from the telephone and knocks on the front door came as a great escape, but back for Tuesday morning and the weekly routine. Over a four week cycle I would have to prepare:- four sermons, four talks for the mother and toddler group, two school assemblies, eight sets of prayers, one family service and one healing service. Not being a born preacher or teacher, I found that careful and hard preparation was the only way to any sort of success. And in those days there was no internet or websites to come to the rescue of the hard-pressed clergyman. The most important thing about sermon preparation was to be sure to write where and when it was preached – that way the same sermon could be used again without boring the same people twice!

Prayer has always been a vital part of the priest's lifeline for survival – as it has for any Christian – but I felt I had special pleading one Tuesday morning as I prepared for the midweek Holy Communion service. "Please God send more than the usual two or three this morning – it would make such a good start to the day!" Ten minutes before the service was due to begin, a coach load of day-trippers stopped outside the church and all fifty joined my little band of regulars. One needs to be careful about asking God for things! Holidaymakers and folk from the convalescent home swelled our congregations and kept a steady flow of people throughout the day coming to see 'our lovely little church'. Kewstoke church was well documented in all the local tourist guides because of its outstanding beauty and setting overlooking the Bristol Channel. However, I became frustrated by the constant accolade of 'lovely little church' – I hoped that it could mean more than that to our visitors. To vent my feelings, I produced a small brochure about the church that concluded with something like 'I hope you have enjoyed your visit. Perhaps it is some time since you went inside your church at home which in its own way you would find just as beautiful as this one'.

The vicar and wife partying. Kewstoke 1985

Talking of beautiful churches, brings me to one of the high spots of my ministry when vicar of Kewstoke. Most clergy get given extra-parochial duties, which in most cases can be a bit of a bind, as there is always more than enough to do in the home patch. Glastonbury with its wonderful abbey is always a place to visit and I had the privilege of doing just that in a special way. I was invited by the abbey authorities to join the rotor of clergy to celebrate the Eucharist in the semi-ruined abbey crypt twice a year. I say it was a magical moment and experience – not in the sense of all the other activities associated with Glastonbury and its alternative life-style crowd – but to celebrate the Holy Mysteries in that unique place of history and unseen Spiritual power really was awe inspiring. The congregation of about twenty usually included communicants from many parts of the world. 'Though we are many, we are one body, because we all share in one bread' had a special significance, as did the sharing of The Peace with these Christians of many different countries. I usually had a small party of Kewstoke parishioners come with me and after the service we would retire to a local hostelry to continue the celebration! It really was a grand way to spend a day.

Pastoral work took a lot of time as well. Late one Saturday evening there was a knock on the front door and in front of me stood a somewhat dishevelled couple asking for help. They had travelled from Birmingham, both having just left their individual spouses, because they now said they were in love with each other. Did I think they had done the right thing? I soon realised that what they really wanted was to be tucked up together for a bit of free love in my free bed! Giving them something to eat and drink, I suggested they return to Birmingham and seek the help of their local priest. Then there were the ladies – two in particular – who periodically came to me about sexual problems with their husbands. It soon became obvious that they did have difficulties, but their solution was by getting a kick out of telling me all the details and trying to embarrass me! Unless I was extremely careful in the way I handled such encounters, all sorts of difficulties and accusations could arise. Of course most people who came for help were genuine and there was great satisfaction when able to point them in the right direction. There is much truth in the situation of someone seeking a solution to their troubles, and being given a listening ear, coming away having solved the problem themselves after being reminded that during the discussion the councillor had said practically nothing – the seeker had done all the talking.

One case caused me particular concern and an awful lot of time. A couple's life had begun to unravel due to the husband, a successful police officer, being falsely accused of some crime. He had become a paralytic whisky drinker and she was finally sectioned into a mental hospital. Their bungalow became a vile smelly den into which the man would retreat for days on end, with several bottles of spirits and no food. A neighbour asked if I could help. To enter the house was like going into the unknown – I never knew what I would find. On several occasions I found the man, hiding in a cupboard or under the bed, completely unconscious and the ambulance would come and take him away to hospital. This went on for some time until one night I failed at first to find him anywhere. I called up Henry Cole for help and we began a detailed search of the house, finally discovering the victim, totally naked, lying unconscious under the eaves of the loft. The ambulance men came and wrapped him in tin foil, but after desperate efforts by the hospital casualty department, he died the same night of hypothermia. His funeral was a very sad occasion, especially when I remembered the photograph on his sideboard of a beautiful lady in long evening dress and a tall handsome man in uniform both ready to go out to a ball. Life seems so unfair for some people.

Working with individuals was always time consuming but I tried to practice the notion that my door was never closed and that personal problems should receive attention immediately. One evening a lady came into church in some considerable distress and desperation. Her conscience had been hurting like mad for a long time and what could she do about it? The RC church isn't the only one to offer the sacrament of absolution and penance in the setting of the confessional and so I explained how it all worked and suggested that this might just be the way forward for her. We didn't have a confessional box so we knelt down side-by-side and she verbally unburdened herself to God before the altar crucifix of Christ and made her confession. I gave her absolution and a simple penance and then she stood up, turned and walked straight out of the church. A few days later I met her again and when I asked her how she was, but not of course referring to her confession, her reply was "I walked out of that church last week just as if I was floating on air – the relief was absolutely amazing."

My weekly stint was always at least seventy hours and it seemed that there was no way in which more activity could be crammed into my schedule. And yet there were times when just that happened. Two or three deaths in a few days could bring piles of work in preparing for the funerals but it was when something extra came along that the pressure was almost overwhelming. The deanery officials had decided that Weston-super-Mare required A Mission. There were to be area activities but each vicar had to arrange something for his own parish. I was not impressed! It soon became evident that what would be appropriate for Kewstoke wouldn't suit Wick St Lawrence, so immediately I had two local missions to organise.

Ever since Claire rang from Durham to loudly proclaim she could speak in tongues, I had felt that the Holy Spirit had not fully, or dramatically, worked in my life nor in my ministry. Every year in church I had prayed that something like the wind and fire of that first Day of Pentecost would fall on the congregation and we would all be transformed into a different, more lively, bunch of Christians. The Holy Spirit wouldn't just be 'The Comforter' of traditional church life, but would be the bringer of all the Gifts of the Spirit that had been the natural (supernatural?) expectations of those early followers of Christ. Doesn't the Gospel of John record Jesus as saying "In truth, in very truth I tell you, he who has faith in me will do what I am doing; and he will do greater things still…" To have this prayer answered was the basis of my planning and scheming for the mission to the people of Kewstoke and my expectations were very high. So it was arranged that the Reverend Denis Ball and his Sacred Dance Group would descend on Kewstoke for a week in the hope that the Holy Spirit would descend as well in no uncertain way. The group were from a well-known charismatic centre in Dorset and they were to present a dancing display in which the gifts (tongues, healing etc) and fruit (love, joy, peace etc.) of the Spirit were to be depicted. Pontins kindly gave us free use of their ballroom and several hundred souls from across the deanery saw a brilliant and spiritual display of dancing.

Then various home groups were arranged when Denis explained how the Spirit worked and how we could claim his presence for ourselves. The final event of any mission is usually a service in which individuals are invited to make some sort of public commitment – 'coming forward' as it is called in Billy Graham speak. Such activity, it seemed to me, was unlikely to be attractive to my congregation – we were far from any such Evangelical actions. Denis, being the sensitive man he was, suggested we invite the individuals in the congregation to come to the altar and there each light a candle. They would not have to speak or say anything. It worked and the altar became a blaze of light and, I hoped, a sign of those flames that descended on the disciples at the first Pentecost in Jerusalem. All I can say is that there weren't any dramatic happenings or changes, but then, who can tell? Seeds are sown, but the fruits often take a long time to be harvested – and often not by the sowers.

For the mission to Wick St Lawrence I invited my Salisbury-days friends Ian Coomber and Alan Gill to come and preach. Alan went down well as he had worked as a farmer before ordination and Ian encouraged everyone to be more open with each other. This had one unusual result. One person who never came to church bared her soul to Ian and me about her deep sexual problem. I hope we were able to help her – God works in mysterious ways.

Missions? I am not sure if they are worth all the work. I think the steady week by week work of the priest and the local church people moving about and meeting people are the activities that brings the Kingdom of God that much closer.

In 1985 Fiona, Graeme and family left Newlyn and moved to a church in Redruth where Graeme was inducted as team rector. This appointment was one of those classic arrangements favoured by some out-of-touch bishops who invite the unsuspecting parson to accept 'The Challenge' of a parish in some difficulty. The problem with Graeme's new charge was that the people were not prepared to change and when he got the thumbs down for his plan to turn the ancient unused Victorian church crypt into a coffee bar for the young Redruth tearaways, he decided the church was beyond redemption. He also received a thumbs down when he burnt a pile of discarded Prayer Books in which the congregation were commanded to pray for Queen Victoria! In the end Graeme's dilemma was resolved when he left in October 1986 and became a Royal Navy chaplain. Life for them all was to change dramatically, starting with a shore posting and married quarters in Plymouth.

1986 was a 'Big O' year for me in the form of my sixtieth birthday. Marian arranged an evening meal at a local pub in Worle, just for the two of us. Later that evening Claire and family were to come and stay in the vicarage. After a while I became somewhat worried about the slow service at the pub and my stomach enquired what had happened to the steak I had ordered. Still waiting for the food to arrive on the table, there came a telephone call to say that Claire had arrived early at the vicarage and couldn't get in to put the children to bed – could we return immediately. The cancellation of my steak was agreed with the management and we set out and returned home. The vicarage was all in darkness, as to be expected, but when I opened the front door and put on the lights, what I saw I most certainly had not expected. Standing shoulder to shoulder throughout the ground floor were one hundred and eighty people!

The trip to enjoy a non-existent steak was part of a large logistical and cunning operation to get me out of the way long enough to allow an army of friends and relatives, together with food to feed the five thousand, to be assembled in the vicarage. People came from all over and from all stages of my life. Claire was the prime mover in setting up this massive party that went on with diminishing energy throughout the weekend – I fear to imagine what the Sunday sermon was like!

One event I remember with great pleasure was a reunion of the seven students from my group of Salisbury days with their wives and children. They came – nineteen in all – some with tents and caravans and some to sleep in our vast vicarage. A group of parish ladies cooked us two grand dinners in the hall, but the high spot –especially for me as I was the celebrant – was a group Eucharist. We invited folk from the parish as well, but I am not sure what they made of some of the variations to the service that we included! One elderly cooking lady found Martin Reynolds a delightful person, he was so kind and helpful and she thought he would make someone a wonderful husband. I didn't enlighten her that Martin was gay! Over the thirty years since that day when we all first met in Salisbury, we have held many reunions in many vicarages as part of an ongoing friendship and source of great support, especially when members have found life hard and difficult.

I woke – half woke – one night to the sound of what I thought was a train rumbling away in the distance. But that just couldn't be as the only line was over the other side of Worlebury Hill. Perhaps it was the wind playing tricks. The next morning I soon realised that there was some activity going on in the hall. People were there with blankets and other bits and pieces. They were refugees from Sand Bay where during the night a combination of high wind and high tide had driven the sea over the wall and flooded about fifty homes. Bristol Channel water is laden with sand so the inundation into the homes, by the front door and out of the back, made a terrible mess. We opened a canteen in the hall and did all we could to help alleviate the suffering, but I wasn't best pleased that I had more or less slept through it all. The shoreline of Sand Bay was later to drastically change as the sea defence had to be strengthened. A high concrete wall was not acceptable, so those experts of water control from Holland – thumbs and all – arrived and pumped thousands of tons of sand out of the sea and up on to the beach. Now the great tidal power of the Bristol Channel is dissipated long before it can reach the houses to wreak further damage.

You will remember the importance I have always put on visiting and sharing a cuppa with people in their homes. There were two occasions during our time at Kewstoke when that cup of tea was particularly memorable – they were taken with the Queen at Buckingham Palace. Why we had the privilege of receiving two invitations in different years to the palace garden party we never found out – but two we did – both times demanded donning our very best finery and joining several hundred others at the home of our monarch. We never actually saw the Queen on either occasions but it's the thought that counts and the grub was terrific!

So over nine years we built up the church in Kewstoke and Wick St Lawrence. We started a healing prayer group and a Bible study home group; we held an annual Bonfire Night party for the village in the vicarage garden and we danced a night away at Christmas time at the local hotel. We organised a group of people to visit anyone from the parish who had sold up home to live in one of the many nursing homes in Weston-super-Mare and another group took responsibility to provide flowers and other extras for Kewstoke day care ward at the new Weston-super-Mare hospital. We introduced a real live donkey for Palm Sunday; released doves of peace at Pentecost; celebrated Christmas with a candlelight service of lessons and carols. We baptised the hatched; we married the matched; we buried the despatched. We confirmed the converted and prayed to heal the sick. We fought off an attempt to close our church school in Worlebury which brought me into conflict with diocesan officials, and after seven years we were tired of the constant presents of builders always trying to keep the vicarage watertight and fit to live in. So the time came when I told the archdeacon we had had enough and wanted to move, not away from Kewstoke, but into a more manageable and modern vicarage.

Our request was readily accepted, but the fulfilment only came after a lot more frustration and work. We searched the parish for a plot on which to build a new vicarage and we inspected several properties for sale but again nothing 'fitted'. Finally we gave up and with the permission of the bishop sought a temporary solution in a house outside the parish. A new house, almost opposite the crematorium in Worle didn't really fit the bill, but as it was only to be a temporary arrangement, we finally left the vicarage and became a bit more normal and I could almost conduct cremations without rising from my bed!

They say that there are none so queer as people. When we moved from the vicarage several people were seriously upset – the pattern of life around the church would never be the same – vicars for years had lives there quite happily so what was different for us? One very close friend and worker at the church absolutely refused to come and have a cup of tea in our new home as she felt almost done out of her birthright. Of course the arrangement wasn't ideal, not living in the village, although we were now much nearer to Wick St Lawrence, and it was only to be until such times as a new vicarage could be found. We did enjoy the luxury of a modern house and the much reduced amount of work to keep it clean and warm.

The impending sale of the vicarage caused great interest, rumour and speculation. It was to become all sorts of things, including a home for the owner of the Weston-super-Mare donkeys who gave rides to children along the sands – even if Jesus only wanted one donkey for Palm Sunday. Finally the sale by auction raised £170,000 and it became the family home of a local hotel owner, much to the relief of us all. The diocese placed several restrictions on the use of the property by the new owner, including one that not more than twenty people could hold a party in the garden. I wonder how often the archdeacon is hiding in the bushes on a Saturday night counting the number of revellers?

At the beginning of 1988 we began to think about where we should live when retirement came in two or three years time. Somehow we felt it would never work to return to old pastures and so we sold Glebe Cottage in Winterbourne Gunner. For fourteen years we had rented it, by gentleman's agreement and absolutely no written contracts, to a string of theological college student families. The arrangement had worked well and now with house prices rising very fast, we realised the money with which to buy a retirement home. But where?

As a general principle, especially at that time, the further west one went the cheaper became the cost of housing, so we made many incursions into various parts of the West Country and Devon in particular.

Unfortunately Marian and I weren't singing from the same hymn sheet, as she wanted a picture postcard village setting and I the edge of a reasonable sized town. She wanted the romance of living under a thatched roof while I could only imagine the fire hazard and increased insurance bill. Her mind revolved happily around large store cupboards and freezers full of food for snowy winter days but mine how quickly could I get to the DIY store. In the end a second visit to Tiverton, in Mid Devon, convinced us that it was quite a nice place and we put our money on a plot of land on the outskirts of the town for a modern estate house – without thatch. The next day Marian was serving a customer in the shop and happened to mention that we were buying a house in Tiverton, which brought the remark "Tiverton – that dreadful rough place!" We consoled ourselves by deciding that if you walk into the centre of any English town at ten thirty on a Saturday night, you mustn't be surprised if you end up with a black eye and a lost wallet.

By October 1988, 29 Bluebell Avenue, Tiverton, was completed and we sought someone to rent it until our retirement – we needed the money to pay the rates and general running costs. That someone came in the form of a public school employee but our new solicitor would have none of this 'contract by a handshake', as we had enjoyed for many years, and so we signed a legal agreement with the school. Our tenant, plus partner and two small boys, moved in. Within three months our neighbours –as they told us later – were thinking very unkind thoughts about this vicar who had unleashed two little monsters into their midst. Sadly, or fortunately, depending on your charitable sensitivities, the partnership couldn't take the strain and the letting came to an end. Now three cheers for solicitors! Ours had written into the agreement a clause that either side had to give nine months notice for early termination. So we now had an empty house with rent coming in enough to pay for the house expenses. Bluebell Avenue would become a bolt-hole over the next year to which we could escape from the pressures of parish life. During the coming months, many a Sunday evening saw us slip out of the vicarage drive in an old Volvo car packed with bits of furniture to make our future home more comfortable. It was like camping out but with built-in heat, light, hot water and loos.

Also at the beginning of 1988 I was making rather regular visits to my doctor, complaining of digestive problems and general skeletal aches and pains. At one time I took to using a stick to alleviate pain in my hip. Then I began to itch around my lower back and several days later I was told I was suffering from shingles. After six weeks off work, my doctor said that shingles thrived on those already suffering from stress, or after some sort of a trauma, and that the time had come for me to slow down and take more rest. Not much chance of that, except I tried to get forty winks in the afternoon. By the beginning of 1989 a house, right next to the church, came on the market which would make an admirable vicarage. But with my stress levels no lower, could we cope with yet another move back to Kewstoke? The archdeacon believed that we could not, as did my doctor, who with my permission wrote to the Bishop of Bath and Wells suggesting that I be given early retirement. Within a few weeks all was settled and I gave the churchwardens and PCC the three months required notice that I was quitting.

The archdeacon quite excelled himself with the package that he arranged for me. I was to be given a lump sum equal to my stipend up to the age of retirement at sixty-five and as it wasn't earnings I didn't pay tax or National Health. Perhaps the church's generosity was born out of the fact that the house at Worle, which we had moved into two years before, sold for £35,000 more than its purchase price.

During our next short visit to Bluebell Avenue – actually there were no bluebells, no trees and the road had several bends – I took a walk out of the burgeoning estate, over the bridge spanning the new dual carriageway North Devon Link Road and up an ascending lane into the silence of the Devon countryside. After about half a mile I turned round to return. What I saw convinced me that we had made the right decision – there laid out before me were the roofs of Tiverton and a church tower nestling in a shallow valley with rolling hills and standing trees providing a protective ring all around the town. I could still see the traffic moving up the new road but that gave me an added dimension to this place we were coming to – it wasn't to be some isolated backwater but a place with good connections with all those people we had come to know and love in many parts of the country. Devon had been a holiday destination on many occasions over the years, and now it was to be our home, and with great expectation I couldn't wait to embrace it.

Back at the ranch there was much to sort out and

arrange. The out-going vicar always has the job of organising other clergy to take the services for the first three months of the interregnum and then I had to make sure there were lay-people to take full responsibility for all the groups and activities. It wasn't easy. Domestically we had already had one recent downsizing of our goods and chattels when we left the vicarage, but there was still a double garage full of furniture with nowhere to go.

I suppose I had always been a bit of a slave-driver to the people of Kewstoke and Wick St Lawrence and I intended to keep up the pressure to the very last moment. At the end of my final services I invited (made?) the people stand up and I commissioned them to carry on the work of the church with as much energy and enthusiasm as they had given during the last nine years.

So what had I achieved in this last part of my fifteen year ministry? Who can say? How long does it take any seeds to germinate and produce the fruit of the earth? Had I sown any seeds at all? Of one thing, however, I am quite sure – I had made, with the backing of many regular churchgoers, a connection between The Church and the people who never, or rarely, came into a building to worship God. The Church was to be part of the community and wasn't just a building where a collection of people, only interested in themselves, gathered on Sundays. The Church was there to love people and to care for them. That was the way the Kingdom of Heaven would come one step nearer to Kewstoke and Wick St Lawrence.

ACT 4

Scene 1

Go west old man

Marian enquired "What does that sign up there say?" To which I made my standard reply "I haven't the faintest idea." We, including Sally our Labrador and Heidi the black cat, had just turned off the M5 at junction 27 and were heading for Tiverton, when we were confronted by an enormous sign by the side of the dual carriageway; YOU ARE ENTERING AN AREA OF SEVERE DROUGHT. PLEASE USE WATER SPARINGLY. So that was the message of welcome as we drove behind the van that held all our worldly goods. An inappropriate metaphor I know, but nothing could dampen our spirits as we travelled the last few miles towards our new home. The physical approach to home has always been of some significance to me. I hated returning from a holiday through the drab surroundings of Croydon or Mitcham or Molesey whilst Horsham and all the other places since hadn't given me that sinking feeling. The countryside on this day was all burnt-up and brittle and brown, yet it was still beautiful and we were going to live in its midst. We had retired, but what exactly did that mean? We were soon to find out.

During the previous months there were other changes taking place in our family. Teddy and Dorothy had already retired and bought a super bungalow looking out over the calm waters of the Moray Firth close by Inverness and the slaughter fields of Culloden; Fiona and Graeme had bought a house in Plymouth so they were already living in Devon.

Bill had successfully applied to the Home Office to become a prison chaplain and was now awaiting his first posting. Criminality is rife right across the country, therefore prisons turn up all over the place – mostly not in very salubrious locations – and so it was with some trepidation we awaiting the news of where we would be travelling to when visiting them in the future. Joy of joy, it was Exeter. None of us could believe our luck! Their move from Bishop's Stortford was complicated due to an accommodation problem. As a result of the recent Great Storm, there were doubts about the structural safety of the chaplain's residence and so Marian and I, always willing to help whenever possible, presented ourselves at Exeter prison's front door enquiring if we could have a word with the chaplain. Having introduced ourselves, we asked the chaplain about the house and did he know if it would be available for Bill and his family. His reply was quite remarkable – he had no idea that a new chaplain was coming and that he would therefore be going somewhere else!! Removing my foot from 'it' was a highly embarrassing operation and unfortunately it turned out to be true that the house would not be available. Instead, Bill and family were to poke up, literally, with a house far too small for comfort and that would not be available until he started work in October. The children needed to be in Devon for the start of the autumn term and so, as I said, we were soon to find out what retirement was all about. The whole family came to stay with us for the first two weeks of our living in Tiverton, with the four children being transported each day to three different schools in Exeter. However, it was only a little, but happy, blip in the process of settling into our new life. On the first evening they were with us, we took seriously that huge sign about being sparing with the water. We reintroduced the wartime order that the bath water should not be deeper than four inches. The four girls managed to circumnavigate this arrangement by deciding that each should have four inches of water, run into the bath continuously and sequentially. Not only was this not keeping to the spirit of corporate co-operation throughout the county of Devon, but also meant that water poured through the newly decorated ceiling into the hall below the bathroom.

What had Tiverton to offer us apart from being in a beautiful, if temporally dry, part of England? We had in the past months explored and sorted out what made it tick. First, places to worship. There are four Anglican churches in Tiverton, ranging from charismatic happy-clappy though traditional Evangelical, 'civic middle-of-the-road' and lastly the Anglo-Catholic church of St Andrew, with its then priest, Father Paul Harrison. Father Paul was to become the third person of the trinity of clergymen to make a huge difference to the way I carried out my ministry. His contribution to my life was to come several months later. If you had to describe how to find St Andrew's Church, the best description would be to look for something like an Odeon cinema or a telephone exchange in Blundells Avenue. It is a square, flat roofed, box made of red concrete blocks – by several hundred years it isn't your traditional church building. Looking in through the glazed front doors, one could see plain off-white walls, wooden pews and a wide elegant stone altar behind a low wooden altar rail. The only other feature to strike the eye immediately was the huge expanse of glass up in the south wall that permitted light to flood into the whole interior. When I first saw this building I immediately fell in love with it – not because I could say "what a lovely little church", but because I could see what a marvellous space it was in which to do all sorts of liturgical movement. It wasn't cluttered up with bits from the past, and people, even in wheelchairs or prams, could move around easily. It had space and light and was the complete antithesis of all the churches I had ever ministered in.

For fairly obvious reasons, the other three town churches didn't get much consideration when deciding where to worship and one in particular was definitely not in the running for two reasons. On some of its front pew desks were large red leather-bound Prayer Books embossed in gold with the words 'Alderman's Copy' and outside near the gate was a small plaque with the words 'dogs not allowed as this is consecrated ground'. Enough said, for Marian and me.

For our first Sunday morning service at St Andrew's I wore an open-necked shirt and a pullover – no dog collar. Nobody knew who we were and yet we were given a wonderful welcome by people in the congregation and Father Paul – the sort of welcome, we were to discover, that was the hallmark of life at St Andrew's.

As I had promised myself, and Marian, I would do nothing about offering my clerical services for at least six months, in an attempt to recharge my overstretched constitution before I made any approach on the subject to Father Paul. My new GP and the local hospital diagnosed me with irritable bowel syndrome and diverticulosis, both of which are synonymous with stress. The doctor recommended that I give up drinking tea and coffee and booze! From that day to this I haven't drunk any tea, coffee or booze and my stomach usually behaves itself quite nicely.

So here was a Monday morning several weeks after retirement – how were things going – how was I coping with this strange new and different life? Remember I had spent the last forty-seven years in the workplace.

First, to walk down Bluebell Avenue was something so different from my experiences during the last fifteen years. Not because it was a different place, but that my relationship with the households that I passed had changed. No longer was I on duty, no longer were these people's souls my responsibility, no longer was I a public figure, no longer could I knock on any one of these doors and say "Hello, I am the vicar, can I come in?" I was just the same as anyone else. It had nothing to do with loss of power or status, just a feeling that things were different. Perhaps it was something to do with my energy still racing a bit and nowhere for it to go, or maybe it was the same as a retired bank manager walking into a bank to cash a cheque.

I quickly learnt a very important lesson about retirement. It soon became apparent how necessary it was to have 'time pegs' during each week on which to hang definite activities and that each day should have its own individual feel.

Monday should feel like Monday and not like Tuesday. This sounds like setting up a weekly programme or regime and surely that is not of the nature of retirement? For some that may be true, but for me retirement wasn't about an extended chilling-out but changing down a gear. Then there was the matter of keeping up standards especially in the house. It would be so easy to become slovenly about appearance, tidiness and yes even personnel hygiene! Over the last fifteen years in Tiverton, all this has meant that we are still active and in no way have we become a burden to our family. We are still a fully functioning household and try to do everything possible to keep it that way.

During those first few retirement months our time was fully taken up with sorting out the garden, decorating and exploring in greater detail the delights of Devon. Visits to our family in Exeter and Plymouth became far more regular and grandma and grandpa were often seen at school plays and concerts in which grandchildren were taking part. My health slowly improved and after about six months I thought it was time to visit Father Paul, having first obtained the Bishop's Permission to Officiate in any church in the diocese of Exeter.

Father Paul was twenty-seven years my junior and attended Salisbury and Wells Theological College a few years after I was ordained. My presence in his study one morning, I suppose, could have been somewhat daunting, even threatening, to the parish incumbent but from the very beginning of our clerical relationship we were like two peas in a pod. Having been schooled in the same theological college was a good start, but Father Paul quickly picked up on what were my needs and how he could arrange things to help me. It may seem odd that all this was going on for someone who was supposed to be retired, but there were factors involved that needed addressing. I had to retire early and therefore I felt a little cheated in not being able to complete my calling. Further, my ministry had been limited to a mere fifteen years and so in a way I felt there was more to be done. What was arranged wasn't so much about allowing me to conduct some services but giving me pastoral care of one part of the parish of St Andrew's. This parish had had an unusual beginning, bound up with the post-war building of a large edge-of-town council estate in the area known as Cowley Moor that had been hived off from the original town parish of St Peter's. St Andrew's started life as a missionary outreach with a converted bungalow as its place of worship. Today, to the majority of the Cowley Moor population, St Peter's with its beautiful traditional church, was the place to go to if you really needed a church – especially at times of hatch, match and despatch. A little colour-washed building wasn't the place to take nice wedding photographs, nor later was a telephone exchange look-alike. The job I was being asked to do was to inform the population that their parish church was St Andrew's and you would be very welcome there at 9.30am next Sunday morning. This meant just one thing – visiting. During the next three or four years I knocked on over seven hundred doors to be given a largely warm welcome by most, even if the congregation didn't increase by more than a few. What was achieved, I think, was that people became aware of St Andrew's; that it was their church and a caring welcome awaited those who could summons up the effort to sit on a pew for an hour on Sunday mornings.

To set me on the road to being the Honorary Assistant Priest, Father Paul dreamed up a special service of commissioning to take place within the Sunday morning Eucharist. He had it all printed out, including my declaration that I would abide by the catholic teaching and traditions of St Andrew's church. After these solemn words I knelt down at the altar rail and received God's blessing, through the Holy Spirit, as Father Paul laid his hands on my head. To me and the rest of the congregation, that was the end of the proceedings, as printed on the order of service. But no, there was something else to come! Father Paul instructed me to stand up, whereupon he knelt down and asked me to give him

God's blessing. It was a moment of great significance to me, as it showed that our work together was to be a shared and equal ministry. Each week after that we met in his study and discussed what we had been doing and I reported on my visiting. They were also times when we could let our hair down about some difficult parishioner we had encountered! As for conducting services, Father Paul was able to be more relaxed about taking time out when duty called him elsewhere and when holidays came round. All baptisms, weddings and funerals from Cowley Moor came my way and it was a really rewarding time – I had all the fun without the hassle of running a parish and a PCC!

I was not able, however, to hide whatever light I had under a bushel and soon I was receiving invitations to fill-in at many other churches in the Tiverton Deanery including about a dozen little country churches in the Exe Valley Team Ministry. How the church would cope without the help of retired clergy is anybody's guess. The C. of E. is well described as 'broad' and each of these churches, with their small congregations out in the sticks, had their own distinctiveness and ways of interpreting the official order of services. These visits were an exercise in theological and liturgical agility, of keeping one's eye ever on the ball, but never forgetting the golden rule so painfully learnt at Salisbury – never try to correct a mistake as nobody ever notices!

One Sunday morning I arrived at a little church to find that about half the congregation of fifteen souls were children, so even if it wasn't billed as a family service, I decided that when it came to the sermon I would ditch my well prepared written words and come down into the nave and just talk to the young ones. I always had one or two children's talks tucked up my cassock sleeve and so I trotted out my party piece and thought what a clever and agile cleric I was. After the service, as usual, I spoke to the people as they left. I asked one little girl if she enjoyed the talk, at which she looked bewildered and turned to a grown-up, who in very broken English, said they were Germans on holiday and none of the children understood our language!

Marian and I attended one unique service – unique, maybe, in the true sense of the word. For several years in Aberdeen and Inverness Teddy, my brother, had been edging towards ordination. His was not the path of a residential theological college but local part-time study and training. In 1990 he was made deacon and the following year ordained priest into the Scottish Episcopal Church in Inverness cathedral. The previous year we had attended Mark's, Teddy's youngest son, priesting in Worcester cathedral. The Bishop of Moray, Ross and Caithness, who was to ordain Teddy, wrote inviting me to preach at my brother's ordination to the priesthood. This was a fantastic offer and one that I accepted with much pleasure but great trepidation. Mark was also to take part in the service so there was the inevitable Episcopal joke at the beginning of the service that it was an all-Strange English take-over of his Scottish diocese. How many times in recent history has an ordination sermon been preached by the younger brother of the candidate, and with the new priest's son taking part as well? It is a Scottish Episcopal Church tradition for members of the congregation, after an ordination service, to kneel before the newly ordained and ask for a blessing – I too received a blessing in this way.

So now there were five dog-collars in the family; Graeme, Bill, Mark, Teddy and me. This family array required a certain recognition but I had to wait another year to bring my plan to fruition.

A gaggle of priests
At back, Bryan Strange. From the left: Graeme Elmore, son-in-law; Mark Strange, nephew; Bill Birdwood, son-in-law, Teddy Strange, brother. Hereford 1992

1992 was very much like the previous three years of retirement with all our commitments of visiting family and friends across the country and having them to stay with us. Church work continued for me, and Marian became more involved with the Tiverton Machine Knitting Club. We were really beginning to get our feet under the local table, although it was inevitable we would never become fully recognised as Devonians. In February 1992 we did, however, become one of a growing group of people to whom came one of the advances of the age – an advance that is not without its downside, I believe – Marian bought her first personal computer. This device was to be married to her knitting machines and so started, for her, a long and sometimes turbulent and frustrating relationship with technology. Over the years of adding all sorts of gismos to that first computer, the art of designing and making knitwear has changed more into a science, but I must confessed also to the production of ever better looking garments. More and more my formal suits have been consigned to the wardrobe as I sport Marian's knitted pullovers.

In June '92 we arranged a holiday with Teddy and Dorothy in a small Herefordshire country cottage. This part of England was new territory for us and we greatly enjoyed the beautiful countryside and towns, such as Ludlow and Hereford, but there was another motive in choosing this part of the land. Mark and his family were in a parish in nearby Worcester and we persuaded Bill, Graeme and families all to come to our cottage for a very specific reason. I had long wanted to have a photo call of all five family dog-collared clerics together. This I achieved one lovely summer's day and now the family photo albums include a record of this strange and unusual quintuplet. The day's proceedings were enlivened by Mark, having borrowed a bishop's mitre from the vestry store cupboard at Worcester Cathedral, by producing photographs that include members of the family resplendent wearing a tall episcopal hat.

Later the same year we had a short holiday with

Marian's cousin Moreen and her friend Maggie, who were very keen on staying in interesting buildings converted for holiday lets and owned by the Landmark Trust. The place they chose had been a Victorian House of Correction in Lincolnshire. Originally such buildings were the institutions for detaining and re-educating the local petty criminals and riff raff, but today the gatehouse to this grim place now comfortably provides holidays for more law-abiding persons.

During this holiday we visited, for the first time, the Fens of Norfolk and the coastline of The Wash. What a strange experience that turned out to be. Navigating by Ordinance Survey, we drove up a narrow flat unfenced road that on the map just petered out, pointing directly out to sea. This is just how we found things except that when we came to the end of the road we were confronted by a bank running at right angles across the land in front of us. It was one of those very still days – no wind at all – with ten tenths low cloud or mist and as we walked to the top of the bank and just down the other side we found ourselves standing facing – well what? Everything was grey and there was no visible demarcation between the land and the sea and the sky. This must have been the original place that gave us the description 'no man's land'. There was an eerie silence and stillness, except that somewhere out there we could hear a bell clanging – presumably one attached to a buoy in the sea beyond – but who could tell? And for whom was the bell tolling? This surely was the spot that Erskine Childers must have visited before he wrote his spy novel about a German invasion of England called 'The Riddle of the Sands'. We were quite relieved to get back into the car and drive back to the material world – through fields of solid red sugar beet and the comfort of our converted prison quarters.

Although we were retired, each year we arranged at least one holiday away but also there were other times when I simply draw a line across a week or two in the diary and stayed at home with no engagements or commitments of any kind. These rests from the usual routine were important and gave us an opportunity to relax and discover more about the attractions of the West Country.

Every two years we visited Dorothy – and Teddy until he died in 1995. Each of these visits to the Highlands of Scotland have been times of discovery of new places and more examples of fantastic scenery, as well as revisiting certain spots that have become firm favourites for us, but not necessarily the same for Marian as for me! The House of Bruar, a few miles to the north of Pitlochry on the A9 towards Inverness, is without doubt one of Marian's most favourite places to visit. This is not an ancient Scottish residence of some famous kilted clansman but a place where a holiday can start disastrously in a financial way. It could be described as the Harrods of the North, with a great selection of tartan style clothing, and is irresistible to Marian who I must say does look rather stylish in a lady's kilt. It also sells rather nice Scotch broth in the restaurant.

My favourite Scottish destination is a small fishing and boating village on the southern shores of the Moray Firth. Findhorn sits at the estuary of a lagoon with fisherman's cottages along the shoreline – most of which I suspect now house others than fishermen. It is the sounds and the light of the place that are so attractive. To sit by the side of the water in this out-of-the-way settlement and listen to the only sound – the lapping of the water and the flapping of rope against mast – is about as relaxing as you could wish for. On a fine day with the sun at your back and looking north, the atmosphere is as pure and clear as it comes and the distant coastline up the final part of the north east side of Scotland seems to go on forever. Add to all this, a package of Dorothy's scrumptious sandwiches, made with Teddy's home-made brown bread, a flask of coffee, and you have the recipe for a wonderful afternoon.

One other location that has won a spot in our hearts and memory is the Benedictine monastery at Plascarden near Elgin. This is a place of quite extraordinary peace and tranquillity, brought about by the beauty of the almost uninhabited green valley in which it is situated, together with the sense of prayer and liturgical worship that hits you as soon as you enter the buildings, especially the recently restored high-roofed chapel. It hasn't become a Northern Buckfast Abbey with its somewhat obvious commercialisation and tourist attraction. There is a small shop, in which you often have to serve yourself with the postcards for sale, but what Plascarden offers is a retreat from the noisy clambering world into a place of prayer and the haunting music of Gregorian chant sung by the monks. Just over the hills in the next valley is a place called Dallas – I have never been to this place but just the name is the antithesis of Plascarden.

Our 1993 holiday in Cornwall ended in disaster when we were staying in a National Trust cottage at Trelissick near Truro. At the time, I was suffering from sore eyes and each morning I applied eye-drops. On about the third morning I went to the bathroom to get my medication but unfortunately instead of picking up the bottle of eye-drops, I chose a bottle of Olbas oil which is a strong version of camphor oil. The pain was so instant that at least I did not attempt to do the same thing with my other eye! The hospital in Truro was not able to help much and so we returned to the eye hospital in Exeter where a doctor was able to save the sight in my damaged eye. To add to our tale of woe, the large bottle of sherry I had bought Marian, as a little compensation for mucking up our holiday, we forgot to pack and left it unopened on the cottage kitchen table. Some lucky souls benefited from my misfortune.

Easter 1994 saw the departure of Father Paul to pastures new and an invitation from the PCC inviting me to officiate at St Andrew's during the interregnum. I agreed with a certain amount of trepidation, as I wasn't quite sure what I was letting myself in for, but also with a sense that this was a kind of consolation prize for having to retire early. I was going to have the chance to minister in this church that from a professional point of view I found so attractive. However, I had to watch out that I didn't get carried away by introducing any new ideas – such antics by stand-in clergy are definitely frowned upon by the hierarchy as it can make things very difficult for the new incumbent. My ten months 'in charge' was a challenge upon all my resources but it was something I thoroughly enjoyed. It did include running a mini Christian Stewardship campaign but with my past experience that wasn't too much of a burden. Even so, nothing is straightforward in this world, especially when things have turned out well!

In January 1995 Father David Fletcher was inducted as priest-in-charge at St Andrew's and my little reign of glory came to an end. Father David's churchmanship was very similar to both Father Paul's and mine, so that aspect of the new broom didn't cause any difficulty. There always is a danger that when only one priest takes on an interregnum the congregation can become too acclimatised to his ways, which is not helpful to the new man. Although I continued to take some services, I made strenuous efforts to see that I melted into the background, leaving a clear run for Father David. One way I attempted this was to stop wearing a dog-collar when I visited people who knew me.

On the morning of December 29th 1995 I received a telephone call from my niece Peta in Inverness telling me that my brother had died. Although it came as a great shock to us, we knew Teddy wasn't a fully well man, having suffered from angina for many years. He once told me that he placed one of those little white tablets that are put under the tongue when chest pains occur, at various strategic points in the church when he took services. He gave of himself unstintingly in his short ministry as a priest in the Scottish Episcopal Church, especially in his pastoral care of the aged. We travelled to his funeral by way of British Rail that took thirteen hours and not to be recommended as a way of travelling to the far north reaches of the British Isles.

The morning of December 29th 1996, exactly one year after Teddy died, was another 'ending' day for me. My brother's death, perhaps, was hastened by giving too much of himself in the service of the Church and for sometime I had decided that I should be careful not to follow suit. Having given Father David several months notice, this first Sunday after Christmas became the last Sunday of my ministry as Honorary Assistant Priest at St Andrew's. The time had come for me to hang up my cassock. Not only was I concerned about overstretching myself, I also wanted to finish my ministry without having become a doddering old priest who just couldn't let go – I have met a few like that and it ought not to be allowed! Of course I let it be known that in a dire emergency I would still be willing to take a service at short notice. I am glad to report that Father David enjoys robust health and only twice in the following years did his wife have to ring me up early on a Sunday morning and say he was prone and unable to move off his bed. When I processed into the church that morning for my last service I was delighted to see Claire, Lisa, Hannah, Alice and Naomi sitting in the front pew with Marian. My final sermon started by telling the story of how that Cross-in-Hand school report, all those years ago, told my parents that Bryan was erratic. I then went on to do the theological bit of my sermon and ending up by suggesting that we the Church should be a little more erratic in its approach to worship and the Christian way of life. What did I mean by that? I meant that I thought the Church had become too set in its ways and that we needed to break out like those men at the first Pentecost when they received the Holy Spirit. The Oxford English Dictionary says that to be erratic is to be itinerant, nomadic, vagrant. We need to be just that – to be willing to go where the Spirit leads. I have always said that it is not the priest or minister who should lead worship but the Spirit and we have to be erratic enough to let that happen. It was with a certain amount of sadness that I received a handsome cheque at what I thought was to be my swansong – well it was as a priest with a dog-collar and dressed up in Eucharistic garb, but unbeknown to me at the time, there was still more to come.

Neither Marian nor I have been drawn to holidaying in exotic or tropical places abroad. Overcrowded beaches with half-naked bodies may have some attraction but are not really for us. Stories of gruesome sanitation facilities fill Marian with horror and disgust and neither of us passed any foreign language exams for School Certificate. Then there have been financial constraints and the necessity to visit far-flung friends and family across the British Isles. However, my sermon on being vagrants and nomadic must have struck a chord in us because in the May of the following year we did decide to go abroad and tour Southern Ireland. This was cheating a bit because the language and the climate are the same – nearly – as England and people sensibly drive on the left-hand side. So we crossed the Irish Sea from Fishguard to Rosslare Harbour and found our previously booked bed and breakfast in New Ross. Every other house and bungalow in Southern Ireland seems to be a B. & B. The next day we made the mandatory visit to the famous glass works at Waterford and spent a fortune on a small cut glass bowl before driving West through Tipperary to our next bed just outside Limerick.

I now know why they say it is a long way to Tipperary – the road surfaces were far below the standard of English highways and there were very few dual carriageways, although I believe that a lot of European money has since greatly improved the superstructure. It is not for nothing that the country is called the Emerald Isle as it certainly is green, lush and beautiful – which is more than can be said of some of the towns and villages, unless you go for brightly colour-washed buildings. Bright purple and orange are bad enough but when they appear next to each other in a row of houses, then things become pretty dire. As there are very few plain brick-faced dwellings the paint suppliers must do a roaring trade.

We based ourselves in Limerick for several days from where we visited the rugged coast around Galway Bay but I didn't kiss the stone in Blarney – there were too many

Americans around to get near it – and that is why I shall never be as eloquent and persuasive as the Irish! Yes, it is true the Irish are extremely friendly and nothing is too much trouble – well in pleasing the tourists at least – and they are all very laid back. In Tralee we bought a crucifix from a local blacksmith made of old iron nails braised together – a most appropriate material to use for such an icon. But perhaps the most memorable place for us was the Roman Catholic Church of the Assumption in Limerick.

What took our fancy was a notice outside this large and rather uninspiring building, advertising a Taizé Mass the following Sunday. Taizé music, from a French monastic community, is modern, yet gentle and deeply spiritual, and has long been a favourite setting of the liturgy for us both. It was a few days before the Sunday service and so we went in to look around. Roman Catholics are especially fond of their candles and all devout and good adherents will light a candle at the drop of a priest's hat. Here, things had been modernised and instead of trays full of burning wax, there were banks of electric light bulbs, each one becoming illuminated by inserting a coin into a box and pressing a timed switch! However, a real candle could be purchased to be lit with many others at the Sunday mass.

We arrived early for the Taizé service on Sunday evening as I wanted to enquire if there was any chance of two Anglicans receiving the sacrament from the hands of a Roman Catholic priest. I was informed by an official that we could because we were all 'friends of Jesus'! This ecumenical approach was further demonstrated when we entered the church to see hundreds of candles alight all round the church – these were those that had been bought during the week by people from countries across the world. It was a truly memorable service. Church of England please note!

After our tour across the west side of Ireland we motored east to Dublin for a further stay of two days. We are never entirely enthusiastic about visiting well-known buildings but we did see Trinity College and the home of the Dáil plus a very modern shopping complex of glass and chromium plate, surely a sign that Ireland has joined this modern age. The last day of our holiday took us south through the high open spaces of the Wicklow Mountains and to a little village called Avoca or Baile Coisc Aingil or Ballykissangel. Yes this was the location for that highly popular series on Television with its cast of Irish rascals. We sampled the shop and the pub that still carried the name Ballykissangel. It is a delightful place and most pleasing to see that it had not become commercialised in the wake of its fame. Our sea voyage home was a great disappointment as we had specially booked on a hydrofoil but it was six hours late, only driving on half power.

During the 1990's we saw our six grandchildren progress through the education system. University and degrees in their chosen subjects was the outcome, apart from Martin who soon after starting university saw his future in modern music. We progressed, from watching these children acting and singing in school entertainments, to becoming taxi drivers and scanning the maps of various university towns and cities as we transported them and their huge quantities of 'stuff' from home to untidy and often squat-like student quarters. By this time Bill, our son-in-law, had been transferred to perhaps the grimmest and hardest prison in the country – that ex French prisoner-of-war establishment high up on remote and desolate Dartmoor. As a portent of things to come, his licensing had to be postponed as the prison was cut-off by snowdrifts.

By 1998 Graeme and Fiona were living in Gibraltar where Graeme was chaplain to Combined Forces stationed on The Rock. We were invited to visit them but this posed a problem as Marian had a great fear of taking her feet off solid ground. Apart from a ten minute flip around a field when a little girl, she had never flown in an aeroplane and I wasn't too keen on flying either. So it was with great trepidation and nervousness that we took off from Gatwick and two hours later landed, safely, on Gibraltar's single stuck-out-in-the-sea runway. There before us was the great white rock that I had not seen for fifty-three years since that day on a troopship en route for India. It looked just as impressive as ever. The chaplain's house was situated some way up the non-vertical side of The Rock, with a large terrace looking out across a spectacular view of the harbour to Spain and in the other direction to the distant coastline of North Africa. There was always much activity to watch on the water, including while we were there a cruise visit by the QE2.

Gibraltar is full of military history and activity, although this has much reduced in recent years. The garrison chapel and the governor's residency in the town are semi-detached in one building, called The Convent, with a soldier from the Gibraltar Regiment standing guard outside, alongside a newly painted pair of old canons (guns not clergymen!) We broke a habit of a lifetime – with good reason of course – by going to church while on holiday for two services conducted by Graeme. The first was a military affair with much heal-clicking and saluting as the old colours of the Gibraltar Regiment were laid up in the chapel in readiness to receiving new colours later from the Duke of Kent. The other service couldn't have been more different – a Harvest Thanksgiving followed by an auction of the packets and tins, no doubt mostly bought at the supermarket, as not much produce is grown in Gibraltar. There were lots of children and they soon got into the swing of the idea of bidding. Unfortunately for the parents their offspring didn't have to pay-up at the end and so for not a tremendous amount of food some £750 was sent to Christian Aid.

No visit to Gibraltar is complete without saying hello to the famous monkeys. These smallish fawny-brown animals live near the top of The Rock and although appearing friendly they can be quite aggressive, especially towards lady's handbags. Then there are the subterranean caves that go deep into the side of the rock and include a huge cavern decked out as a theatre. Within the face that glowers at Spain, the British have in time past constructed several miles of caverns and galleries with portholes from which to point and fire large-bore guns at the old Spanish enemy. All these attractions we 'did' with the aid of a taxi and its driver who stopped long enough at all the essential places. The guns of Gibraltar make a connection with the place of my childhood, Heathfield. It was General Elliot who in 1779 successfully defended Gibraltar against the Spanish after they had lain siege to the British colony for four years. He defeated the enemy and later became Lord Heathfield. In tribute to his service to England a tower was built in his honour in the grounds of his home, Heathfield Park, and named Gibraltar Tower. In my childhood days the tower was in some state of disrepair and locally had the character of being no more than yet another Sussex folly.

One other attraction on Gibraltar that required our attention was the cable-car that ran from near the town centre right up to almost the highest point of The Rock. This method of transport held for Marian all the terrors of flying and in some ways even more so. That little cabin with hardly anything between oneself and a sheer drop of several hundred feet, suspended on a wire, didn't hold any attraction for either of us, but somehow we were driven on to take the plunge – not literally we hoped – pay our money and overcome our fears. The views were absolutely staggering, so long as you didn't look down! Then there was that strange piece of engineering – a huge slab of concrete, the size of several football pitches, lying steeply up against the side of the Rock. This edifice was constructed as a method of catching rain, which when it fell, drained into a gully at the bottom. Desalination plants now provide drinking water and insure against the vagaries of the weather.

We made several trips into Spain, despite the Spanish officials' attempts to make the transition over the border as uncomfortable and long-winded as possible. For one trip it took us an hour to slowly pass through customs en route to a Spanish supermarket. This emporium was the largest I have ever seen with sixty checkouts that the supervising cashier travelled up and down on roller-skates and wearing a pink miniskirt. We also tasted the delights of Spanish fish suppers washed down with free replenishments of red wine. It was a very good holiday and we enjoyed tagging on to the social life of Graeme and Fiona, but the heat and the mosquitoes didn't do anything to encourage thoughts of going abroad again for holidays and flying is really only for the birds.

Our trip home gave us a demonstration of how the elements can still outwit human technology. Gibraltar has only one airport runway and so if the wind decides to blow hard across – and not along – this landing path, then all flying ceases. This meteorological condition was to be our lot when we arrived at the airport to return home, resulting in a long bus trip up to Jerez, near Cadiz, and famous for sherry and golf. We were in no mood to enjoy a round of either of these pleasures as the hours of waiting mounted up with only ghastly Spanish sandwiches being offered as compensation for the delay. When finally approaching Gatwick, ten hours late, our captain informed us that he wasn't sure if he could land as fog was causing some difficulties at ground level. This uncertainty, added to our frustration, did nothing to endear flying to us. Finally we did land at Gatwick in the middle of the night and then waited an hour for our luggage to appear ignominiously on the carousel – which must be the ugliest piece of public utility ever invented. Airplanes – no thanks!

Sunday July 19th 1998 was to be a very important day for me. There had been a demand for St Andrew's Church to provide a wider and more appropriate range of worship for children and families. Somehow the information leaked out that I had conducted Family Services at Kewstoke and so I was asked if I would be willing to follow suit in Tiverton. By this time I had reached the grand old age of seventy-two, but was a white-haired man of such great antiquity the right person to address the spiritual needs of young people? To be quite honest I believe that I was, for the simple reason that I was prepared to get down to their level – literally – speaking to kids sitting around on the floor. A large carpet became my pulpit. The format of the services was the same as I had successfully developed at Kewstoke and so with a small group of adult helpers we launched the next stage of my ministry, remembering that I had already retired twice!

Although we had a pre-determined format for all the services, each one really started at my desk with a blank piece of paper. I kept to three important principles for these services. They should be structured but not scripted – in other words there was a set format and everyone knew the part they had to play but prayers, talks and all the words connecting the service together were ad lib. Then there was the question of language. Church worship – and especially Anglican – is full of words that people don't understand and so often there are non-theological words which really make comprehension so much easier. As one simple example illustrates, 'saying sorry' is far more understandable than 'repentance'. Church leaders and theologians take far too much for granted when describing the Christian life, especially to the uninitiated. After one Rogation Day service I spoke to a young mum who hadn't attended. I told her what a smashing afternoon we had enjoyed with a short service of blessing on the farm, followed by games for the children and a lovely tea. I asked her why she missed out on such a happy occasion and she replied "well I didn't know what a Rogation Service was." Communication is something that needs a great deal of attention and I was determined to give it my best attention. The third principle I tried to abide by was that in any act of worship the leader is not the person out at the front (the 'sharp end' as I have always called it) but the Holy Spirit. That may sound rather esoteric, but like many things related to the Spirit, there is a kind of physical and human manifestation – it is being sensitive to the needs of the moment and a preparedness to act differently to an unexpected situation or opportunity. To be bound to a script doesn't allow the Spirit to work! It was because the Spirit was allowed to work that in one Family Service we were all singing a song that hadn't been previously selected, because it exactly reflected what someone had just said. To share my solidarity with the young, I always wore an open necked shirt and pullover – no cassocks or other clerical garb was to be seen.

And so the years trundled on, as did the decades, as did the centuries and finally as did the millenniums. Many years ago I can remember wondering if I would ever make the year 2000. At a much younger age seventy-four seemed terribly old and way off in the far distant future, but that was now my age and I did see in the third millennium. At the time, there was much discussion as to whether the new era started on 1st January 2000 or 2001, but the world celebrated the 2000th birthday of Christ on the former date, irrespective of the niceties of calendar calculations.

Marian and I joined Claire and Bill and many friends of theirs in Exeter to see in the New Millennium. Being a somewhat 'religious' lot we included a short time of reflection on the true reason for all the fuss and celebration. I read the following lines concerning the person of Jesus. (For those whose theological knowledge is a bit rusty, 'the Word' is a Biblical way of describing Jesus.)

In the beginning was the Word,
and the Word was with God,
and the Word was God.
He was in the beginning with God;
all things were made through him,
and without him was not anything made that was made.
In him was life,
and the life was the light of men.
The light shines in the darkness,
and the darkness has not overcome it.

The true light that enlightens every man
was coming into the world.
He was in the world,

and the world was made through him,
yet the world knew him not.

He came to his own home,
and his own people received him not.
But to all people who received him,
who believed in his name,
he gave power to become children of God;
who were born, not of blood
nor of the will of the flesh
nor of the will of man, but of God.

And the Word became flesh and dwelt among us,
full of grace and truth;
we beheld his glory,
glory as of the only Son from the Father.

(John 1: RSV version)

It was a time to celebrate and renew our hopes for the future which we certainly did as we wined and dined and kissed and hugged and enjoyed a most fantastic fireworks display over the City of Exeter.

The following March I received an invitation to go to Westminster Hall in London. No, this wasn't to be a meeting of clerics but of past and present members of the Decca Navigator Co. The Decca transmissions had come to the end of their useful life – a life foreshortened by the onset of the Global Positioning System. Satellite dishes and tiny receivers had replaced the more cumbersome Decca equipment and now even walkers over Dartmoor could pinpoint their position to within speaking distance. To mark this demise after fifty-five years of service to travellers, we were invited to come together to remember and celebrate what had been achieved. It was with a certain amount of trepidation that Marian and I walked into the gathering. Remember it was twenty-seven years since I left Decca and so a sea of white hair shouldn't have surprise me – but it did! After a morning of personal reminiscences and reminders of how the equipment had developed over the years, we had time to speak to past friends and colleagues.

Perhaps the day for me was encapsulated in an encounter I had with one of the senior engineers with whom I had worked for many years. I looked around the hall to see if I could locate one John Vickers. Sure enough, sitting there on a bench I saw John and I went up to him, put out my hand and said "hello John." A hand was not reciprocated but "I'm not John, I think you want my father, sitting right here beside me." As I said, there was a lot of white hair about and on closer inspection a lot of smaller crinkled bodies! We had a good laugh together and John began asking me questions about my life after leaving Decca. A few months later, I heard that John had died. When we arrived home, I began to think back – and I am not really very good at 'going back' – I got to thinking about that conversation and my years with Decca Navigator. Today there is much talk about pressure at work and not without good reason. It is a pressure that builds up because management and people in charge have their minds on one thing – getting their pound of flesh from employees. My years at Decca had nothing anywhere approaching that attitude. Management's object was to get the job done which is totally different from what happens today. There were no individual targets set for each person – we worked as a team to complete the task and produce equipment for the customer on time. This engendered a spirit of respect up and down the management structure and personal gain came second to corporate job satisfaction. Rarely did anyone go sick with stress, even if we did work all the hours God gave us. Every effort was made to ensure that all staff was aware of the fruits of their labours. The women wirers on the bench in my department were given a flying demonstration in the company's aircraft of the equipment they helped to develop and produce. Yes, it was a sad day when we said farewell to the Decca Navigator but I remembered I told the Bishop of Winchester that my twenty-five years in electronics would be the most important thing I had done in preparation for my life in the sacred ministry. Good relationships and recognition of the worth of people come top of the agenda for success in all walks of life.

The year 2000 continued to be a year of celebration with our Golden Wedding falling on 29th July. We planned a small family gathering but because Graeme and Fiona were engaged in returning home from Gibraltar and also, rather inconveniently for them, because Fiona was having a spinal operation in Southampton, we delayed the party until September. On the day itself, Marian, her bridesmaid Moreen, and I had a lunch at one of our favourite watering holes up on the North coast of Devon. We kept the occasion very low key and in September we had a family lunch at the famous Devon beauty spot of Bickleigh Mill. This delightful establishment sits by the River Exe with its bridge reputed to be the inspiration for the song Bridge Over Troubled Waters.

The three women in my life. From the left: Bryan Strange, Fiona Elmore, daughter; Marian; Claire Birdwood, daughter. In a pub, Salisbury 1999.

This association was not indicative of our married life – we had had a wonderfully smooth passage for which we were celebrating and giving grateful thanks. Marian's other bridesmaid, Beri, had travelled all the way from Canada to enjoy the party.

The following year was a relatively quiet time, continuing our annual preoccupations of visiting family and friends and entertaining them as they came to stay in glorious Devon. We included two visits to the newly constructed Eden Project down in Cornwall and one to the Lost Gardens of Heligan. Eden is an experience not to be missed with those enormous biome structures housing vegetation of all the world's different climates. These jet age greenhouses are constructed in old clay workings and when first viewed from the road above them, they don't look all that big against the surrounding land. Then you see the ant-like humans down there walking into the biomes and realise how immense they are. Heligan is quite different – a huge working garden recaptured from seventy years of neglect and demonstrating all aspects of low technology horticulture. For this visit we had booked into bed and breakfast nearby that Claire and Bill recommended. The big attraction was a huge four-poster bed that sounded most romantic! Unfortunately our visit was the first outing after Marian had armed herself with a digital camera to use in conjunction with her laptop computer. Instead of our bed being covered in romance, it was covered with wires and gizmos that I thought was a waste of the extra money I had spent for the four-poster!!

By this time I had passed my three-quarters of a century and our thoughts turned to a future where the energy and agility would begin to wane – if it hadn't already started. For some years we had worked on the principle that at all times, however old one became, every effort should be made to keep up standards and not let property and possessions – and ourselves – fall into a state of decrepitude. What steps could we take to make life easier and prolong our ability to stay in 29 Bluebell Avenue? First we changed all the outside woodwork for plastic and double glazing – no more climbing up ladders to paint; the front garden wooden fence and hedge were removed and replaced with a double brick wall with rock plants; all the grass was removed and shingled; all the beds and borders were edged with bricks; the kitchen was completely restyled and modernised. All we need now, sometime in the future, is the Stenner lift to take us up the stairs to bed!

The big event of 2002 was the wedding of one of our grandchildren. September 7th saw a great gathering of the family and friends of Hannah and Ben in St David's Church Exeter. For me, it was a particularly memorable day as I was up at the 'sharp end' – I conducted the wedding service. It was a delight to officiate but I must say that I found it a daunting experience. I felt – quite wrongly no doubt – that all eyes were on me and not on the bride and groom. It was another marker that my active ministry in public worship was running out of steam.

By the beginning of 2002 Marian and I had started to look for some new pastures green, particularly in the brain activity department. We have always believed that in older age so long as the brain is able to relate to the world around, then however much the body has slowed up or worn out, we are still the same person. And like the body, brain exercise and stimulation are vital to keep going. We found our answer and new interest by joining the University Of The Third Age. This worldwide organisation has local branches, including Tiverton. The arrangement is that like-minded elderly people meet in small groups to pursue their particular interests. Gardening, local history, rambling, acting, foreign languages – we chose creative writing and computers. Then each month all groups join together for a luncheon meeting with speaker. Although the title of U3A sounds a little academic, I am pleased to say that examinations are not included in the activities! Just to show how entrenched one can become in a particular life-style, I remember the first creative writing group meeting we attended. About seven of us were assembled in the leader's sitting room and about to start. I had been in a similar situation countless times before for home groups and Bible study, and so as I looked around I wondered who would say the opening prayers!! I certainly was in need of some refreshing new activity! The computer group was really for Marian's benefit, as I have a love-hate relationship with modern technology. Marian wasn't so enthusiastic about the writing group, but we agreed that because, in the past, we had spent so much time apart due to my work, we would each choose a group and perhaps suffer a bit together!

The monthly speaker meeting produced one talk that had us really excited. A Plymouth University professor spoke on the Adventure of Old Age. It really was most stimulated and at the end we all felt like teenagers again and ready for the next fifty years. One story he related concerned a lady who went to her doctor with an extremely painful left knee. After an examination and questioning the GP said "Well my dear, I am afraid it's your age." This diagnosis is very common, and really an affront, for all sorts of aches and pains suffered by we 'crinklies'. The lady's response to this piece of medical news was, "well that is very interesting doctor, but can you explain why my right knee is perfectly OK, it being exactly the same age as my left knee?" I shall remember 2003 as the year in which I received some minor plumbing work on one of the arteries to my heart. Slight angina had reared its ugly head in the previous year and after some internal photographic work, a very nice man in Exeter hospital placed a metal tube inside the offending artery to keep the flow of blood up to scratch. Ain't science wonderful! Even with this necessary repair, I felt that after five years of taking Family Services the time had really come to hang up my cassock – this would be my third, and final last time and I would actually be carrying out my decision. So on July 20th over sixty children and parents gathered in St Andrew's church hall for the fifth birthday service and my last. After the service I was presented with a large number of gift tokens to spend in various shops, but perhaps more importantly, a large folder made up of pictures, writings and photographs contributed by the children, thanking Father Bryan for the good times we had shared together over the last five years.

In my resignation piece, printed in the church magazine, I said that although my public ministry was at an end, there still was a ministry that I would continue to exercise. This was the ministry of 'How are you? – and a hug'. To show a real interest in people and their well-being, together with some physical contact has always been an important part of my ministry and I intend to keep going with that for as long as I have breath to speak and the strength to put my arms round someone!

Perhaps the time has come to reflect a little on my life and record what are the important landmarks that have shaped the path I have taken. There are four decisions that probably above all else have been paramount in the way life has panned out for me. These decisions have not been mine but are the results of asking four questions and getting affirmative answers to them all. The first question was to ask His Majesty King George the Sixth if I could serve in his Royal Air Force. I wasn't ordered to put on the blue uniform as I volunteered to become a Brillcream Boy. Fortunately he – well one of his minions – agreed that I was fit enough in wind and mind to help defend the realm against the enemy. That decision set the scene for my future in many different ways, as my story has related. My time in the RAF launched me into a wider world than the green fields of Sussex; gave me a basic training in electronics; a taste for travel; a taste for a certain young lady who became my wife.

The next question was to ask the Decca Navigator Co if I could work for them. I didn't reply to a job vacancy advertisement but just enquired if a place could be found for me. The answer was yes. Working for Decca gave me a tremendously satisfying job, even if towards the end I realised it was not to be my final 'calling'. But it gave me something far more important – it gave me stability and the financial basis on which to bring up the children and enjoy a happy family life. It also gave me an understanding of the meaning and necessity of empathy with other people and developing their skills as the way to fulfil their needs.

The third question was to ask Marian Burford if she would become Marian Strange. Again the answer was yes. Although at the time I thought I was taking a bit of a risk asking a medical person to share my life, without Marian I would not have achieved anything that I have achieved. In our life together she has been totally constant in her support of all the twists and turns that have come my way and the decisions that I have had to make. No that's not quite right – in all the questions we have had to ask and in all the decisions that we have had to make. Even more vitally, especially in later years, is the fact that when I had some difficulty in making a decision, how Marian saw the way forward has always turned out to be right. She could always see what I thought might be a risk, wasn't a risk at all. This decision-making has been underpinned for both of us by asking for divine guidance in difficult situations. To ask God for guidance, and then to get on and act, has always given us the assurance that we are on the right course.

The final question was to ask the Church of England if they would ordain me into the priesthood. Again the answer was in the affirmative – an answer that was to change our lives totally.

You will note that none of the decisions were mine, but the questions were. Surely life is all about asking questions – and knowing the right questions to ask?

So, how to end a story that's not ended? Life still goes on! Perhaps to record a wonderful holiday Marian and I enjoyed in 2003.

It was during that glorious summer and autumn when the sun shone for days and weeks almost uninterrupted and the temperature passed a record 38 degrees. A brilliant summer turning into a golden dry autumn.

Holidays for many years have been a combination of

visiting friends and relatives and a time for Marian and me to be on our own. Sussex and the north of Scotland have for long provided locations for holidays as they are home to nearly all our relatives and friends – apart from those who have gravitated to the West Country – and both in different ways are places of great natural beauty. The Highlands of Scotland and the South Downs of Sussex are topographically very different but both lift up the spirit from the lowlands of everyday life.

It has long been a joke in the family that as soon as Christmas dinner is over I begin planning next year's holiday. Marian always says that I shouldn't throw away my life but live just for the day! For me, planning and looking forward have always been activities giving great pleasure. Unanswered questions, worry and uncertainty are overcome by making decisions as quickly as possible!

The year 2003, however, dawned differently. My impending angioplasty put pay to any forward thinking until after June. Following the successful widening of the offending artery, the way was made clear for my blood to flow more easily and the way made clear to plan our holiday. In many respects this holiday turned out to be a kind of re-run, in miniature, of events and experiences that have happened during my life. Some activities during our 2003 holiday were repeats of many years past; some were new, yet very firmly connected with the past.

Travelling east to Sussex – for that was our destination this year – we turned round a corner just outside Salisbury and there, as always, was that most slender and splendid of spires reaching nearer to heaven above than any other in England. In the shadow of that great cathedral the theologians of the Church of England had struggled with me, thirty years ago, to bring me nearer to heaven on ground level. Salisbury was also a turning point in my spiritual life and I never go to that city without offering up a quick one in thanksgiving for all that was revealed to me there.

Our first home visiting stop was with Ron and Phyllis

Cousins in Pulborough – they were our next-door neighbours over fifty years ago when we bought our first houses in West Molesey. Strange how some friendships last whilst others just fade away. From Pulborough we made a visit to Horsham and were again amazed at yet more construction sites, changing the little 1950's market town even closer to a clone of so many other towns in England with their standard issue of supermarkets. Of course the Causeway, with its row of Tudor houses either side of the road down to St Mary's Church will never change. Inside the church that had nurtured me into ordination we met the duty guide who turned out to be the man who lived next door to my father-in-law thirty years ago.

Going east again, we travelled over that flat marshland that had been my cross-country course at Lewes County School – now bisected by the hard and dry tarmacadam of a dual carriage causeway and just round the corner the tunnel driven through the prehistoric chalk of the South Downs. Is nothing sacred any more?

As we headed further east towards the uplands of Wealden Sussex, there across the fields near the village of Halland, still stood the Decca Navigator mast of the transmitting station I had helped to update over fifty years ago. I fear that this symbol of times gone-by – remember the Decca system had met its death a year or two past – was now suffering the ignominy of supporting common-or-garden mobile phone aerials. I hope the Dean and Chapter of Salisbury Cathedral haven't allowed such infestation into that beautiful spire! Long ago Halland, for our family, became famous for another reason. Here there is a perfectly good and adequate pub but which for Claire is definitely off-limits. During one of our caravan holidays at East Hoathly, she and Fiona with other youngsters, went in one day to have a drink. Claire, being eighteen and the oldest, but looking the youngest, was refused a glass of beer. What worse could befall a girl of eighteen?

On through Heathfield – no time to stop as we wanted to get to our destination – to Northiam where we were to spend a week in a fifteenth century Sussex thatched cottage. Northiam lies on the southern edge of the Rother Levels and is the last outpost of East Sussex before my homeland – the County of Kent. It is also the proud possessor of a railway station, with steam trains operating on the Kent and East Sussex Railway. During our week's holiday we were stopped at the level crossing and there in the station was a wonderful steam engine all gleaming and hissing violently with steam. I quickly borrowed Marian's digital camera to take a picture, aimed and pressed the button; nothing happened. By the time I got things sorted out the train had gone. Oh for the days of the Box Brownie!

We visited the place where this whole story started – Cranbrook. It was our purpose to find the shop that seventy-seven years ago had housed Strange Electrical Co Ltd and was the address of my birth. I knew the approximate location of the premises, so we enquired of a shopkeeper if she could help us. No, but she knew a lady who could. This lady, further down the street, couldn't help either, but she knew a man who could!

So we met Peter Ryan – even further down the street. Peter, it soon became obvious, could readily hold the title of 'Mr Cranbrook'. Yes, he knew which had been my father's shop. "I don't actually remember it myself as Strange Electrical" he confessed "but I know it was where the solicitors office is now – I was born about a hundred yards from where you were born." I then asked him how old he was. "I was born in 1926." Then to my question, what date, he replied "February 22nd."After seventy-seven years two men, born within spitting distance of each other, on the same day and in the same year, had met by sheer chance! When I told Peter Ryan that my father's sojourn in Cranbrook hadn't fulfilled his hopes for a profitable business, he explained to me the reason why the town hadn't been blessed with electricity. Like many small towns across the country at that time, the place of my birth included its own gas works – gas produced by burning coal. This enterprise was owned by local shareholders. Electricity? Certainly not!

Then we visited Heathfield where my father's shop had been a success for over fifty years. No more an electrical retail establishment, it had been shut down by the directors who followed my father and is now a cafe and second-hand 'bits and pieces' business. The present owner found it difficult to believe that her storeroom once produced thousands of aircraft parts that helped to provide the peace we now enjoy. Where my father sat and prepared estimates of how much wire would be required to distribute electric light around a client's house, now stood a young girl preparing a salad for her client.

Unfortunately the present occupiers of Mudros were not in when we knocked on the door. I saw that the air raid shelter had gone but the garden shed constructed by my father still remains – a monument to his good workmanship. The window still remained – now PVC and double glazed no doubt – from where I watched those beautiful trains before Doctor Beeching had his wicked way with the Cuckoo Line. New square boxes of a small trading estate have wiped off the face of the earth the last vestige of that bygone age of curving lines, platforms and semaphore signals, and waiting trains for late rising schoolboys.

The final holiday visit into the past was a trip to Tunbridge Wells and my grandfather's shop. This is still an electrical business owned and run by a former employee of my father. Over a cuppa in the small upstairs office we heard how the company had changed. The name Strange has now gone forever as far as the retail electrical business is concerned, although it remains as a separate electrical contracting company in Tunbridge Wells. The present owner of the shop hunted around in several cupboards for something he wanted to show us. Finally he produced a photograph of a group of men that he said was taken at the firm's annual outing around 1950. There amongst the forty-odd men was my grandfather, father and uncle Frank. Many of the others I recognised from those days of my youth and of the time my father offered me a job. In some ways it is sad that I am not in that photograph as well but we left the shop very gratefully clutching this record of bygone days.

Travelling home across the counties of southern England, I had a strong feeling that although the past was once the present and the future, it is not the place in which to spend too much time. As we drove down the M5 to the Tiverton road at Junction 27, I felt that I was coming home because to me home is now and all the expectations of what is still to come.

Sitting writing these last words of the story it has struck me that if the good burghers of Cranbrook hadn't been so bloody minded about electricity, nearly all this you have just finished reading would never have happened!

EPILOGUE

I haven't travelled alongside the whole course of the River Exe in a single journey, but we all know that it is one river and what starts on Exmoor ends in the sea at Exmouth.

My life, and all our lives, are like the River Exe; it has a birth and a death and then there is the bit in the middle. Like all rivers, like all lives, it is this part in the middle that sees so much change and just as two rivers are never the same, so our lives are all different. We all have individual rivers of life – our journeys, on the way, are all different, all even a bit erratic.

Life is like the River Exe...
it's seed – it's spring of life
lies deep in a dark womb
on the heights of Exmoor,
fertilised by the rain
penetrating from the skies.
It's born a weak gurgling creation
of new life
protected by the gentle slopes
and strong stones of mother earth,
as it starts its journey
to death in the sea.

Soon a fast moving stream
full of vigour
flowing ever faster
as it gets into the stride of life,
dashing round all obstacles:
gathering strength and demanding

notice by the rest of the world,
becoming broader and more mature.
Slowing – a little – to flirt with Tiverton
and to earn money for Bickleigh.
Onwards to the flatlands of Stoke Canon
and a more measured life
but still able to leave its mark
over the surrounding land.
It comes to the peak of its influence
as it grandly embraces the City of Exeter.
Flowing ever on, ever on,
perhaps less energetic now,
towards its ultimate place
Exmouth and the sea.
Here there is a uniting of river
and the vast ocean beyond.
Here the Exe finally gives up
its land-locked being, joining
the waters of countless other rivers,
never destroyed, but changed
to share in a greater experience.
Life is like the River Exe.